Rechtsgeschichtliche Forschungen

Edited by

Prof. Dr. Andreas Deutsch
Prof. Dr. Stephan Dusil
Prof. Dr. Saskia Lettmaier

Volume 1

Stephan Dusil

Researching Medieval Canon Law around 1900

The Life and Work of Viktor Wolf Edler von Glanvell (1871–1905)

Nomos

The Deutsche Nationalbibliothek lists this publication in the Deutsche Nationalbibliografie; detailed bibliographic data are available on the Internet at http://dnb.d-nb.de

ISBN 978-3-7560-1136-0 (Print)
978-3-7489-4252-8 (ePDF)

British Library Cataloguing-in-Publication Data
A catalogue record for this book is available from the British Library.

ISBN 978-3-7560-1136-0 (Print)
978-3-7489-4252-8 (ePDF)

Library of Congress Cataloging-in-Publication Data
Dusil, Stephan
Researching Medieval Canon Law around 1900
The Life and Work of Viktor Wolf Edler von Glanvell (1871–1905)
Stephan Dusil
147 pp.
Includes bibliographic references and index.

ISBN 978-3-7560-1136-0 (Print)
978-3-7489-4252-8 (ePDF)

Online Version
Nomos eLibrary

1st Edition 2023

Acknowledgements

About ten years ago, while researching pre-Gratian canonical collections, I first came across Viktor Wolf Edler von Glanvell and his edition of Deusdedit's collection. I was intrigued by this meticulous edition and also by his exceptional life with its dramatic ending, namely his death in the mountains. The aim of this study is to shed light on Wolf von Glanvell and his academic œuvre, and thus to highlight the beginning of systematic research in medieval canon law in the second half of the nineteenth century.

A previous version of this study was submitted as a master thesis for the degree of *Juris Canonici Licentiatus* at KU Leuven (2021). I am very grateful to Professor Dr. Matthias Pulte (Mainz) for supervising this study, especially for his support and advice. I am also indebted to Dr. Johan Ickx (Rome) who wrote the second opinion. Earlier versions of this book were read by Prof. Melodie Eichbauer, PhD (Fort Myers), Prof. Dr. Johannes Liebrecht, and Prof. Dr. Andreas Thier (both Zurich). All of them provided valuable feedback. I am also much indebted to the members of the "Canon Law Friday Zoom" for their discussions with me. In Graz, Prof. Dr. Anita Ziegerhofer and Dr. Dr. Reingard Rauch were helpful interlocutors. My staff at Tübingen—especially Maximilian Knaak— helped me during the publication process. Dr. Magda Hayton (Springfield, Missouri) undertook the arduous task of copy-editing the text. I am also grateful to the staff members of various archives and libraries for their helpfulness and willingness to search their holdings and to provide me with material, especially when travel was hampered due to corona-restrictions, and to permit publication of their material. I want to express my gratitude especially to Dr. Andreas Golob, Graz, and Yann Potin, Paris. The publisher, Nomos, saw the publication process through in a professional way.

At family dinners, Wolf von Glanvell and his alpine adventures were often vividly discussed, including his equipment, his nights spent in shepherds' huts and tents, and his ascents. I dedicate this study to our tent- and mountain-loving children: Élise, Enrik, and Konrad.

Tübingen, 2023 April 19
Stephan Dusil

Table of Contents

1. Introduction: Approach to a Bio-Bibliographical Study

Around 1900, Viktor Wolf Edler von Glanvell was a mountaineer who reached more than 1500 peaks, including 200 first ascents. In addition to being an outstanding alpinist, he was also a promising legal historian who researched medieval canon law. While his edition of Deusdedit's canonical collection may still be known, at least among specialists, his other works have fallen into oblivion.

This study aims to shed light on Wolf von Glanvell as scholar. Therefore, it reconstructs his academic biography (Chapter 2.) and scrutinizes his publications, both his textual editions and his studies on the medieval law of the church. It not only assembles those pieces of information that shed light on the "making of" his studies, but also analyses their content, methodology, and reception—contemporary as well as current (Chapters 3.-6.). Finally, this study contextualizes his research within the general research carried out in the end of the nineteenth century and asks the questions: In what respect is Wolf von Glanvell a typical representative of canon law research around 1900? In what respect did he try out new approaches (Chapter 7.)?

This study follows a bio-bibliographical approach, that of the German "Werkbiographie," and thus places Wolf von Glanvell and his œuvre against the background of his time. It links his biography with his studies and tries to unearth the—obvious or hidden, direct or indirect—influences that affected his work: influential books, dominant colleagues, authoritative ideas.[1] To achieve such a comprehensive picture, his works must be read

1 On "Werkbiographien" see, for instance, Joachim Rückert, "Review of 'Bernd-Rüdiger Kern, Georg Beseler. Leben und Werk, 1982,'" in: ZRG.GA 104, 1987, 399–405; André Depping, *Das BGB als Durchgangspunkt. Privatrechtsmethode und Privatrechtsleitbilder bei Heinrich Lehmann (1876–1963)* (Beiträge zur Rechtsgeschichte des 20. Jahrhunderts 34), Tübingen: Mohr Siebeck, 2002, 1–9; Ralf Seinecke, *Das Recht des Rechtspluralismus* (Grundlagen der Rechtswissenschaft 29), Tübingen: Mohr Siebeck, 2015, 6: "Diese Methode [i.e."werkbiographische Methode"–SD] beschränkt sich nicht auf die sachliche Analyse von Begriffen und die Rekonstruktion von wissenschaftlichen Theorien. Stattdessen unterstreicht sie die vorausgesetzten Axiome, biographischen Momente und politischen Anschauungen der untersuchten Theoretiker." Wilhelm Bleek, *Geschichte der Politikwissenschaft in Deutschland*, München: Beck, 2001, 20: "Wissenschaftsgeschichte als Wissenschaftlergeschichte fragt nach der familiären und

against other contemporary works of the late nineteenth century. At the same time, this study makes extensive use of unprinted, archival material, which permits a close-up view of Wolf von Glanvell as an academic. This material includes letters to and from colleagues, reports in which he delineated the progress of his work, and evaluations composed by colleagues about him. This combination of macro and micro approaches allows for a greater understanding of Wolf von Glanvell both as representative of the late nineteenth century and as individual author.

Wolf von Glanvell was a famous alpinist, and this aspect of his life is well-researched, even if he has not been the subject of a monograph.[2] Contrary to his alpine achievements, however, his academic merits have received little attention. In the several studies focusing on canonists and the history of canon law in Austria and at the University of Graz, where he studied and taught, references to him are either relegated to a side note[3] or are based on contemporary reviews of his works.[4] An in-depth reading of

sozialen Herkunft von Hochschullehrern, nach deren Bildungsweg, Studienfächern, Universitäten und akademischen Lehrern. Wissenschaftliches Werk und akademische Biographie werden solchermaßen in einen engen Bezug gesetzt." As a current example for "Werkbiographien" serve Isabelle-Christine Panreck, *Klaus von Beyme. Eine Werkbiographie*, Wiesbaden: Springer, 2021, esp. at 21–25; and Johannes Liebrecht, *Brunners Wissenschaft. Heinrich Brunner (1840–1915) im Spiegel seiner Rechtsgeschichte* (Studien zur europäischen Rechtsgeschichte 288), Frankfurt am Main: Klostermann, 2014.

2 Cf. the literature mentioned on 13 n. 7.

3 Richard Puza, "Kirchenrechtslehrer an der Juridischen Fakultät der Universität Graz aus zwei Jahrhunderten," in: ZRG.KA 70, 1984, 237–270, at 263–264 (having used archival documents); Kurt Ebert, "Die Pflege der Rechtsgeschichte an der Grazer Universität im 19. Jahrhundert," in: Einzelne Probleme der Rechtsgeschichte und des römischen Rechts. Referate der internationalen Arbeitskonferenz für Rechtsgeschichte und Römisches Recht (Szeged 18.-20. September 1969) (Acta Universitatis Szegediensis de Attila József nominatae, Acta Juridica et Politica 17), Szeged 1970, 249–260, at 256; Kurt Ebert, "Die Pflege der Rechtsgeschichte an der Universität Graz im Zeichen der Historischen Schule," in: ZRG.GA 87, 1970, 239–286, at 256–257. A history of the Faculty of Law of the University of Graz with regard to canon law is missing. The series "Geschichte der Rechtswissenschaftlichen Fakultät der Universität Graz" contains only one volume on legal history, namely Gunter Wesener, Geschichte der Rechtswissenschaftlichen Fakultät der Universität Graz, vol. 1: *Römisches Recht und Naturrecht* (Publikationen aus dem Archiv der Universität Graz 9/1), Graz: Akademische Druck- und Verlagsanstalt, 1978.

4 Nikolaus Grass, "Die Kirchenrechtslehrer der Universität Graz und ihre Bedeutung für die Erforschung des klassischen kanonischen Rechts," in: Studia Gratiana 8, 1962, 195–304, at 253–259; another publication by Nikolaus Grass, "Österreichische Kanonistenschulen aus drei Jahrhunderten," in: ZRG.KA 41, 1955, 290–411 does not mention Wolf von Glanvell.

Wolf von Glanvell's scholarship against the intellectual background of the late nineteenth century is still lacking, especially one that scrutinizes the secluded assumptions and fundamental conditions that shaped his research, including the context of canon law research in general around 1900.[5] This book is an attempt to fill this gap in the scholarship. If it also serves as a prolegomenon to a history of canon law research in the nineteenth and early twentieth centuries in general, it fulfills another goal; but this is not its primary purpose.

5 A history of canon law research ("Wissenschaftsgeschichte") is almost completely missing; there are some remarks by: Peter Landau, "Evangelische Kirchenrechtswissenschaft im 19. Jahrhundert," in: Zeitschrift für Evangelisches Kirchenrecht 48, 2003, 1–16 (reprint in: Peter Landau (ed.), *Grundlagen und Geschichte des evangelischen Kirchenrechts und des Staatskirchenrechts*, Tübingen: Mohr Siebeck, 2010, 253–268); Carlo Fantappiè, *Storia del diritto canonico e delle istituzioni della Chiesa*, Bologna: Il Mulino, 2011, 236–244; Péter Erdö, *Geschichte der Wissenschaft vom kanonischen Recht. Eine Einführung* (Kirchenrechtliche Bibliothek 4), ed. Ludger Müller, Berlin: Lit, 2006, 138–148; and also Constant Van de Wiel, *History of Canon Law* (Louvain Theological & Pastoral Monographs 5), Leuven: Peeters, 1991, 162–166. In addition to these overviews, some more specific studies have been conducted, for instance: Charles Donahue Jr., "Roman Canon Law in the Medieval English Church: Stubbs vs. Maitland Re-examined After 75 Years in the Light of Some Records from the Church Courts," in: Michigan Law Review 72, 1974, 647–716 on the Stubb Maitland-debate concerning whether "Roman canon law" was binding to English courts, and also Charles Donahue Jr., *Why the History of Canon Law is Not Written*, London: Selden Society, 1986, esp. at 3–16; Stefan Ruppert, *Kirchenrecht und Kulturkampf. Historische Legitimation, politische Mitwirkung und wissenschaftliche Begleitung durch die Schule Emil Ludwig Richters* (Ius ecclesiasticum 70), Tübingen: Mohr Siebeck, 2002 and, based on his PhD, Stefan Ruppert, "'Nach Canossa gehen wir nicht.' Kirchenrecht und Kulturkampf," in: Zeitschrift für evangelisches Kirchenrecht 49, 2004, 689–717; Andreas Anter, *Max Weber und die Staatsrechtslehre*, Tübingen: Mohr Siebeck, 2016, at 47–66 on Max Weber and Rudolf Sohm; Charles de Miramon, "L'invention de la Réforme grégorienne: Grégoire VII au XIXe siècle entre pouvoir spirituel et bureaucratisation de l'Église," 2017 on Gregory VII and the creation of a "Gregorian Reform" in the nineteenth century; Christof Rolker, "Fournier's Model and Its Merits," in: Christof Rolker (ed.), New Discourses in Medieval Canon Law Research. Challenging the Master Narrative (Medieval Law and Its Practice 28), Leiden: Brill, 2019, 4–32; Péter Erdö, "Die Forschung der Geschichte des kanonischen Rechts: ein Dialog zwischen Theologie und Rechtsgeschichte," in: ZRG.KA 91, 2005, 1–16 is silent on this question. Nonetheless, recent historiographical studies on the research of Germanic law have been published by Frank L. Schäfer, *Juristische Germanistik. Eine Geschichte der Wissenschaft vom einheimischen Privatrecht* (Juristische Abhandlungen 51), Frankfurt am Main: Klostermann, 2008; Liebrecht, *Brunners Wissenschaft* (2014); and Johannes Liebrecht, *Die junge Rechtsgeschichte. Kategorienwandel in der rechtshistorischen Germanistik der Zwischenkriegszeit* (Beiträge zur Rechtsgeschichte des 20. Jahrhunderts 99), Tübingen: Mohr Siebeck, 2018.

Fig. 1: Viktor Wolf Edler von Glanvell (1902)

2. Academic and Alpinist: The Life of Viktor Wolf Edler von Glanvell

2.1. *Wolf von Glanvell as Canonist*

Viktor Wolf Edler von Glanvell was born on September 4, 1871 as son of the officer Ignaz Wolf von Glanvell (1832–1898)[6] and Therese, née Braunhofer (1845–1930).[7] He received his primary education in Klagenfurt and Graz at the "Volksschule" (1877–1881) and attended high school in Graz, namely the

6 Ignaz Wolf was an officer in the Austrian army ("Major" at the latest). Due to his merits, he was ennobled at the end of his career, as was customary in nineteenth-century Austria (so-called "systemmäßiger Adel"). In 1879, Ignaz Wolf was allowed to add "Edler" to his name and he chose a fictitious "Praedikat," namely "von Glanvell," apparently derived from the river Glan in Klagenfurt. The other "Praedikate" he proposed were "von Wörthern" and "von Liddorf." His coat of arms shows, among other things, a wolf, a silver river, and a golden star. For his ennoblement, see: Wien, Österreichisches Staatsarchiv, AVA, Adel, Hofadelsakten, Wolf, Ignaz, Major, Adelsstand (Wien, 1879 January 24). On ennoblements in general, see Peter Frank-Döfering, *Adelslexikon des österreichischen Kaisertums, 1804–1918*, Wien: Herder, 1989, 642–643. On the genealogy of his family, see Arno Kerschbaumer, *Beamte, Unternehmer, Offiziere. Familien der "Zweiten Gesellschaft" aus Innerösterreich*, Graz, 2018, 273–274.

7 The biography is based on his Curriculum Vitae (dated to 1897 July 25), in: Wien, Österreichisches Staatsarchiv, AVA, Unterricht-Allg., Ktn. 915.37, PA Wolf-Glanvell. A biographical sketch is also published in: Grazer Volksblatt 1905 May 9 (Morgenausgabe), 4. The following short biographies focus mainly on his alpine achievements: Georg Vavra, "Wolf von Glanvell, Viktor Edler," in: Österreichisches Biographisches Lexikon (1815–1950), vol. 16, Wien: Verlag der Österreichischen Akademie der Wissenschaften, 2021, 327–328; Hans-Günter Richardi, *Die Erschließung der Dolomiten. Auf den Spuren der Pioniere Paul Grohmann und Viktor Wolf-Glanvell in den Bleichen Bergen*, Bozen: Athesia, 2008, 148–200; Franz Wolkinger, "Univ.-Prof. Dr. Victor Wolf Edler von Glanvell," in: Alpenverein Graz. Nachrichten 2005 (Heft Nr. 4), 6–7; N.N., "Glanvell, Viktor Wolf von," in: Franco De Battaglia / Luciano Marisaldi (ed.), Enciclopedia delle Dolomiti, Bologna: Zanichelli, 2000, 75–77; H. Kiene, "Erschließer der Dolomiten (7): Dr. Viktor Wolf von Glanvell," in: Dolomiten. Der Bergsteiger in den Dolomiten, 11. Mai 1989, Nr. 106; Lieselotte Buchenauer, "Dr. Viktor Wolf Edler von Glanvell," in: Österreichische Alpenzeitung 100, 1982, 80–83; Fritz Schmitt, "Viktor Wolf von Glanvell. Bezwinger des bizarrsten Campanile," in: Der Bergsteiger 1982 (Heft 7), 44–45; but also Karl Doménigg, *Ein Bergsteigerleben. Einer von der 'Gilde zum groben Kletterschuh,'* Wien: Österreichische Bergsteiger-Zeitung, 1949 with many references to Wolf von Glanvell; Günther Freiherr von Saar, "Nachruf," in: Österreichische Alpenzeitung 27, 1905, 121–126. Some pieces of information can be found online, for instance:

"Kaiserlich-Königlich I. Staatsgymnasium."[8] He graduated in July 1889 with honors ("mit Auszeichnung") and entered the Karl-Franzens-Universität in Graz. He studied at the "rechts- und staatswissenschaftlichen Fakultät" (winter term of 1889/90–August 10, 1893) and in addition to courses on contemporary law, such as administrative and procedural law, he attended many courses on legal history. His teachers were Arnold Luschin von Ebengreuth, Friedrich Thaner, and August Tewes. He also heard lectures on economics, and, more importantly, dedicated time—especially in the first year—to courses offered by the Philosophy Faculty, namely courses on Austrian history, diplomatics, and the history of the Middle Ages, thus laying the groundwork for his future career as a canonist.[9] He completed his studies and received his "Doctoren-Diplom" on May 23, 1894.[10] Wolf von Glanvell dedicated another year to a "Fachstudium"[11] before receiving a research fellowship for a stay in Rome (October 1895–February 1896). During this time, he prepared his first publication on a canonical collection of the Gregorian era, namely the Vatican Codex Vat. lat. 1348.[12] When he returned to Graz, he studied the history of legal institutions from the perspective of canon law, focusing on agricultural, commercial and inheritance

---

http://www.alpinwiki.at/portal/navigation/erst-besteiger/erstbesteigerdetail.php?erstbesteiger=6697. He first name is partly written with "c," partly with "k."

8 Wolf von Glanvell supported the "Verein zur Unterstützung armer und würdiger Schüler am k. k. I. Staatsgymnasium" with donations (see Grazer Volksblatt 1886 July 7, 7; Grazer Volksblatt 1891 June 28, 7; Grazer Volksblatt 1892 December 25, 14; Grazer Volksblatt 1897 January 1, 7), but also by auditing this "Verein" (see Grazer Volksblatt 1901 January 6 (Morgenausgabe), 7; Grazer Volksblatt 1902 January 1 (Morgenausgabe), 6; Grazer Tagblatt 1903 January 3, 3–4; Grazer Volksblatt 1903 December 31 (Abendausgabe), 2).

9 See Graz, Universitätsarchiv, Jur. Fak., Nationale Viktor Wolf von Glanvell (winter term of 1889/90–summer term of 1893). Winter term of 1889/90: "Österreichische Geschichte" (Franz Krones von Marchland) and "Urkundenlehre" (Anton Julius Chroust); summer term of 1890: "Urkundenlehre" and "Diplomatische Übungen" (both: Chroust); winter term of 1890/91: "Urkundenlehre" (Chroust); winter term of 1891/92: "Geschichte des Mittelalters" (Arnold Busson).

10 See the "Rigorosenprotokolle:" Graz, Universitätsarchiv, Jur. Fak., Rigorosenprotokolle, vol. 8., No 145: "Judizielle Fächer" (Österreichisches Civil- und Strafrecht, Handels- und Wechselrecht, österreichischer Civil- und Strafproceß) 1893 December 9, "Staatswissenschaftliche Fächer" (Allgemeines und österreichisches Staatsrecht, Völkerrecht und politische Oekonomie) 1894 March 9, "Rechtshistorische Fächer" (Römisches, kanonisches und deutsches Recht) 1894 May 22.

11 The content of this "Fachstudium" remains unclear. It may have prepared him for his academic career.

12 On the codex Vatican City, Biblioteca Apostolica Vaticana, vat. lat. 1348, see 31–40.

law, publishing "Negotia inter vivos" in 1898 and "Letztwillige Verfügungen" in 1900.

His first book, the "Negotia inter vivos," together with his study of Vat. lat. 1348 served as the basis for his "Habilitation" in 1897/98. Both publications were examined by Friedrich Thaner and Arnold Luschin von Ebengreuth, legal historians at University of Graz, who accepted them as sufficient. Wolf von Glanvell passed a "Colloquium" some days before Christmas and gave his "Probevortrag" in January 1898, which he devoted to costumary law in the Church ("Das kirchliche Gewohnheitsrecht").[13] From March 1898 he was "Privatdocent" at the University of Graz with the *venia legendi* for "Kirchenrecht."[14]

His first academic term was the summer term of 1898. He designed two courses on the history of canon law, namely an exegetical course on selected topics of the *Corpus Iuris Canonici* and a "Repetitorium des canonischen Rechts" (both two hours weekly). In the first course, he focused on those parts of the *Liber Extra* that deal with private and public law, such as the laws pertaining to tithing or patronage. He aimed to link aspects of canon law with respective elements of Roman and Germanic law in order to compare them: "An die Ausführung der in dem einzelnen Titel enthaltenen Rechtssätze, soweit sie aus sonst vorhandenen kirchlichen Normen sich ergibt, würde ich jedesmal ein vergleichenden Hinweis auf das römische und das deutsche Recht anschließen."[15] The second course was also based on the idea of contextualizing canon law, namely in the social condition of the late Middle Ages. Wolf von Glanvell aimed to highlight moral aspects of canon law and its economic relevance, for instance with regard to the prohibition of interest: "Es würde da bei der Behandlung des canonischen Zinsverbotes insbesondere sich ein näheres Eingehen auf die Handels- und

13 "Colloquium:" 1897 December 21; "Probevortrag:" 1898 January 21. See also the invitation to the "Probevortrag" in Graz, Universitätsarchiv, Jur. Fak., Z. 292 ex 1897/98. On the discussion of customary law in the Church, see 93.

14 The document is transmitted in: Wien, Österreichisches Staatsarchiv, AVA, Unterricht-Allg., Ktn. 915.37, PA Wolf-Glanvell. See also Graz, Universitätsarchiv, Jur. Fak., Z. 305 ex 1897/98: Faculty of Law in Graz to the Ministery requesting confirmation of the decision to grant the *venia legendi* to Wolf von Glanvell (1898 January 24). The "Personalakte" (Graz, Universitätsarchiv, Personalakte Wolf von Glanvell) consists of only one folio with some personal information and is therefore of no further interest. The archive of the diocese Graz-Seckau does not have any records concerning Wolf von Glanvell (kind mail by the archive, 2022 September 22).

15 Wien, Österreichisches Staatsarchiv, AVA, Unterricht-Allg., Ktn. 915.37, PA Wolf-Glanvell ("Vorlesungsprogramm," dated to 1897 July 25).

Verkehrsverhältnisse des Mittelalters in ihrem Widerstreit gegen die canonistischen Ansichten ergeben."[16] Following his methodological programme, he read various courses on the history of legal institutions in the *Corpus iuris canonici* between 1898 and 1901.[17]

His teaching abilities were positively summarized in a report sent to the Austrian Emperor, who decided on Wolf von Glanvell's further career: "Seit seiner Habilitation hat er in jedem Semester zwei- bis dreistündige Vorlesung über einzelne Partien seines Faches und Repetitorien aus denselben abgehalten, welche Vorträge sich einer regen Theilnahme der Studierenden zu erfreuen hatten."[18] And, indeed, Wolf von Glanvell was a well-received teacher in Graz, judging by the number of students he attracted: in the summer term of 1899, he had some 75 students;[19] in the summer term of 1900, 247 students attended his classes, in the winter term of 1900/01 still 47.[20] In October 1899, he was appointed a member of the "rechtshistorische Staatsprüfungscommission." Wolf von Glanvell—according to a later report of a faculty commission—"prüft nicht blos canonisches sondern auch deutsches Recht in deutscher und italienischer Sprache."[21]

16 Wien, Österreichisches Staatsarchiv, AVA, Unterricht-Allg., Ktn. 915.37, PA Wolf-Glanvell ("Vorlesungsprogramm", dated to 1897 July 25: "Der Zweck dieser Vorlesung wäre, die leitenden Gedanken im Gebäude des canonischen Rechtes darzulegen mit specieller Hervorhebung des Verwaltungsorganismus der Kirche und der volkswirtschaftlichen Bedeutung des ganzen canonischen Rechtes. Es würde da bei der Behandlung des canonischen Zinsverbotes insbesondere sich ein näheres Eingehen auf die Handels- und Verkehrsverhältnisse des Mittelalters in ihrem Widerstreit gegen die canonistischen Ansichten ergeben.").

17 He read: "Exegese ausgewählter Stellen des Corpus iuris canonici (unter besonderer Berücksichtigung der Wucherlehre") in the winter term of 1898/99, "Exegese ausgewählter Stellen des corpus iuris canonici (II. Die letztwilligen Verfügungen nach Kirchenrecht)" in the summer term of 1899, and, more general, "Kirchliches Privatrecht (mit Exegese ausgewählter Stellen des Corpus iuris canonici)" in the winter term of 1900/01. See also 18 and Appendix 2.

18 Wien, Österreichisches Staatsarchiv, AVA, Unterricht-Allg., Ktn. 915.37, PA Wolf-Glanvell (Z. 35251: Minister of Education Wilhelm von Hartel to the Austrian Emperor, 1901 November 6).

19 Wien, IÖG, Nachlass Sickel, Letter from Viktor Wolf von Glanvell to Theodor von Sickel, 1899 May 8.

20 Wien, Österreichisches Staatsarchiv, AVA, Unterricht-Allg., Ktn. 915.37, PA Wolf-Glanvell (Z. 316: report of a commission of the faculty (Thaner, Tewes, and Hanausek) on Wolf von Glanvell, s.d. (1900?)).

21 Wien, Österreichisches Staatsarchiv, AVA, Unterricht-Allg., Ktn. 915.37, PA Wolf-Glanvell (Z. 316: report of a commission of the faculty (Thaner, Tewes, and Hanausek) on Wolf von Glanvell, s.d. (1900?)). See also: Wien, IÖG, Nachlass Sickel, Letter from Viktor Wolf von Glanvell to Theodor von Sickel, 1899 May 8 and Grazer

Once he was appointed "Privatdocent," his mother allowed him to become engaged to Maria Theresia Luschin von Ebengreuth (1877–1968), a niece of his mentor, the Graz professor of legal history, Arnold Luschin von Ebengreuth (1898). He married his fiancée on July 20, 1901, in the neo-Gothic "Herz-Jesu-Kirche" in Graz.[22] A former teacher of the groom, the "Religionsprofessor" Dr. Josef Starn, celebrated the wedding ceremony; most of the marriage witnesses were academic colleagues: Arnold Luschin von Ebengreuth, Friedrich Thaner, and the professor of Roman law, Gustav Hanausek (1855–1927), as well as the former Austrian officer, Anton Schaffer Ritter von Schäffersfeld (1835–1910).[23] Some weeks later, he and Mary moved into an apartment in the Morellenfeldgasse 36, located in the same urban quarter each had lived in previously.[24]

1901 was an important year for Wolf von Glanvell: he not only got married, but he was also appointed "Extraordinarius" (similar to the rank of Associate Professor) at Graz University. On November 21, the Emperor, Franz Joseph, appointed him "Extraordinarius ad personam" to take effect on April 1, 1902, including the "systemmäßige Bezüge."[25] The faculty in

---

Volksblatt 1899 November 5, 4 (brief note of his nomination). Wolf von Glanvell was fluent in French, English and Italian (see his own Curriculum Vitae, dated to 1897 July 25, in: Wien, Österreichisches Staatsarchiv, AVA, Unterricht-Allg., Ktn. 915.37, PA Wolf-Glanvell).

22 On this church from the end of the nineteenth century: Maximilian Liebmann, "Bewährung im österreichischen Kulturkampf," in: Karl Amon / Maximilian Liebmann (ed.), Kirchengeschichte der Steiermark, Graz / Wien / Köln: Styria, 1993, 256–308, at 280–283.

23 Trauungsbuch II 1896–1902 of the parish "Herz-Jesu" in Graz, Signature 1575, fol. 224 (online: https://data.matricula-online.eu/de/oesterreich/graz-seckau/graz-herz-jesu/1575/?pg=228). Brief note: Grazer Tagblatt 1901 July 21 (Morgenausgabe), 5: "Unter sehr großer Betheiligung eines vornehmen Publicums fand gestern um halb 12 Uhr vormittags in der Herz Jesu-Kirche die Trauung des Universitätsdocenten Herrn Dr. Victor Wolf Edlen v. Glanvell mit Fräulein Marie Luschin-Ebengreuth statt."

24 They moved in on October 10, 1901, according to the "Meldezettel" (StadtA Graz, Meldezettel "Wolf Edler von Glanvell, Victor"). According to the wedding registration (see n. 23), Wolf von Glanvell lived in "Alberstrasse 19" (his parents' home), Mary Luschin von Ebengreuth in "Schumanngasse 3."

25 The monthly salary amounted to 370 Kronen according to the "Todfalls-Aufnahme" (Graz, Steiermärkisches Landesarchiv, Bezirksgericht Graz-I, Verlässe P-XIV-202/1905, 6), which corresponds approximately to the salary mentioned in a draft of a letter by Minister von Hartel (3600 Kronen and 840 Kronen "Activiteitszulage" annualy: Wien, Österreichisches Staatsarchiv, AVA, Unterricht-Allg., Ktn. 915.37, PA Wolf-Glanvell (Z. 35251, 1901 December 2); the same amount is mentioned in Graz, Universitätsarchiv, Jur. Fak., Z. 508 ex 1901/02).

Graz requested that Wolf von Glanvell lecture on canon law and teach a course on "Rechtsenzyklopädie."[26] The Minister of Education accepted this request: Wolf von Glanvell was ordered to teach "Spezialkollegien ihres Nominalfaches," five hours per week in each semester, and an additional course "Encyklopaedie der Rechts- und Staatswissenschaften," two hours weekly.[27] Therefore, Wolf von Glanvell taught—among other courses—a "Repetitorium des Kirchenrechts" in the summer term, as well as "Ordensrecht," ecclesiastical marriage law, and the already mentioned courses on institutional history.[28] In the academic self-administration of his faculty, he was elected as the contact person for scholarships ("Stipendienreferent").[29]

In addition to his teaching, Wolf von Glanvell devoted himself to the edition of Deusdedit's canonical collection.[30] He was entrusted with this task in 1900 and dedicated much time to transcribing manuscripts, identifying sources, and completing the edition. In early 1903, he spent several weeks in Rome with his wife (and also his mother) to study the manuscripts of Deusdedit's canonical collection and to visit Italy, including the Blue Grotto in Capri.[31] Two years later, on March 22, 1905 at "3/4 8 Uhr früh," Mary gave birth to their daughter, Irmingard Maria Teresia Lidwina, who was baptised three days later in the local parish, the "Herz Jesu-Kirche."[32] But she would not get to know her father for very long…

26 Wien, Österreichisches Staatsarchiv, AVA, Unterricht-Allg., Ktn. 915.37, PA Wolf-Glanvell (Z. 566, 1902 February 3). See also Graz, Universitätsarchiv, Jur. Fak., Sitzungsprotokolle, vol. 3, Protokoll 1900 November 23, 1901 December 10, and 1902 January 27.

27 Wien, Österreichisches Staatsarchiv, AVA, Unterricht-Allg., Ktn. 915.37, PA Wolf-Glanvell (Z. 3604, draft, 1902 February 14); Graz, Universitätsarchiv, Jur. Fak., Z. 598 ex 1901/02.

28 See Appendix 2.

29 Election: Graz, Universitätsarchiv, Jur. Fak., Sitzungsprotokolle, vol. 3, Protokoll 1902 July 10; in the minutes of his faculty's meetings, he is often mentioned, see: Graz, Universitätsarchiv, Jur. Fak., Sitzungsprotokolle, vol. 3, Protokoll 1904 May 11, 1904 October 28, 1904 December 9, 1905 February 10, 1905 March 3, and 1905 March 14.

30 See 41–59.

31 On this journey, see the remarks by Richardi, *Erschließung*, 189–190 and below 49. His request for leave in February and March 1903 obviously refers to this trip (see Graz, Universitätsarchiv, Jur. Fak., Z. 1520 ex 1902/03).

32 Taufbuch II 1901–1911, Signature 1500 of the parish "Herz-Jesu" in Graz, fol. 147, https://data.matricula-online.eu/de/oesterreich/graz-seckau/graz-herz-jesu/1500/?pg=152. Baptism: March 25, 1905.

2.2. Wolf von Glanvell as Alpinist

At a very young age, Wolf von Glanvell started to discover the Dolomites of South Tyrol, which are now part of Italy, but were Austrian in his day. His mother and his mountain loving aunt spent their vacations at Lake Prags ("Pragser Wildsee"), a gorgeous lake in the Prags Dolomites. Local mountain guides—such as Josef Appenbichler, and Michel and Sepp Innerkofler—introduced him to rock climbing: its technique, appropriate equipment, and safety measures. At first, he climbed as a "tourist" with the aid of local guides; later, he reached summits without professional help ("führerlose Besteigungen").[33]

After discovering the mountains around Lake Prags, he extended his climbing area to the rest of the Dolomites in the 1890s. By the end of that decade, Wolf von Glanvell was a well-versed and well-known, even famous, Austrian rock-climber. In total, he climbed about 1500 summits, of which about 200 were first ascents. His regularly published "Tourenberichte" bear witness to his success.[34] He was even known abroad, as an English society invited him to join a Himalayan expedition—a prestigious offer which he had to decline due to academic obligations.[35] As a summer project in 1905, he planned to further extend his climbing area by exploring the Western Alps, namely the Swiss Alps, and to ascend Mont Blanc, but his early death destroyed this plan.[36]

Wolf von Glanvell admired the Prags Dolomites, but he also fell in love with Val Travenances, a small valley a few kilometers south of the Prags Dolomites. In the late 1890s, he spent time there exploring the Fanes group, among other mountains. Tourism in the Dolomites was in its infancy around 1900 and rock climbing was quite adventurous. A trip undertaken in 1897 illustrates the efforts made by Wolf von Glanvell and others: On July 18, 1897, accompanied by Josef Appenbichler, he set out from Lake Prags early in the morning and reached a shepherd's hut ("Kaser") in the middle of the Val Travenanzes in the evening. They shared the hut with the local

---

33 Richardi, *Erschließung*, 148–164; Vavra, "Wolf von Glanvell," passim.

34 See Appendix 1.

35 Note in Grazer Volksblatt 1905 May 9 (Morgenausgabe), 4.

36 About the planned tours in Switzerland, see von Saar, "Nachruf," 125 ("[...] denn von nun ab wollte er sich der Schweiz zuwenden, um in Eis und Schnee womöglich dieselbe Meisterschaft zu erwerben wie im Fels"). On the Mont Blanc-plan, see the information in the following newspapers: Freie Stimmen 1905 May 19, 9 and Neues Wiener Tagblatt 1905 May 9, 8.

shepherds and started to explore the Fanes group the next morning.[37] One year later, Wolf von Glanvell returned with Günther Freiherr von Saar to climb the "Fanisturm" (August 12, 1898).[38] It was in this valley, not far from the "Kaser" where he first stayed, that the Wolf-Glanvell-Hütte was later built to commemorate him as an explorer of this part of the Dolomites.[39]

Wolf von Glanvell was also the founder and leader of an informal group of rock climbers, called "Gilde zum groben Kletterschuh."[40] Its members included Günther Freiherr von Saar, Karl Doménigg, Gottlieb Stopper, Leo Petritsch, and others.[41] In the winter, they met in Wolf von Glanvell's apartment in Graz to plan their summer trips.[42] In the summer, they often met in Neu-Prags (near Lake Prags) where they were welcomed by Anton Oberhammer, the mountain loving leader of the local community, and pitched their tents near the mountains they intended to ascend. Often, the male members of this fraternity were joined by their wives and fiancées, such as Mary Wolf von Glanvell and Titty (Klementine) Angerer,[43] who stayed in a women's tent, not only cooking and fixing climbing gear, but also climbing themselves.[44] Mary Wolf von Glanvell and Titty Angerer, for instance, were the first women to reach the summit of the Campanile di Val Montanaia, a spectacular 300-meter finger of rock (August 21, 1903).[45] Just one year earlier, their partners—Wolf von Glanvell and Günther von Saar—were the first to set foot on this "terribly wild rock mass," as one newspaper put it.[46]

37 Wolf von Glanvell, "Aus der Fanis-Tofanagruppe," 339–345.

38 Wolf von Glanvell, "Aus der Fanis-Tofanagruppe," 345–349.

39 See 105–107.

40 "Gilde zum groben Kletterschuh" roughly translates as "Fraternity of rugged climbing shoes."

41 Richardi, *Erschließung*, 165–166.

42 Remark by Karl Doménigg / Günther Freiherr von Saar, "Zur Erschließung der Karnischen Voralpen [II]," in: Zeitschrift des deutschen und österreichischen Alpenvereins 37, 1906, 380–396, at 380.

43 Titty Angerer was later married to Günther Freiherr von Saar, see Peter Grimm, "Saar, Günther Freiherr von," in: Neue Deutsche Biographie 22, 2005, 316–317.

44 Richardi, *Erschließung*, 164–169.

45 The ascent on the Campanile di Val Montanaia is mentioned in the following newspapers: Salzburger Volksblatt 1903 August 31, 6; Salzburger Chronik 1903 September 3, 6 (headline "Von tollkühnen Touristinnen"); Neues Wiener Tagblatt 1905 March 20, 8; Neue Freie Presse 1903 August 3, 6; Innsbrucker Nachrichten 1902 October 13, 9.

46 Cf. Günther Freiherr von Saar, "Zur Erschließung der Karnischen Voralpen [I]," in: Zeitschrift des deutschen und österreichischen Alpenvereins 36, 1905, 383–400, at

In the winter, Wolf von Glanvell did a lot of sports, practicing gymnastics and fencing; he also went skiing and even led ski-tours.[47] Institutionally, he was associated with the Graz section of the "Österreichischer Touristenclub." He was elected second secretary of this section in 1895,[48] and later became member of the executive board without a specific function (1902).[49] He also served as an instructor at a "Bergführer-Instructionscursus" and introduced interested hikers to "Alpine Ausrüstung, Bekleidung und Verproviantirung" and "Bergführerwesen im Allgemeinen."[50] In 1901, he became member of the Graz "Turner-Bergsteiger."[51] Wolf von Glanvell also initiated a "Wintersport-Klub" as a subgroup of the "Österreichischer Touristenclub" (1904/05), which enabled him and others to enjoy alpine pleasures in both summer and winter.[52] Against this background, it is perhaps not surprising that one of his last publications is entitled "Winterfahrt."[53]

Wolf von Glanvell's alpine achievements—his breathtaking ascents, his endurance, and his meticulous descriptions of the Dolomites—are not the focus of this book.[54] Nevertheless, it is important to remember him as a pioneer of mountaineering around 1900 who reached the summits not for military reasons (such as geographical surveys), but for his own pleasure. In this respect, the old-fashioned term "Hochtourist" offers a succinct description of what he did: he climbed on mountains for fun. In pitching tents in the untouched nature, in his hiking and mountaineering, his reaching out for new, unexplored summits or searching for a new climbing path, Wolf von Glanvell is a representative of a phenomenon in the nineteenth and

---

399. "Furchtbar wilden Felskoloß:" Neue Freie Presse 1903 August 3, 6. Ascent: 1902 September 17.

47 Cf. Neues Wiener Tagblatt 1904 December 12, 12 and Neues Wiener Tagblatt 1904 December 17, 8. He also played tennis, cf. Grazer Volksblatt 1904 June 7 (Abendausgabe), 2 publishing the results of a tennis tournament Wolf von Glanvell attended.

48 Grazer Tagblatt 1895 January 15, 4; Österreichische Touristenzeitung 15, 1895, 57.

49 Grazer Volksblatt 1902 December 2 (Morgenausgabe), 2.

50 1895 January 22–30, cf. Österreichische Touristenzeitung 15, 1895, 62–64.

51 Note: Grazer Tagblatt 1901 October 27 (Morgenausgabe), 5.

52 Neue Freie Presse 1904 December 21 (Morgenblatt), 9–10; Neue Freie Presse (Morgenblatt) 1905 January 13, 8; Allgemeine Sport-Zeitung 1905 January 15, 38. See also the obituary by von Saar, "Nachruf," 123 ("erster Fahrwart des Wintersportklubs") and Karl Doménigg, "Ein Getreuer des Oesterreichischen Touristenklubs. Dem Andenken Viktor Wolf-Glanvells," in: Österreichische Turistenzeitung 57, 1937, 9–10.

53 Wolf von Glanvell, "Winterfahrt," in: Österreichische Touristenzeitung 25, 1905, 41–42.

54 His alpine achievements have already been described elsewhere, see 13 n. 7. On his alpine publications, see 27–30 and Appendix 1.

early twentieth centuries: mountaineering as leisure sport.[55] Whereas in the eighteenth century, mountaineering was an activity for extraordinary scientists—the Mont Blanc, for instance, was first reached in 1786—, it turned into a pleasure sport at the end of the nineteenth century. The mountains lost their fearsome appearance and more and more men and women turned uphill: they left the secure valleys to explore Alpine pastures, glaciers, and the brittle rock of the mountains—just for fun. The long decade between 1850 and 1865 comprised the pinnacle of mountaineering in Switzerland—even the Matterhorn was successfully ascended in 1865; in the following decades, mountaineers turned eastwards exploring the Austrian Alps and the Dolomites. In addition to this, rock climbing as it was practiced by Wolf von Glanvell—in and of itself and no longer in the service of hiking and mountaineering—became increasingly famous. And the Dolomites became a playground for rock climbers.

The different "Alpenvereine," often founded in the 1860s, such as that of Austria in 1862, provided the institutional framework for mountain activities by supplying information, organizing trips, guiding groups, or offering cabins for overnight stays. Wolf von Glanvell did all of this: he offered a detailed description of the Dolomites for all kinds of tourists in his "Dolomitenführer" (1898), introduced beginners to mountaineering, published captivating accounts of his adventures, and discussed how to open up the Val Travenanzes to tourism by building a cabin.[56] In this regard, Wolf von Glanvell was a child of his time.

This is also true in another regard: mountaineering was a sport of the better-off, of members of the middle or upper class, and often of academics, and one may, without any hesitation, count Wolf von Glanvell among this social group: "Es waren Herrenbergsteiger, Adelige, Akademiker, die dennoch wochenlang in Zelten hausten, im Fels biwakierten oder im Heu der Almhütten nächtigten."[57] The long-term wilderness trips of Wolf von

55 On alpinism and the evolution of mountaineering, see Peter Grupp, *Faszination Berg. Die Geschichte des Alpinismus*, Köln / Weimar / Wien: Böhlau, 2008, 25–78; Andrea Hungerbühler, *"Könige der Alpen." Zur Kultur des Bergführerberufs*, Bielefeld: Transcript, 2013, 54–57; Manuel Burkhard, *Der Mönch und seine Berge. Pater Placidus Spescha (1752–1833) als Pionier und Vertreter des modernen Alpinismus* (Berner Forschungen zur Regionalgeschichte 19), Nordhausen: Traugott Bautz, 2016, at 34–47; Tait Keller, *Apostles of the Alps. Mountaineering and Nation Building in Germany and Austria, 1860–1939*, Chapell Hill: University of North Carolina, 2016, 17–118.

56 See 105–107.

57 Schmitt, "Viktor Wolf von Glanvell," 44.

Glanvell and his companions, like Scouts, reflects a longing for closeness to nature that was quite typical in the early twentieth century. Moreover, the nights spent in shepherds' huts allowed direct contact between social groups that normally never met in the late Austrian Empire: noble academics and simple shepherds. They shared a fire and roof (and also the fleas in the hay).[58]

It remains vague, however, whether another typical element of mountaineering around 1900 also applies to Wolf von Glanvell. Mountaineering was often associated with cultural conservatism and anti-modernism; mountaineers fled urban areas to return to nature, to escape from dirty, filthy towns and the pollution of the industrialized cities.[59] There is no doubt that Wolf von Glanvell slept in flea-infested huts and humble tents and that he enjoyed nature, but whether or not he also shared this inner attitude remains unknown.

Many of the most daring mountaineers of the nineteenth and early twentieth centuries fell to their deaths in the mountains, and so, too, did Wolf von Glanvell at a young age. On the weekend of May 6 and 7, 1905, he went climbing, as he often did on weekends. He left Graz on Saturday to exercise in the Hochschwab, some 50 km north of Graz, in preparation for his summer trips. Some friends joined him, and they spent the night from Saturday to Sunday at the "Fölzhotel" in Aflenz. They left early on Sunday morning and reached the Mitteralm where they split up: one group decided to take an easier, less challenging path; the other group, consisting of Wolf von Glanvell, Leo Petritsch,[60] and Gottlieb Stopper,[61] took a more difficult route up the rock face.[62] Although the two groups were far apart, they could observe each other. Suddenly, the group on the smoother path spotted something falling. Rocks? Or ... their comrades...? When Wolf von Glanvell and the others did not join them at the designated meeting point,

58 Obviously, the fleas were a torture: von Saar, "Zur Erschließung der Karnischen Voralpen [I]," 387: "Begrenzt ist der Raum, unbegrenzt jedoch die Menge der Flöhe!"

59 See, on the one hand Hungerbühler, *"Könige der Alpen,"* 64, on the other hand, with more critical reflections, Ben Anderson, *Cities, Mountains and Being Modern in fin-de-siècle England and Germany*, London: Palgrave Macmillan, 2020.

60 Leo Petritsch (1873?-1905) was "Finanz-Prokuratur-Konzipient" and "Privatdozent" at Karl-Franzens-Universität; brief biography: Grazer Volksblatt 1905 May 9 (Morgenausgabe), 4.

61 Gottlieb Stopper (1872–1905) was "Landesrechnungsoffizial." Short biography: Grazer Volksblatt 1905 May 9 (Morgenausgabe), 4.

62 According to Grazer Volksblatt 1905 May 9 (Morgenausgabe), 4.

they descended to reach out for a rescue mission. Wolf von Glanvell's wife, Mary, rushed to Aflenz on Monday, accompanied by Stopper's sister. By the time they arrived, a rescue team had already found her husband's body: bare, smashed, and with broken limbs, he had only a torn-off rope around his hips. Later, the broken bodies of Stopper and Petritsch were found. How could this accident happen? Wolf von Glanvell was known to be a very careful climber. Was it too early in the year and the rock still wet and fragile? Or did a herd of chamois cause a rock fall, hitting the group?[63] We still do not know. What is certain is that the life of a renowned alpinist, of a promising canonist, and of a young father came to an end at the rock face of Fölzstein that spring.[64]

63 This possibility was mentioned in: Grazer Volksblatt 1905 May 9 (Abendausgabe), 2.

64 The death of the three alpinists was widely reported in the news; it was mentioned in the following German-language Austrian newspapers (based on a research in https://anno.onb.ac.at; other newspapers, especially Italian and German ones, were not systematically included): Agramer Zeitung 1905 May 10, 5; Arbeiterwille (Organ des arbeitenden Volkes der Alpenländer) 1905 May 10, 3; Das interessante Blatt 1905 May 8, 1; Das Vaterland (Morgenblatt) 1905 May 9, 5; Das Vaterland 1905 May 10, 3; Deutsches Südmährerblatt 1905 May 12, 3; Freie Stimmen May 19, 9 and 1905 May 20, 7; Grazer Volksblatt 1905 May 9 (Morgenausgabe), 4, 1905 May 10 (Morgenausgabe), 3, and 1905 May 9 (Abendausgabe), 2; Kärntner Zeitung 1905 May 10, 5; Mährisches Tagblatt 1905 May 10, 6 and 1905 May 9, 7; Mährisch-Schlesische Presse 1905 May 10, 4; Marburger Zeitung [Maribor] 1905 May 9, 5; Neue Freie Presse 1905 May 9 (Morgenblatt), 9–10 and 1905 May 10 (Morgenblatt), 7; Neue Schlesische Zeitung 1905 May 14, 2; Neues Wiener Tagblatt 1905 May 9, 8 and 1905 May 10, 7–8; Neuigkeits-Welt-Blatt 1905 May 10 (2. und 3. Bogen), 1905 May 11 (3. Bogen), and 1905 May 11 (3. Bogen); Oesterreichische Kronen-Zeitung 1905 May 10, 5; Österreichische Land-Zeitung 1905 May 13, 12; Österreichische Touristenzeitung 1905 May 16, 126; Prager Tagblatt 1905 May 9, 10; Reichspost 1905 May 10, 5; Salzburger Chronik 1905 May 10, 5; Salzburger Chronik 1905 May 9, 5; Salzburger Volksblatt 1905 May 9, 3–4; Tagespost [Linz], 1905 May 10, 3; Volksblatt für Stadt und Land 1905 May 12, 3; Voralberger Tagblatt 1905 May 11, 3; Wiener Zeitung 1905 May 9, 2; Znaimer Wochenblatt 1905 May 10, 8. The death was also mentioned in: Rivista Mensile del Club Alpino Italiano 24, 1905, 203 (with obituary). German newspapers were just browsed randomly; death notices, for instance: Münchner Neueste Nachrichten 1905 May 9 (Morgenausgabe), 4 and 1905 May 10 (Morgenausgabe), 5; Allgemeine Zeitung 1905 May 10, 6.

Fig. 2: Viktor Wolf Edler von Glanvell (1902)

Epilogue. Shortly before his death, Wolf von Glanvell composed a poem.[65] A premonition? Or just a reflection of the melancholic "Zeitgeist"?

Einst ward ein Lied gesungen
Da droben hoch im Wald,
Nun ist der Ton verklungen,
Verloren und verhallt.

Doch dem, der's Liedchen sang,
Nicht mehr die Sonne glüht,
Er ruht am Bergeshang,
Wo's Edelweiß erblüht.

Allnächtig dann im Mondenschein,
Da klingt's herab ins Tal,
Wird wohl ein Gruß gewesen sein:
Ade, ihr Liebsten all.

65 Cited according to: N.N., "Wandern, Bergsteigen und das Lied," in: Österreichische Touristenzeitung 39, 1919, 150–152, at 151.

3. Alpine and Popular Scientific Publications

Although Wolf von Glanvell died quite young, he was a prolific author. Five academic publications, including three books, a popular scientific article, and a good number of alpine publications bear witness to his energy. Although the focus of this book is on his academic publications, the other works will also be presented, albeit briefly, in order to give a fuller picture of his life as an author.

In 1890, at the age of nineteen, Wolf von Glanvell shared his knowledge of Prags Dolomites with a wider public in his first book "Führer durch die Pragser Dolomiten."[66] In this book, he offered a thorough description of the region, including its mountains, paths, geographical measurements, and other information of interest to those traveling in the area. This regional guide was complemented by a more general guide titled "Dolomitenführer," published just eight years later, in which—similar to his first guide—he offered a description of the entire Dolomites.[67] He addressed both the mountaineering tourist as well as the tourist admiring the mountains from the bottom of a valley: "Bestimmt ist es [das Buch–SD] für alle Arten von Touristen, mögen sie nun im bequemen Landauer durch die Thäler fahren, gemüthlich über Jöcher bummeln oder mit Eispickel und Kletterschuh bewehrt zu den schroffen Zinnen hinanklimmen."[68]

---

66 Wolf von Glanvell, *Führer durch die Pragser Dolomiten*, Wien: K.K. Hof- und Universitätsbuchhandlung R. Lechner, 1890. Review: [J.A.], in: Mittheilungen des deutschen und österreichischen Alpenvereins 7 [17], 1891, 135; [J.M.], in: Österreichische Touristenzeitung 10, 1890, 155.

67 Wolf von Glanvell, *Dolomitenführer. Mit einer Übersichtskarte der Dolomiten im Massstabe 1:300.000*, Wien: Gerold, 1898. On this book, see: Richardi, *Erschließung*, 32–35.

68 Wolf von Glanvell, *Dolomitenführer*, III. Positive reviews, for instance, can be found in: Österreichische Touristenzeitung 18, 1898, 179, and also in: Allgemeine Sport-Zeitung 1899 January 1, 45–46: "Ein interessantes, ausführliches Buch, das sowohl erfahrenen, wie auch minder geübten Touristen zu empfehlen ist. Der Verfasser hat mit kundigem Blick das Wichtigste hervorgehoben, Unnützes bei Seite gelassen. Man erkennt in dem Buche deutlich seine Absicht, zwar kurz gefasst, aber doch vollständig zu sein, und dies ist ihm auch durchweg gelungen." For a slightly more critical review, as this book is aimed at the advanced climber, not the beginner, see: Der Gebirgsfreund 1898 September, 85.

In addition to this rather technical description of the Dolomites and possible expeditions there, he also published lively and colorful descriptions of his alpine adventures. It was primarily the "Österreichische Touristenzeitung" that published his descriptions of the tours he completed in various regions, including those in the Prags Dolomites,[69] the Sexten Dolomites,[70] the Dolomites of Val Gardena,[71] and in the Fanis-Tofana-Group,[72] among others.[73] Wolf von Glanvell also shared his knowledge of ropes (material, length, weight, and knots) with the reader,[74] and combined his legal expertise with his love for the mountains. He published a longer

69 Wolf von Glanvell, "Aus den Pragser Dolomiten," in: Österreichische Touristenzeitung 11, 1891, 1–5, 13–16, 25–28 and 12, 1892, 37–42, 49–51, 65–69, 77–81 and 13, 1893, 17–19, 29–31, 53–54, 69–71, 141–144, 169–172, and 15, 1895, 1–5, 25–29, and 17, 1897, 99–102.

70 Wolf von Glanvell, "Aus den Sextener Dolomiten," in: Österreichische Touristenzeitung 15, 1895, 269–273, 281–285 and 16, 1896, 53–56, 65–68, 81–85, 109–112.

71 Wolf von Glanvell, "Aus den Grödener Dolomiten," in: Österreichische Touristenzeitung 16, 1896, 213–218, 237–242 and 17, 1897, 13–17, 25–28.

72 Wolf von Glanvell, "Aus der Fanis-Tofanagruppe," in: Zeitschrift des deutschen und österreichischen Alpenvereins 35, 1904, 338–380.

73 Wolf von Glanvell, "Der Haunold. Eine topographisch-touristische Studie," in: Österreichische Touristenzeitung 13, 1893, 205–209, 217–221; Wolf von Glanvell, "Die Croda da Lago," in: Österreichische Touristenzeitung 14, 1894, 261–265; Wolf von Glanvell, "Die Thürme von Vajolett," in: Österreichische Touristenzeitung 15, 1895, 161–166, 173–176, 185–188; Wolf von Glanvell, "Die Croda di pausa marza 2503m," in: Österreichische Touristenzeitung 17, 1897, 261–265. A study of these "Tourenberichte" as a literary genre could also be of academic interest. They offer a certain view of the local population, admiring especially their strength and endurance, since the equipment was often carried to the final destination by locals in exchange for some money (von Saar, "Zur Erschließung der Karnischen Voralpen [I]," 386: "um drei bis vier Lire pro Tag tragen die Leute 30–40 kg schwere Lasten wohin man will", and again at 394: "... und nehmen einen ortskundigen Mann als Träger und Begleiter mit. Als verdorbenes Stadtkind verlangt er natürlich 7 Lire pro Tag, gegen 3 Lire seiner bäuerlichen Landsleute in Cimolais."). Whether they also reveal a slight form of colonialism in the Austrian Empire is a question that cannot be answered here. This idea is supported by the fact that they paid the shepherds to share their hut with them; a younger shepherd once received a "tip" for preparing their hay bed and was therefore called "Kammerdiener," which is also a play on words for the humble chamber in a hut (Wolf von Glanvell, "Aus der Fanis-Tofanagruppe," 350: "Nachdem wir noch den Jüngsten der Hirten, einen ganz intelligenten Badioten namens Ferdinand, gegen ein kleines Trinkgeld als 'Kammerdiener' für die allergröbsten Arbeiten aufgenommen hatten, traten wir ins Freie...."). In any case, it is quite striking that many of Wolf von Glanvell's reports end in a mountain cabin, a restaurant, or a bar, obviously to demonstrate the safe return of the mountaineer and to juxtapose the wild mountains with tame civilization.

74 Wolf von Glanvell, "Die Technik des Seiles," in: Österreichische Touristenzeitung 12, 1892, 151–153, 162–164.

study on tourism and law ("Touristik und Recht") in which he elaborated on the conflicts between tourists and landowners (1894).[75] Do landowners have the right to prevent unauthorized access? Can tourists use the various kinds of public (or even private) paths? And what would happen if someone acquired the plot of land where the "Three Peaks of Lavaredo" are located and demanded a fee to climb them?[76] The ensuing and apparently lively discussion on this topic sparked a second article on legal aspects of alpinism, namely on acquiring ownership of huntable animals, whether birds of prey or chamois.[77]

Wolf von Glanvell shared his legal knowledge not only with alpine colleagues, but also with a wider public. In early 1901, he gave a public introductory lecture on marriage law in Graz.[78] He provided an overview of the different legal systems in the Austrian Empire, discussed secular and canon law, prohibitive and impeding impediments, betrothal and marriage, including the dissolution of a marriage (divorce, separation from bed and

75 Wolf von Glanvell, "Touristik und Recht," in: Österreichische Touristenzeitung 14, 1894, 153–155, 165–168, 177–180, 189–192.

76 Wolf von Glanvell, "Touristik und Recht," 180: "Jemand erwirbt von dem bisherigen Eigenthümer das Terrain, auf welchem sich die bekannten Drei Zinnen in den Dolomiten befinden. [...] Der betreffende neue Erwerber hätte nun den Einfall, das Betreten seines Gebietes, also auch das Besteigen der Drei Zinnen, rundweg zu verbieten, wozu er als Eigenthümer vollständig berechtigt wäre [...]; oder er würde eine Besteigung nur gegen eine Art von Entrée erlauben." Wolf von Glanvell discussed the economic consequences for the local guides and for tourism in general, but could not develop a legal solution, since a servitude ("Wegeservitut") would take 30–40 years to come into being, and the "Grosse Zinne" was not climbed until 1869. Such a climbing fee exists today in the Himalayas, albeit for different reasons.
Brief note of this article in the Rivista mensile del Club Alpino Italiano 14, 1895, 492: "Turistica e Diritto. É un lungo articolo che si occupa di strade, proprietà di terreni e catasto, beni demaniali, riserve di caccia, ecc., in rapporto al movimento dei turisti; sonvi numerosissime citazioni di leggi, decreti, decisioni giudiziarie, scritti che trattano l'identica questione, fra i quali trovammo ricordati quelli del nostro 'Bollettino' sulle proprietà dei ghiacciai. Crediamo però che la questione come è trattata dal sig. Wolf von Glanvell possa in gran parte valere solo per le Alpi Austriache, dove esistono ancora molti privilegi feudali e consuetudini antiche tuttora osservate."

77 Wolf von Glanvell, "Ueber das Eigenthum an den jagdbaren Thieren. Ein Nachwort zu 'Touristik und Recht,'" in: Österreichische Touristenzeitung 15, 1895, 73–76, 89–92.

78 Grazer Volksblatt 1901 January 6 (Morgenausgabe), 7: "Privatdocent D. Victor Wolf Edler von Glanvell: Ueber Eherecht. Freitag den 1., 8., und 15. Februar im Mädchen-Turnsaale Marschallgasse Nr. 11." See also the announcement: Grazer Volksblatt 1901 February 8, 3.

board).[79] These lectures were later published in the new journal "Das Wissen für alle," which aimed at deeper education and broader knowledge ("vertiefte Bildung und reicheres Wissen") for the whole population, as it was once advertised.[80]

In addition to alpine and popular scientific publications, he also authored purely academic publications, namely editions of medieval texts and works on institutional history. They are, of course, the focus of this study.

79 For brief summaries of the three presentations, see: Grazer Tagblatt 1901 February 4 (Abendausgabe), 2; Grazer Tagblatt 1901 February 11 (Abendausgabe), 5; Grazer Tagblatt 1901 February 18 (Abendausgabe), 2.

80 Wolf von Glanvell, "Österreichisches Eherecht," in: Das Wissen für alle. Volksthümliche Vorträge und populär wissenschaftliche Rundschau 1, 1901, 701–704, 724–728, 744–747, 763–767. This publication was advertised in: Neues Wiener Journal 1901 March 24, 21: "[...] Der Beweis ist damit erbracht, daß diese Wochenschrift einem allgemeinen und wirklichen Bedürfnisse entspricht, dem Bedürfnisse nach vertiefter Bildung und reicherem Wissen, das sich in allen Kreisen und Schichten der Bevölkerung in der lebhaftesten Weise geltend macht." On this journal, see Klaus Taschwer, "Das Wissen für Alle. Annäherungen an das populärwissenschaftliche Zeitschriftenwesen um 1900," in: Relation. Medien–Gesellschaft–Geschichte 4, 1997, 17–50.

4. Editions of Medieval Canon Law

4.1. The Edition of the Manuscript Vat. lat. 1348

4.1.1. Discovering a Manuscript in the Vatican Library

On Monday, October 7, 1895, Wolf von Glanvell, a young scholar of 24 years, arrived in Rome. Only a month before, the Austrian "Ministerium für Cultus und Unterricht" had granted him a "Roman Fellowship" for a five-month research stay in Rome.[81] A few days later, on October 11, Theodor von Sickel (1826–1908), the founder and director of the "Istituto Austriaco di studii storici" (Austrian Historical Institute) in Rome, introduced him to the Vactican Library and the Vatican Archives. Wolf von Glanvell intended to study manuscripts pertaining to Eastern canon law and the canonical process as well as pre-Gratian canonical collections.[82] Friedrich Maassen and Johann Friedrich von Schulte had already studied collections up to the

81 According to Wolf von Glanvell's first "Arbeitsbericht" (Roma, Istituto Storico Austriaco, Archiv I 3, Glanvell 1, 1–2 ("Arbeitsbericht der ordentlichen Mitglieder des Istituto Austriaco degli Studi Storici, Dr. Victor Wolf von Glanvell für die Arbeitsperiode vom 10. October bis 10. November 1895," 1895 November 14). The notice of granting (Zl. 20.104/1895, dating to 1895 September 5), however, is not preserved in Wien, Österreichisches Staatsarchiv, AVA, Unterricht-Allg., Karton 705 (friendly information of the archive, 2021 April 23). Such a "Roman Fellowhip" was granted to scholars working on the history of the Middle Ages and the centuries that followed, esp. "politische Geschichte, Kirchen-, Cultur-, Rechts-, Kunstgeschichte u.s.w.," cf. Statut für das Istituto austriaco di studii storici in Rom, esp. § 4, in: Verordnungsblatt für den Dienstbereich des Ministeriums für Cultus und Unterricht 1893 (1893 October 15), 294–296. The previous statutes dated to 1883: Provisorisches Statut, betreffend die Errichtung von Stipendien zum Betriebe wissenschaftlicher Studien in Rom (römische Stipendien), in: Verordnungsblatt für den Dienstbereich des Ministeriums für Cultus und Unterricht 1883 (1883 August 1), 200–202.

82 Cf. Wien, IÖG, Nachlass Sickel, Letter from Viktor Wolf von Glanvell to Theodor von Sickel, 1895 June 21: "... außer Arbeiten auf dem Gebiete des canonischen Prozesses möchte ich mich auch mit dem orientalischen (griechischen) Kirchenrecht beschäftigen, worüber nach der Meinung des Herrn Professor Dr. Thaner in Rom sehr viel Material zu finden sein dürfte." Procedural law was later researched and edited by the Austrian professor Ludwig Wahrmund (1860–1932), see 85.

ninth century and from the post-Gratian period, respectively,[83] but they left a gap that Wolf von Glanvell strove to fill, namely the tenth, eleventh and first half of the twelfth centuries. In the weeks that followed, he browsed the repertories of the Vatican Library to familiarize himself with its holdings and to identify a manuscript worthy of study:

> "Um nun eine Übersicht über das vorhandene Material zu erhalten, was natürlich vor allem notwendig war, gieng ich nun die vielbändigen Inventare der Vaticana, Ottoboniana, Regina, Palatina, Urbina und Capponiana genau durch, notierte mir alles brauchbar scheinende und ließ mir dann die einzelnen Codices kommen, um dieselben dann zu bestimmen, und ein oder das andere Stück eventuell zu bearbeiten."[84]

According to his first "Arbeitsbericht" to the Austrian Historical Institute, he examined manuscripts that represented a kind of "best hits" of pre-Gratian material, namely the *Collectio Hispana Gallica Augustodunensis* (Vat. lat. 1341), the *Collectio Hibernensis* (Vat. lat. 1349), a "Collection in 20 Books" (Vat. lat. 1350), the *Collectio Caesaraugustana* (Vat. lat. 4976 and Vat. lat. 5715), the *Collectio Dionysio-Hadriana* (Vat. lat. 7222), the *Tripartita* (Reg. lat. 973), the *Decretales* of Pseudo-Isidore (Reg. lat. 976 and Reg. lat. 1038), the *Collectio Anselmo Dedicata* (Vat. lat. 4899, Pal. lat. 580, and Pal. lat. 581), the *Collectio Duodecim Partium* (Pal. lat. 584), the *Collectio Dacheriana* (Ottobon. lat. 261), the *Collectio Avellana* (Ottobon. lat. 1105), and the *Epitome Hispana* (Ottobon. lat. 3295), among others. He also discovered an unknown collection of canons in the manuscript Vat. lat. 1348 which aroused his interest.[85]

---

83 Friedrich Maassen, *Geschichte der Quellen und der Literatur des canonischen Rechts im Abendlande bis zum Ausgange des Mittelalters*, vol. 1, Graz: Leuschner & Lubensky, 1870; Johann Friedrich von Schulte, *Die Geschichte der Quellen und Literatur des Canonischen Rechts von Gratian bis auf die Gegenwart*, vol. 1: *Einleitung. Die Geschichte der Quellen und Literatur von Gratian bis auf Papst Gregor IX.*, Stuttgart: Ferdinand Enke, 1875.

84 Roma, Istituto Storico Austriaco, Archiv I 3, Glanvell 1, 1–2 ("Arbeitsbericht der ordentlichen Mitglieder des Istituto Austriaco degli Studi Storici, Dr. Victor Wolf von Glanvell für die Arbeitsperiode vom 10. October bis 10. November 1895," 1895 November 14).

85 Roma, Istituto Storico Austriaco, Archiv I 3, Glanvell 1, 2 ("Arbeitsbericht der ordentlichen Mitglieder des Istituto Austriaco degli Studi Storici, Dr. Victor Wolf von Glanvell für die Arbeitsperiode vom 10. October bis 10. November 1895," 1895 November 14): "Auf diese Weise habe ich studiert Cod. Vatican. lat. 1341, 1348, 1349, 1350, 4899, 4976, 5715, 5920, 7222; Cod. Vatican. Regina 973, 976, 1038; Cod. Vatican. Palatina 152, 580, 581, 584; Cod. Vatican. Ottoboniana 238, 261, 474, 1105, 3295 und

In October and November 1895, he made a transcription of this manuscript and identified the origin of the canons, namely Pseudo-Isidore's writings, Burchard's *Decretum*, Ivo's collections, and penitentials. This was an arduous task, since the canons were often based on different parts of a *fons materialis* or even on different *fontes*, i.e. sources; in addition to this, the inscriptions included above the canons were repeatedly flawed:

> "Ich ging dabei in der Weise vor, dass ich auch stets bestrebt war aufzuzeigen, wo sich der Text der betreffenden Stelle gedruckt finden lässt, eine Arbeit, welche z.B. bei Stellen, die aus verschiedenen Sätzen eines Kapitels oder gar verschiedener Werke (oft mehrerer Autoren) compiliert sind, keine Geringe ist. Dazu kommt noch der Umstand, dass die Quellenangaben meiner Sammlung sehr oft unrichtig sind, was—um nur eine anzuführen—bei den mit 'Ex registro Gregorii' bezeichneten Kapiteln fast ausnahmslos der Fall ist, indem diese meist aus allerlei anderen Briefen, nur nicht denen Gregors VII. stammen."[86]

The edition of the collection was hampered by the fact that the *fontes* of some canons had not yet been printed—Wolf von Glanvell had to study other manuscripts to identify their origin.[87]

By the end of 1895, he had completed his study of Vat. lat. 1348 and moved on to another subject. Father Heinrich Denifle, OP (1844–1905),

---

mich dann entschlossen, den Cod. Vatican. lat. 1348, über welchen sich meines Wissens in der Literatur keinerlei Notizen vorfin-den, zu bearbeiten." Some notes on Wolf von Glanvell's research in Rome: Karl Rudolf, "Geschichte des Österreichischen Historischen Instituts in Rom von 1881–1938," in: Römische Historische Mitteilungen 23, 1981, 1–137, at 56. The Biblioteca Apostolica Vaticana has no record of Wolf von Glanvell as a library user (kindly communicated by the Vatican Library, 2021 June 1).

86 Roma, Istituto Storico Austriaco, Archiv I 3, Glanvell 2, 1 ("Arbeitsbericht der Mitglieder des Istituto Austriaco degli Studi Storici in Rom, Dr. Victor Wolf Edlen von Glanvell für die Arbeitsperiode vom 10. November bis 27. December 1895," 1895 December 27).

87 Roma, Istituto Storico Austriaco, Archiv I 3, Glanvell 3, 1 ("Arbeitsbericht der ordentlichen Mitglieder des Istituto Austriaco degli Studi Storici in Rom, Dr. Victor Wolf Edlen von Glanvell für die Arbeitsperiode vom 10. Januar bis 10. Februar 1896," 1896 February 9): "Die Bestimmung einiger canones des Cod. Vatic. lat. 1348 bot zum Schluss insofern unerwartete Schwierigkeiten, als deren Text in keinem der hier vorhandenen Druckwerke aufzufinden war und daher für die Stücke, welche sämmtlich bloß die vage Bezeichnung 'ex ordine Romano' führen, auf Handschriften zurückgegriffen werden musste, zumal die hauptsächlich in Betracht kommende Publication–Mabillon's 'Iter italicum'–vollständig im Stiche ließ."

theologian and archivist at the Vatican Archives,[88] had pointed out an unexplored text by Raymond of Penyaforte, the seminal canonist of the early thirteenth century and compiler of the *Liber Extra*.[89] Wolf von Glanvell searched the entire Borghese-library, some 350 manuscripts, for the codex —but to no avail. Denifle therefore assumed, as Wolf von Glanvell wrote in his "Schlussbericht," that the codex must have simply disappeared ("der betreffende Codex müsse eben unter der Hand weggekommen sein").[90]

Wolf von Glanvell ended his quest for codices on February 8, 1896, and returned to Graz. The result of four months in Roman libraries was a description and analysis of one pre-Gratian canonical collection.[91] He intended to promptly publish his results and thereby contribute to the discussion of canon law before Gratian:

> "Der von mir eingehend bearbeitete Cod. Vatic. lat. 1348, welcher eine fünfbücherige Canonessammlung ca. aus dem Jahre 1100 enthält, ist bisher wohl gänzlich unbekannt gewesen; in wenigen Monaten gedenke ich mit der Zusammenfassung der Ergebnisse der Bestimmung der einzelnen Canones und der Vergleichung mit mehr oder minder verwandten Sammlungen so weit zu sein, um die ganze Arbeit—vielleicht

---

88 On Denifle, see Michael Schmaus, "Denifle, Heinrich Suso," in: Neue Deutsche Biographie 3, 1957, 595–597 and the contributions in: Andreas Sohn / Jacques Verger / Michael Zink (ed.), *Heinrich Denifle (1844–1905). Un savant dominicain entre Graz, Rome et Paris. Ein dominikanischer Gelehrter zwischen Graz, Rom und Paris*, Paris: Académie des Inscriptions et Belles-Lettres, 2015.

89 On Raymond, see Jörg Müller, "Raymundus de Penyafort," in: Michael Stolleis (ed.), Juristen. Ein biographisches Lexikon. Von der Antike bis zum 20. Jahrhundert, München: Beck, 1995, 511–512; Dennis Theiß, "Raimund de Peñaforte (1175/80–1275)," in: Albrecht Cordes et al. (ed.), Handwörterbuch zur Deutschen Rechtsgeschichte, 2nd edition, vol. 4, Berlin: Erich Schmidt, 2022, 1000–1002.

90 Roma, Istituto Storico Austriaco, Archiv I 3, Glanvell 4, 1 ("Schlussbericht des Mitgliedes des Istituto Austriaco degli Studi Storici in Rom Dr. Victor Wolf Edlen von Glanvell," 1896 March 9).

91 Roma, Istituto Storico Austriaco, Archiv I 3, Glanvell 3, 1 ("Arbeitsbericht der ordentlichen Mitglieder des Istituto Austriaco degli Studi Storici in Rom, Dr. Victor Wolf Edlen von Glanvell für die Arbeitsperiode vom 10. Januar bis 10. Februar 1896," 1896 February 9). According to a "Journal über die Arbeitszeit vom 12. October 1895 bis zum 8. Februar 1896" added to this "Arbeitsbericht," he spent most of his time in the Vatican Library, but also in the Biblioteca Casanatense, the Biblioteca Vittorio-Emmanuele, and the Biblioteca Alessandrina. Only one day was free: "1. Februar 1896: Ausflug nach Tagliacozzo." The remark by von Saar, "Nachruf," 122 that Wolf von Glanvell visited the Abruzzo, may refer to this trip. On his way back from Rome to Graz, he stopped in Florence, Bologna, and Ravenna (Wien, IÖG, Nachlass Sickel, Letter from Viktor Wolf von Glanvell to Theodor von Sickel, 1896 April 10).

durch die k. Academie der Wissenschaften—publicieren zu können. Und ich hoffe, es wird damit ein neuer und nicht unwichtiger Beitrag zur Kenntnis der vorgratianischen Canonessammlungen geliefert sein."[92]

4.1.2. The Edition: Method, Results, Reception

Two years later, Wolf von Glanvell presented the results of his research in the Vatican Library to a wider audience. As planned, he published an analysis of Vat. lat. 1348 in the "Sitzungsberichte der philosophisch-historischen Classe der kaiserlichen Akademie der Wissenschaften" (1897).[93] He offered an incipit-explicit-edition of this pre-Gratian canonical collection, including a formal description of the manuscript, and the *fontes materiales* of the canons. He supplemented his presentation of this collection with some observations on the intention of the compiler. According to Wolf von Glanvell, the collection was compiled around 1100—1106 at the latest—and contained a reform collection divided into five books with almost modern views ("Reformsammlung im besten Sinne des Wortes mit fast modernen Anschauungen").[94] It was heavily based on writings by Pseudo-Isidore, but also on Burchard's *Decretum*, Anselm of Lucca's collection, and the *Collectio Anselmo Dedicata*, and it was interdependent with a smaller collection called the *Collectio septem partium*.[95]

Where does this study belong within the context of research at the end of the nineteenth century? Wolf von Glanvell was inspired by Paul Fournier, a renowned French legal historian (1853–1935), who devoted his academic life to the study of medieval canon law.[96] In 1894, Fournier published a seminal study on the "Collection in 74 Titels" (*Diversorum patrum sententiae*),

---

92 Roma, Istituto Storico Austriaco, Archiv I 3, Glanvell 4, 1 ("Schlussbericht des Mitgliedes des Istituto Austriaco degli Studi Storici in Rom Dr. Victor Wolf Edlen von Glanvell," 1896 March 9).

93 Wolf von Glanvell, "Die Canonessammlung des Cod. Vatican. lat. 1348," in: Sitzungsberichte der philosophisch-historischen Classe der kaiserlichen Akademie der Wissenschaften 136, Wien 1897 as "II. Abhandlung" (1–55). Short note on this publication in: Deutsche Zeitschrift für Kirchenrecht 8, 1898, 123 and 9, 1900, 425–426.

94 Wolf von Glanvell, "Canonessammlung," 55.

95 A digital copy of the manuscript is available at https://digi.vatlib.it/view/MSS_Vat.lat.1348.

96 Brigitte Basdevant-Gaudemet / Rafael Domingo, "Paul Fournier (1853–1935)," in: Olivier Deschamps / Rafael Domingo (ed.), Great Christian Jurists in French History, Cambridge: Cambridge University Press, 2019, 309–323, esp. 311–318. On Fournier and his influence: Rolker, "Fournier's Model and Its Merits," 4–32.

which served as a model for Wolf von Glanvell. In an "Arbeitsbericht" for the Austrian Historical Institute, Wolf von Glanvell briefly presented the newly discovered collection Vat. lat. 1348 and explained how it should be analyzed:

> "[Ich habe] mich dann entschlossen, den Cod. Vatican. lat. 1348, über welchen sich meines Wissens in der Literatur keinerlei Notizen vorfinden, zu bearbeiten. Der besagte Codex enthält außer einem bis auf Paschal II. reichenden Papstkataloge und eine 'Cronica Ysidori' eine mäßig große Canones-Sammlung in 5 Büchern, welche nach Anlage und Tendenz offenbar den von P. Fournier so genannten Reformsammlungen beizuzählen ist, und welche ich in der Art zu behandeln gedenke, wie die z.B. Fournier (Mélanges Bd. XIV, pg. 147–222, 285–290)[97] mit einer anderen Sammlung derselben Epoche gethan hat."[98]

Fournier structured his analysis of the "Collection in 74 Titles" as follows: He began with an introduction and the state of the art (147–150), described the manuscripts (150–154), and offered an incipit-explicit-edition, including the *fontes materiales* (154–186). Fournier also analyzed the sources of the collection (187–190) and its structure and content (190–191), before gathering observations on its origin (place and date of compilation) (191–202), its originality (202–203), and its influence and reception (203–222). Wolf von Glanvell chose exactly the same structure for his edition: introduction and state of the art (in his case: "unbekannt," "neu") (1), description of the manuscript (2–3), incipit-explicit-edition with *fontes materiales* (3–50), sources (i.e. *fontes formales*) (50–52), content and structure (52–54), falsely attributed canons (54), place and date (54–55), reception and main character (55).

How are we to assess Wolf von Glanvell's work in the light of late nineteenth-century scholarship and more recent reassessments? First, by choosing the distinguished French master Paul Fournier as his model, Wolf von Glanvell analyzed the codex Vat. lat. 1348 according to the methodolog-

97 Wolf von Glanvell referred to: Paul Fournier, "Le premier manuel canonique de la réforme du XIe siècle," in: Mélanges d'archéologie et d'histoire de l'École française de Rome 14, 1894, 147–223, 285–290 (reprint: Paul Fournier, *Mélanges de droit canonique*, vol. 2, ed. Theo Kölzer, Aalen: Scientia Verlag, 1983, as Nr. 19 (551–633)).

98 Roma, Istituto Storico Austriaco, Archiv I 3, Glanvell 1, 1 ("Arbeitsbericht von Victor Wolf von Glanvell für die Arbeitsperiode vom 10. October bis 10. November 1895," 1895 November 14). He repeated the reference to Paul Fournier and his method in his printed edition of this collection, see Wolf von Glanvell, "Canonessammlung," 1.

ical standards of the late nineteenth century.[99] By the standards of the time, his edition is a fine piece of work, even though he omitted four canons,[100] misread some words,[101] and erred in the identification of some sources.[102]

Second, his assumption that the collection was of Italian origin turned out to be correct. Wolf von Glanvell hesitated to locate it in Florence, even though the manuscript stemmed from a monastery there:[103] "aber daraus zu schliessen, das ein dortiger Mönch der Verfasser war, wäre doch wohl zu gewagt."[104] Research today is less cautious, since the repetitive *aliud*—instead of *De eodem*—is a known Florentine feature.[105] The method by which he dated this collection is, however, still commonly used: the *terminus post quem* is determined by the most recent canon, that of Gregory VII (1073–1085);[106] the *terminus ante quem* is determined by the end of the pontificate

---

99 Today, one might prefer a complete edition to an incipit-explicit-edition, and one would also add the *fontes formales*, the formal sources of the canons. For the reception of Fournier's contribution, see, for instance, the review in: AKKR 75, 1896, 174–175, at 175: "vortreffliche Orientirung."

100 Herbert Hees, "Zur Collectio quinque Librorum (Cod. Vat. lat. 1348)," in: BMCL 4, 1974, 63–64.

101 For corrections, see: Joseph Motta, "I rapporti tra la Collezione canonica di S. Maria Novella e quella in Cinque Libri. Firenze, Bibl. Naz. Conventi Soppressi MS A.4.269 e Bibl. Vaticana, Vat. lat. 1348," in: BMCL 7, 1977, 89–94, at 90–91. A modern description of the manuscript is offered by: Stephan Kuttner / Reinhard Elze, *A Catalogue of Canon and Roman Law Manuscripts in the Vatican Library*, vol. 1: *Codices Vaticani latini 541–2299* (Studi e Testi 322), Città del Vaticano: Biblioteca Apostolica Vaticana, 1986, 106–108 and Joseph Motta, *Liber canonum diuersorum sanctorum patrum siue Collectio in CLXXXIII titulos digesta* (MIC B/7), Città del Vaticano: Biblioteca Apostolica Vaticana, 1988, xli–xlii. Some remarks on this manuscript also by Giorgio Picasso, *Collezioni canoniche Milanesi del secolo XII*, Milano: Vita e Pensiero, 1969, 33.

102 Cf. Hubert Mordek, *Kirchenrecht und Reform im Frankenreich. Die Collectio Vetus Gallica, die älteste systematische Kanonessammlung des fränkischen Gallien. Studien und Edition* (Beiträge zur Geschichte und Quellenkunde des Mittelalters 1), Berlin / New York: De Gruyter, 1975, 201 n. 529.

103 Vat. lat. 1348, fol. 13r: *Iste liber est monasterii sancte marie de angelis de florentia.*

104 Wolf von Glanvell, "Canonessammlung," 55.

105 Linda Fowler-Magerl, *Clavis Canonum. Selected Canon Law Collections Before 1140. Access with data processing*, Hannover: Hahn'sche Buchhandlung, 2005, 102.

106 On this canon (1.37.1; from a synod in 1074), see Motta, *Liber canonum*, xliii; John Gilchrist, "The Reception of Pope Gregory VII into the Canon Law (1073–1141) (part 2)," in: ZRG.KA 66, 1980, 192–229, at 206, and also Arturo Bernal Palacios, "La redacción breve del c. 'In die ressurectionis' en las colecciones canónicas pregracianas," in: Peter Landau / Jörg Müller (ed.), Proceedings of the Ninth International Congress of Medieval Canon Law, Munich, 13–18 July 1992 (MIC C/10), Città del Vaticano: Biblioteca Apostolica Vaticana, 1997, 923–952, at 926.

of Paschal II (1098–1118), since the catalogue of popes that followed the collection—written in the same hand as the collection—names Paschal, but omits the years of his regency. Similarly, the catalogue of emperors ends with Henry IV (1056–1106). Wolf von Glanvell concludes that the manuscript was written "wohl vor 1106 oder spätestens in diesem Jahr."[107] His *terminus post quem* is fully accepted and his *terminus ante quem* is more or less accepted.[108]

Third, by editing the collection in Vat. lat. 1348, Wolf von Glanvell unwittingly opened a can of worms: the Italian canonical collections of around 1100, their reworkings, realignments, abbreviations, and excerpts still puzzle historians. In his analysis, Wolf von Glanvell pointed to a certain *Collectio septem partium* and a "Pistojeser Sammlung" that were related to his manuscript. The first is easy to identify: it is the manuscript Vat. lat. 1346 which contains the "Collection in 7 Books."[109] The other collection is more difficult to pin down. Wolf von Glanvell offered no information that can be used to identify it, stating only: "Eine vollständige Abschrift derselben besitzt Herr Professor Dr. Friedrich Thaner."[110] Nevertheless, the only manuscript from the Chapter Library in Pistoia which fits thematically is C. 135, a copy of the "Collection in 3 Books."[111]

Wolf von Glanvell discovered a close relationship ("ein inniger Zusammenhang") between Vat. lat. 1346 and Vat. lat. 1348, as they shared many canons.[112] He was aware, however, that further research was needed to determine the exact nature of their relationship: "Welche von beiden Samm-

107 Wolf von Glanvell, "Canonessammlung," 55.

108 Lotte Kéry, *Canonical Collections of the Early Middle Ages* (History of medieval canon law 1), Washington D.C.: Catholic University of America Press, 1999, 217: "written during the pontificate of Paschal II (1099–1118)."

109 Wolf von Glanvell referred to Ferdinand Walter, *Lehrbuch des Kirchenrechts aller christlichen Confessionen*, 13th edition, Bonn: Adolph Marcus, 1861, 234 (as Nr. 29): "Eine ungedruckte Sammlung in sieben Büchern, die unter Paschalis II., also zwischen 1102 und 1118, verfaßt ist. Sie ist insbesondere aus Anselmus, dann aus der dem Anselmus dedicierten und aus der eben genannten Sammlung in drei Abtheilungen gezogen." and also to Augustin Theiner, *Disquisitiones criticae in praecipuas canonum et decretalium collectiones seu Sylloges Gallandianae dissertationum de vetustis canonum collectionibus continuatio*, Rome: Collegium Urbinum, 1836, 345–355.

110 Wolf von Glanvell, "Canonessammlung," 52.

111 Kéry, *Canonical Collections*, 117 (C. 101: *Capitula Angilramni*), 141 (C. 125: *Decretum Burchardi*), 103 (C. 130: Pseudo-Isidore, *Decretales*), 270 (C. 135: *Collectio 3 Librorum*), 141 (C. 140: *Decretum Burchardi*).

112 Wolf von Glanvell, "Canonessammlung," 51.

lungen jedoch die ältere ist, ob die vorliegende oder die 'coll. septem part.,' und ob sie nicht vielleicht gar beide auf eine dritte zurückzuführen seien, lässt sich, so lange die 'coll. septem part.' nicht eingehend untersucht worden ist, nicht behaupten."[113] Subsequent research has indeed shed light on this thorny issue. Wolf von Glanvell's hunch that the two collections might have a common ancestor has been confirmed: Vat. lat. 1348 is a reworking of the "Collection in 183 Titles," also known as *Collectio Santa Maria Novella*, which also influenced the "Collection in 7 Books" in Vat. lat. 1346.[114]

Wolf von Glanvell also correctly pointed to the relation between Vat. lat. 1348 and the "Collection in 3 Books" (this is the "Pistojeser Handschrift"), since the latter is also based on the *Collectio Santa Maria Novella* (among other *fontes formales*, of course).[115] And he even suggested a connection between Vat. lat. 1348 and Gratian's *Decretum*: "dass die Quelle zweier Stellen aus Gratian's Decrete von bisher unbekannter Provenienz in meiner Sammlung zu suchen ist."[116] This was, of course, a bit of an exaggeration, but not too far-fetched: the "Collection in 3 Books" served as a major source for Gratian, which may explain Wolf von Glanvell's impression that his collection influenced Gratian.

In hindsight, the first work of the young scholar Wolf von Glanvell was a skillful, up-to-date, and thorough analysis of an unknown canonical collection.[117] Despite these qualities, it was condemned to a shadowy exis-

113 Wolf von Glanvell, "Canonessammlung," 52.

114 See, for instance, Paul Fournier / Gabriel Le Bras, *Histoire des collections canoniques en occident. Dépuis les fausses décrétales jusqu'au décret de Gratien*, vol. 2, Paris: Sirey, 1932 (reprint 1972), 135; Fowler-Magerl, *Clavis Canonum*, 232, and especially Peter Landau, "Die Quellen der mittelitalienischen Kanonessammlung in sieben Büchern (MS Vat. lat. 1346)," in: Kathleen G. Cushing / Richard F. Gyug (ed.), Ritual, Text and Law. Studies in Medieval Canon Law and Liturgy presented to Roger E. Reynolds (Church, Faith and Culture in the Medieval West), Aldershot: Ashgate, 2004, 255–268, esp. at 267. The "Collection in 183 Titles" is edited by Motta, *Liber Canonum* (1988).

115 On this connection, see Motta, *Liber canonum*, xliv–xlvi.

116 Wolf von Glanvell, "Canonessammlung," 52.

117 Cf. Johann Baptist Sägmüller, "Review of 'Wolf von Glanvell, Studien aus dem kanonischen Privatrecht' and 'Wolf von Glanvell, Die Kanonessammlung des Cod. Vatican. lat. 1348,'" in: Theologische Quartalschrift 83, 1901, 626–629, at 629: "Auf Grund guter, methodisch geführter Untersuchung kann er [Wolf von Glanvell] sagen, ..." Friedrich Thaner reported to the Faculty of Law (Graz, Universitätsarchiv, Jur. Fak., Z. 303 ex 1897/98, 1897 November): "Das Hauptverdienst dieser Arbeit besteht darin, daß ungeachtet der ungenauen und theilweise irreführenden Quellenangaben im Codex selbst, die wirklichen Quellen zu den einzelnen Kapiteln (nahezu 700) aufgefunden und so genau bezeichnet sind, daß sich der vollständige In-

tence. The reason is obvious: the manuscript Vat. lat. 1348 stands alone. Neither other copies of the collection nor any other collections based on Vat. lat. 1348 were ever discovered—it thus languished in a library.[118] "Le seul intérêt qu'elle présente," declared Fournier / Le Bras in 1932, "est de faire connaître les matériaux dont disposait, à la fin du règne de Grégoire VII, un canoniste italien, probablement toscan, en même temps que ses tendances et ses préoccupations."[119] When choosing a manuscript in the reading room of the Vatican Library, Wolf von Glanvell picked a marginal collection without any noticeable influence in the Middle Ages. This may explain why his edition did not receive much scholarly attention.[120] Nonetheless, his edition remained the sole scholarly work on Vat. lat. 1348 for almost 100 years; only in 1988 did Joseph Motta publish a new edition, namely a list of canons, as an appendix to his edition of the "Collection in 183 Titles."[121]

halt der Sammlung aus demselben rekonstruieren läßt. Eine solche Arbeit erfordert nicht bloß großen Aufwand an Zeit und Mühe, sie kann auch ohne große Belesenheit und einen ziemlich hohen Grad an Spürsinn überhaupt nicht zum Ziele führen. Dass der Verfasser diese Gaben besitzt, ist für ihn umso empfehlender, als gerade für das canonische Recht noch vieles handschriftliche Material in Bibliotheken und Archiven unverwerthet begraben liegt. Derselbe unterließ es nicht, die Sammlung nach allgemeinen gut gewählten Gesichtspunkten zu characterisieren und wenn auch gegen Einzelheiten Widerspruch zu erheben ist, so kann sein Urtheil doch im Großen und Ganzen als zutreffend bezeichnet werden." Arnold Luschin von Ebengreuth reported a similar impression to the Faculty: Graz, Universitätsarchiv, Jur. Fak., Z. 304 ex 1897/98 (s.d.). See Appendix 4 and Fig. 3.

118 Hubert Mordek, "Systematische Kanonessammlungen vor Gratian: Forschungsstand und neue Aufgaben," in: Stephan Kuttner / Kenneth Pennington (ed.), Proceedings of the Sixth International Congress of Medieval Canon Law, Berkeley, California, 28 July-2 August 1980 (MIC C/7), Città del Vaticano: Biblioteca Apostolica Vaticana, 1985, 185–201, at 193 used—in a different context—the term "hochmittelalterliches Dornröschendasein" to describe the non-reception of a canonical collection.

119 Fournier / Le Bras, *Histoire des collections canoniques II*, 135.

120 The edition by Wolf von Glanvell is used, for instance, by Howard Adelson / Robert Baker, "The Oath of Purgation of Pope Leo III in 800," in: Traditio 8, 1952, 35–80, at 40 n. 18.

121 Motta, *Liber canonum*, 303–324.

4.2. The Edition of Deusdedit's Collectio canonum

The second medieval text edited by Viktor Wolf von Glanvell was Deusdedit's canonical collection, the *Collectio canonum*. Deusdedit was a Benedictine monk in Tulle (Limoges), before he was appointed cardinal priest of the church *Sanctorum Apostolorum* in Eudoxia (today's San Pietro in Vincoli) some time prior to November 1, 1078. He died on March 1, 1098 or 1099. He was a poet and the author of some *carmina*, and, above all an outspoken defender of the reform movement in the Church, which he argued for in the *Libellus contra invasores et symoniacos* (around 1097), as well as in his *Collectio canonum* (before 1087).[122]

Deusdedit's collection was one of the "famous" collections of the Gregorian reform and it was therefore studied from a very early date. The *Correctores Romani*, for instance, used the collection for their reworking of the *Decretum* of Gratian in the sixteenth century, Cesare Baronius exploited it for his *Annales ecclesiastici*, and Giovanni Domenico Mansi used it for his history of councils.[123] Friedrich Carl von Savigny referred to Roman law fragments in Deusdedit's collection[124] and Theodor von Sickel used the manuscript for his book "Das Privilegium Otto I. für die römische Kirche."[125] Compared to other, especially minor collections, it attracted the interest of many scholars long before 1900.[126] The reason for this was the close tie between Deusdedit and Gregory VII presumed by researchers in the nineteenth century: whether Deusdedit used the register of pope

122 Peter Christian Jacobsen, *Die Carmina des Kardinals Deusdedit* (Editiones Heidelbergenses 31), Heidelberg: Winter, 2002; Ernst Sackur, *Deusdedit Presbyteri Cardinalis Libellus contra invasores et symoniacos et reliquos scismaticos*, in: Monumenta Germaniae Historica, Libelli de lite 2, Hannover: Hahn'sche Buchhandlung, 1892, 292–365. On Deusdedit: Stephan Dusil, *Wissensordnungen des Rechts im Wandel. Päpstlicher Jurisdiktionsprimat und Zölibat zwischen 1000 und 1215* (Mediaevalia Lovaniensia I/47), Leuven: Leuven University Press, 2018, 93–95.

123 See Wolf von Glanvell, *Die Kanonessammlung des Kardinals Deusdedit*, vol. 1: *Die Kanonessammlung selbst*, Paderborn: Schöningh, 1905, XVII–XVIII.

124 Friedrich Carl von Savigny, *Geschichte des römischen Rechts im Mittelalter*, vol. VII, Heidelberg: J. C. B. Mohr, 1851, 75–77.

125 Theodor von Sickel, *Das Privilegium Otto I. für die römische Kirche vom Jahre 962*, Innsbruck: Wagner, 1883, 61–64, 77.

126 Compare the bibliography of the collection of Deusdedit (Kéry, *Canonical Collections*, 230–233) with those of other collections.

Gregory VII was a much debated question in the 1880s,[127] and Ernst Sackur even presented Deusdedit as the author of the famous *Dictatus Papae*, a polemical position paper by Gregory VII.[128] The conflict between the Catholic Church and the state in the second half of the nineteenth century during the "Kulturkampf" obviously aroused the interest of historians in its medieval counterpart, the so-called "Investiture Controversy" between Pope Gregory VII and Emperor Henry IV. It is very likely that Deusdedit's collection became the object of increasing scholarly interest in the wake of this conflict.[129]

---

127 Samuel Löwenfeld, "Canonsammlung des Cardinals Deusdedit und das Register Gregors VII.," in: Neues Archiv der Gesellschaft für ältere deutsche Geschichtskunde 10, 1885, 309–329, esp. at 314.

128 Ernst Sackur, "Der Dictatus papae und die Canonsammlung des Deusdedit," in: Neues Archiv der Gesellschaft für ältere deutsche Geschichtskunde 18, 1893, 135–153. On the *Dictatus Papae*: Andreas Thier, "Dictatus Papae," in: Albrecht Cordes et al. (ed.), Handwörterbuch zur Deutschen Rechtsgeschichte, 2nd edition, vol. 1, Berlin: Erich Schmidt, 2008, 1043–1045.

129 See, for instance, Ulrich Stutz, "Review of 'Wolf von Glanvell, Die Kanonessammlung des Kardinals Deusdedit,'" in: Deutsche Literaturzeitung 26, 1905, 2273–2277, at 2274: "Diese Werke haben ihm [Deusdedit] gerade in neuester Zeit [...] zu besonderer Beachtung auch durch Nichtkanonisten verholfen." For a list with publications on Deusdedit's *Collectio Canonum*, see: Kéry, *Canonical Collections*, 230–233. It seems that Deusdedit's collection was less appreciated in the second half of the twentieth century. Horst Fuhrmann, *Einfluß und Verbreitung der pseudoisidorischen Fälschungen. Von ihrem Auftauchen bis in die neuere Zeit* (MGH Schriften 24/2), vol. 2, Stuttgart: Hiersemann, 1973, at 524 did not appreciate it ("roh," "streckenweise primitiver Eindruck," "nicht den Grad systematischer Information wie die Collectio canonum des Anselm von Lucca"); in a similar vein, Hubert Mordek, "Kanonistik und Gregorianische Reform. Marginalien zu einem nicht-marginalen Thema," in: Karl Schmid (ed.), Reich und Kirche vor dem Investiturstreit. Vorträge beim wissenschaftlichen Kolloquium aus Anlaß des achtzigsten Geburtstages von Gerd Tellenbach, Sigmaringen: Jan Thorbecke, 1985, 65–82, at 69: "etwas plumpe Werk des eifrigen Deusdedit." Recent research has re-evaluated Deusdedit's collection and its methodological approach, see Christoph H. F. Meyer, "Ordnung durch Ordnen. Die Erfassung und Gestaltung des hochmittelalterlichen Kirchenrechts im Spiegel von Texten, Begriffen und Institutionen," in: Bernd Schneidmüller / Stefan Weinfurter (ed.), Ordnungskonfigurationen im Hohen Mittelalter (VuF 64), Sigmaringen: Jan Thorbecke, 2006, 303–411, at 327–331; Dusil, *Wissensordnungen*, 93–94, 153–161. Obviously, a canonical collection is subject to the ups and downs of scholarly interest just like any other source or subject.

4.2.1. The Making of Deusdedit's Edition

A key figure in nineteenth-century research on Deusdedit was Theodor (von) Sickel (1826–1908), a German-Austrian historian, whose main expertise was the "ancillary sciences," namely paleography and diplomatics. Educated at the Paris "École des chartes" and the Milan "Scuola di paleografia," among other institutions, he became first extraordinary and then, in 1867, ordinary professor of paleography at the University of Vienna. From 1873, he was in charge of the "Institut für Österreichische Geschichtsforschung" in Vienna. After the opening of the Vatican Archives in 1881, von Sickel founded the "Istituto Austriaco di studii storici" (Austrian Historical Institute) in Rome, which he directed from 1891 to 1901.[130] His study of the "Privilegium Otto I." was partly based on the only entire copy of Deusdedit's collection, namely Vat. lat. 3833, and it offered a thorough description of this manuscript.[131] Von Sickel's intention was to see that a new edition of Vat. lat. 3833 was produced, as the first edition by Pius Martinucci in 1869 had been much criticized as insufficient and flawed.[132]

Von Sickel attempted to realize this new edition using the resources available to him as director of the Austrian Historical Institute in Rome.[133] A fellow of the Institute in 1893/95, Dr. Josef Teige,[134] made a transcription of the Vatican codex, but by 1897 he had not yet completed his edition. Meanwhile, another scholar had asked the librarians of the Vatican Library for access to Vat. lat. 3833, and they, in turn, urged Theodor von Sickel to complete his edition.[135] However, when Teige delivered his preliminary

130 On Sickel, see Winfried Stelzer, "Sickel, Friedrich Adolf Theodor Ritter von," in: Neue Deutsche Biographie 24, 2010, 309–311; Wilhelm Erben, Theodor Sickel. Denkwürdigkeiten aus der Werdezeit eines deutschen Geschichtsforschers, München / Berlin: Oldenbourg, 1926.

131 von Sickel, *Privilegium Otto I.*, 61–64.

132 Pius Martinucci, *Deusdedit Presbyteri Cardinalis Tituli Apostolorum in Eudoxia Collectio Canonum*, Venice: Typographia Aemiliana, 1869; criticism: Wolf von Glanvell, *Kanonessammlung des Kardinals Deusdedit*, XLV–XLVII.

133 The following information is based on a letter from Theodor von Sickel to the "Savigny-Kommission" (Wien, AÖAW, Savigny-Kommission, Karton 1 / Mappe 26, 1900 January 3).

134 Josef Teige (1862–1921), staff at the Austrian Historical Institute 1893–1895, later director of the municipal archive in Prague; cf. V. Petrbok, "Teige, Josef," in: Österreichisches Biographisches Lexikon (1815–1950), vol. 14, Wien: Verlag der Österreichischen Akademie der Wissenschaften, 2013, 229–230.

135 This scholar who intended to edit Deusdedit's collection remains unidentified.

work, including a first transcription to von Sickel in January 1899, there was no final edition.[136] At this time, von Sickel desperately sought a new editor. Berthold Bretholz,[137] later director of the "Landesarchiv" in Brno, declined von Sickel's offer to work on the edition, as did Harold Steinacker,[138] who was later appointed professor in Innsbruck. In April 1899, von Sickel even asked the former fellow of the Institute, Wolf von Glanvell, but he asked for more time than von Sickel had foreseen; consequently, the director of the Institute stopped negotiating with him.[139]

In his distress, von Sickel turned to the "Savigny-Kommission" in Vienna.[140] The "Kommission für die Savigny-Stiftung" was a "Spezialcommission" of the philosophical-historical class of the Academy of Science in Vienna, or, in other words, a sub-commission that maintained contact with the "Savigny-Stiftung" in Berlin and proposed projects worthy of support. The "Savigny-Stiftung" was named after the well-known German jurist and legal historian, Friedrich Carl von Savigny (1779–1861), and its purpose was to support research in the

---

136 The quality of Teige's transcription is criticized by Wolf von Glanvell, *Kanonessammlung des Kardinals Deusdedit*, XLIX–L; in a similar vein: Wien, IÖG, Nachlass Sickel, Letter from Viktor Wolf von Glanvell to Theodor von Sickel, 1900 December 1 ("Was Teiges Arbeit selbst anlangt, so ist meines Erachtens deren Wert ein ziemlich zweifelhafter; wie mir Stichproben gezeigt haben, enthält sie nahezu alle die charakteristischen Fehler, welche der [better: die] Druckausgabe (von Martinucci) aufweist, so dass ich mich des Verdachtes nicht recht erwehren kann, Teige habe im großen und ganzen einfach Martinucci abgeschrieben.") and 1900 December 29.

137 Berthold Bretholz (1862–1936) was historian, staff member of the "Österreichisches Institut für Geschichtsforschung" and the "Monumenta Germaniae Historica," later director of the "Landesarchiv" in Brno, cf. Rudolf Schreiber, "Bretholz, Berthold," in: Neue Deutsche Biographie 2, 1955, 601–602. See also Rudolf, "Geschichte des Österreichischen Historischen Instituts," 67–69; Alphons Lhotsky, *Geschichte des Instituts für Österreichische Geschichtsforschung 1854–1954* (Mitteilungen des Instituts für Österreichische Geschichtsforschung, Ergänzungsband 17), Graz / Köln: Hermann Böhlau Nachfolger, 1954, 187–188.

138 Harold Steinacker (1875–1965) was a historian who completed research studies in Rome 1899–1901, and became later professor in Innsbruck; cf. Manfred Stoy, "Steinacker, Harold Eugen Adolf," in: Neue Deutsche Biographie 24, 2013, 159–161. He published one article on Deusdedit: Harold Steinacker, "Die Deusdedithandschrift (Cod. Vat. 3833) und die ältesten gallischen libri canonum," in: Mittheilungen des Instituts für österreichische Geschichtsforschung Innsbruck, VI. Ergänzungsband, Innsbruck: Wagner, 1901, 113–144. Some remarks also by Rudolf, "Geschichte des Österreichischen Historischen Instituts," at 69–71.

139 Cf. the following letters: Wien, IÖG, Nachlass Sickel, Letter from Viktor Wolf von Glanvell to Theodor von Sickel, 1899 May 8, 1899 May 27, 1899 June 3.

140 Letter by Theodor von Sickel to the "Savigny-Kommission" (Wien, AÖAW, Savigny-Kommission, Karton 1 / Mappe 26, 1900 January 3).

history of law.[141] This support included making the surplus income it accrued through interest on its investments available to the Academies in Vienna, Munich, and Berlin on a rotating schedule.[142] In February 1899, von Sickel wrote to Heinrich Siegel, professor of Germanic law in Vienna and member of the "Savigny-Kommission," who, unfortunately, passed away in early June without answering von Sickel's letter.[143] At the same time, however, the "Savigny-Kommission" was also considering a new edition of Deusdedit's collection.[144] At the end of 1899, at the request of the philosophical-historical class, the Academy in Vienna decided to grant 2000 marks "für die Vorarbeiten zu einer durch den Privatdocenten der Universität Graz, Dr. Victor Wolf von Glanvell, zu besorgenden Ausgabe der Canonensammlung des Cardinals Deusdedit."[145] The editor who would see the project through to completion, Wolf von Glanvell, was thus appointed. The project was thereby successfully

141 For some remarks on the "Savigny-Stiftung" which is—at least at first glance—under-researched, see: Werner Ogris, "Zum Erscheinen von Band 125 der Zeitschrift der Savigny-Stiftung für Rechtsgeschichte," in: ZRG.GA 125, 2008, XXXI–XLIX, at XXXIII–XXXIV; Werner Ogris, "Die Savigny-Stiftung 1863–???," in: ZRG.GA 126, 2009, XXXVI–XLVI, esp. at XLII; Richard Meister (ed.), *Geschichte der Akademie der Wissenschaften in Wien 1847–1947* (Österreichische Akademie der Wissenschaften. Denkschriften der Gesamtakademie 1), Wien: Adolf Holzhausens NFG., 1947, 313–314, 346–347. An overview of funded projects is given by: Georg Bruns, "Die Savigny-Stiftung," in: ZRG.GA 1, 1880, III–XIX; Heinrich Brunner, "Die Savigny-Stiftung seit 1880," in: ZRG.GA 22, 1901, III–XV (Wolf von Glanvell at XI-II); Ulrich Stutz, "Die Savigny-Stiftung seit 1901," in: ZRG.GA 46, 1926, IX–XXII (Wolf von Glanvell at XIII and XIV). The Savigny-Stiftung was founded in 1863 and it supported, among other projects, the "Zeitschrift für Rechtsgeschichte" (which was hence renamed "Zeitschrift der Savigny-Stiftung für Rechtsgeschichte").

142 In the beginning, the Academies could dispose of it on a biennial basis, but from 1881 onwards it rotated yearly.

143 Heinrich Siegel (1830–1899) was a legal historian and professor of Germanic law in Vienna, cf. Stephan Dusil, "Siegel, Heinrich Joseph," in: Neue Deutsche Biographie 24, 2010, 338–339.

144 The reason why the "Savigny-Kommission" also considered a new edition remains unknown. Some sparse information is given by Rudolf, "Geschichte des Österreichischen Historischen Instituts," 69–70. Letters from Wolf von Glanvell sent to Theodor von Sickel do not clarify this point, cf. Wien, IÖG, Nachlass Sickel, Letter from Viktor Wolf von Glanvell to Theodor von Sickel, 1899 July 24 and 1900 May 24.

145 Wien, AÖAW, Protokoll der Sitzung der Gesamtakademie 1899 December 15 (A. 545). See also the request of the "philosophisch-historischen Klasse" to the "Gesamtakademie:" "... den weiteren Betrag von 2000 Mark für die Deusdedit Ausgabe, für welche noch die betreffende Persönlichkeit zu bestimmen sein wird, zu widmen." (Wien, AÖAW, Protokoll der Sitzung der philosophisch-historischen Klasse 1900 January 3 (C. 1517)); surprisingly, Viktor Wolf von Glanvell is not named in the later minutes.

transferred from the Austrian Historical Institute to the "Savigny-Kommission" and the Austrian Academy of Science. Therefore, Arnold Luschin von Ebengreuth drafted a letter to be sent to von Sickel: "... die Erklärung, daß das römische Institut den Gedanken an eine eigene Deusdedit-Ausgabe aufgegeben hat, [wird] zur Kenntnis genommen [...] und außerdem [wird] der Dank für die wohlwollende Förderung ausgesprochen [...], welche einer von der Akademie unternommenen Ausgabe in Aussicht gestellt worden ist."[146]

Wolf von Glanvell was quite hopeful that the edition would be completed by July 1903 and published a year later: "Soweit ich die Arbeit übersehe, hoffe ich das druckfertige Manuscript bis Ende Juli 1903 an den Verleger gelangen [zu] lassen und etwa 1 Jahr später das fertige, gedruckte Werk vorlegen zu können."[147] As it was an arduous task to edit the collection and analyze it from a legal point of view, Theodor von Sickel first thought of a team of two scholars, one to edit and one to interpret. He had Kamil Krofta[148] in mind for the first task, but Krofta declined because of his

146 Letter from Arnold Luschin von Ebengreuth to the Academy (Wien, AÖAW, Savigny-Kommission, Karton 1 / Mappe 26, 1900 March 8).

147 Viktor Wolf von Glanvell to the Savigny-Kommission (Wien, AÖAW, Savigny-Kommission, Karton 1 / Mappe 7, Akte 426/1900, 1900 June 22). See further Wien, AÖAW, Protokoll der Sitzung der philosophisch-historischen Klasse 1900 July 4 (C. 1534): "Der Sekretär verliest eine Zuschrift des Privatdocenten Herrn Dr. Victor Wolf von Glanvell, worin dieser erklärt, dass er bereit sei, die ihm von der Kaiserl. Akademie übertragene juristische Bearbeitung der Canonen-Sammlung des Cardinals Deusdedit zu übernehmen und gleichzeitig der Kaiserl. Akademie für das ihm damit erwiesene Vertrauen dankt." and Wien, AÖAW, Protokoll der Sitzung der philosophisch-historischen Klasse 1900 October 17 (C. 1537): "Der Secretär bringt der Classe ein Dankschreiben des Herrn Dr. Victor Wolf von Glanvell in Graz für die ihm aus der Zinsenmasse der 'Savigny-Stiftung' zugesprochene Summe von 1200 Mark (behufs Collationierung der vaticanischen Handschrift der 'Collectio Canonum' des Cardinals Deusdedit in Rom) zur Kenntnis." On the whole nomination, see also Wien, AÖAW, Protokoll der Sitzung der Gesamtakademie 1900 January 25 (A. 546) (2000 marks for the edition) and the official confirmation letter from the Academy to Wolf von Glanvell (Wien, AÖAW, Savigny-Kommission, Karton 1 / Mappe 7, Akte 426/1900, 1900 June 12) and the minutes of the meeting of the "philosophisch-historischen Klasse" (Wien, AÖAW, Protokoll der Sitzung der philosophisch-historischen Klasse 1900 April 4 (C. 1527)).

148 Kamil Krofta (1876–1945) was a historian and diplomat who studied in Prague and Vienna; in 1899–1901, he was a scholar of the Austrian Historical Institute in the Vatican Archives. He became a professor of Czech history and later envoy to the Vatican and Berlin and Minister of Foreign Affairs (1936–1938). He participated in the Resistance during the German occupation of Czechoslovakia and was later incarcerated in Terezín. Cf. Kučera, "Krofta, Kamil," in: Österreichisches Biographi-

own work on the Monumenta Bohemiae Vaticana.[149] As a result, the "Savigny-Kommission" decided to transfer both tasks to Wolf von Glanvell ("daß wir Herrn Dr. Victor Wolf von Glanvell auch die Vorarbeiten für die Textherstellung übertragen.")[150] Wolf von Glanvell was henceforth in charge of both the text and its interpretation. To verify Teige's transcription, Wolf von Glanvell had planned to travel to Rome in the fall of 1900, but—with the help of Theodor von Sickel—the Vatican Library offered to take pictures of the entire codex. Luschin von Ebengreuth wrote: "Bei dieser Sachlage räth Herr Sectionschef von Sickel selbst Herrn von Wolf die Reise vorerst zu unterlassen und lieber die ganze Handschrift durch den Photographen aufnehmen zu lassen."[151] In addition, von Sickel offered to send Teige's transcription to Graz. Wolf von Glanvell considered the proposal and postponed his trip: Teige's transcription arrived in Graz in early December,[152] and shortly thereafter 145 photographs of the complete manuscript (format: 11 ½ x 17 ½ inches) taken by P. Lucchesi, the authorized Roman photographer.[153]

Wolf von Glanvell worked on the edition for the next three and a half years. According to the reports that he wrote to the "Savigny-Kommission," he was first occupied with producing his own transcription of the text of Vat. lat. 3833, which he completed at the end of July 1901.[154] He then planned to check his preliminary text against the codex in the Vatican Li-

sches Lexikon (1815–1950), vol. 4, Wien: Verlag der Österreichischen Akademie der Wissenschaften, 1969, 287.

149 Letter from Kamil Krofta to Theodor von Sickel (Wien, AÖAW, Savigny-Kommission, Karton 1 / Mappe 7, Akte 426/1900, 1900 July 6).

150 Arnold Luschin von Ebengreuth to the "Savigny-Kommission" (Wien, AÖAW, Savigny-Kommission, Karton 1 / Mappe 7, Akte 426/1900, 1900 July 21).

151 Arnold Luschin von Ebengreuth to the "philosophisch-historischen Klasse" (Wien, AÖAW, Savigny-Kommission, Karton 1 / Mappe 7, Akte 426/1900, 1900 October 31).

152 Viktor Wolf von Glanvell to the "philosophisch-historischen Klasse" indicating that he had received the "15 Hefte der Teige'schen Abschrift des Deusdedit" (Wien, AÖAW, Savigny-Kommission, Karton 1 / Mappe 7, Akte 426/1900, 1900 December 3 and Wien, IÖG, Nachlass Sickel, Letter from Viktor Wolf von Glanvell to Theodor von Sickel, 1900 December 1).

153 See the "Bericht über die Vorarbeiten" (Wien, AÖAW, Savigny-Kommission, Karton 1 / Mappe 7, Akte 428/1901, s.d. (presumably spring 1901)) and also Wolf von Glanvell, *Kanonessammlung des Kardinals Deusdedit*, L; further: Wien, IÖG, Nachlass Sickel, Letter from Viktor Wolf von Glanvell to Theodor von Sickel, 1900 October 14 and 1900 December 1.

154 Wolf von Glanvell's "Vorläufiger Bericht" (Wien, AÖAW, Savigny-Kommission, Karton 1 / Mappe 7, Akte 409/1902, 1902 March 12).

brary and also to transcribe the variant readings found in the fragmentary copies of Deusdedit's collection, such as those transmitted in Biblioteca Casanatense 2010 (B V 17) or Vatican Library, Vat. lat. 1984.[155] To this end, the Savigny-Kommission dispersed another portion, namely 800 marks, of the previously awarded 2000 marks (1901).[156] However, according to the surviving records, Wolf von Glanvell travelled to Rome only in the spring of 1903. Meanwhile, he was occupied with the identification of the *fontes materiales* of Deusdedit's collection and assessing their transmission in other collections. Wolf von Glanvell wrote to the "Savigny-Kommission" in 1902:

> "Der Nachweis, woher die einzelnen Stücke genommen sind, erscheint um so nothwendiger, als nur so ein Überblick über Deusdedits-Quellenkreis gewonnen und nur dadurch allfällige Ergänzungen und Berichtigungen des im vaticanischen Codex überlieferten Textes vorgenommen werden können; ganz abgesehen davon, dass nur aus dem Vergleiche mit der sonstigen Überlieferung der einzelnen Stücke erhellt, wo Deusdedit (beabsichtigte oder unabsichtliche) Änderungen einfließen ließ."[157]

In the spring of 1902, he had identified three quarters of the *fontes*, "allerdings sind gerade die unangenehmsten Stücke übriggeblieben, an welchen ich eben fortarbeite."[158]

155 Wolf von Glanvell's "Bericht über die Vorarbeiten" (Wien, AÖAW, Savigny-Kommission, Karton 1 / Mappe 7, Akte 428/1901, s.d. (presumably spring 1901)). His request to send the codex transmitted in the Biblioteca Casanatense to Graz, was declined (see Graz, Universitätsarchiv, Jur. Fak., Z. 202 ex 1902/03).

156 The Savigny-Kommission decided to grant 800 marks (Wien, AÖAW, Savigny-Kommission, Karton 1 / Mappe 7, Akte 428/1901, 1901 March 28); the "philosophisch-historische Klasse" adopted the motion (Wien, AÖAW, Protokoll der Sitzung der philosophisch-historischen Klasse 1901 April 24 (C. 1554) and informed the Gesamtakademie (Wien, AÖAW, Protokoll der Sitzung der Gesamtakademie 1901 May 2 (A. 559)). Note in the Almanach der kaiserlichen Akademie der Wissenschaften 51, Wien 1901, 321–322.

157 Cf. Wolf von Glanvell's "Vorläufiger Bericht" (Wien, AÖAW, Savigny-Kommission, Karton 1 / Mappe 7, Akte 409/1902, 1902 March 12).

158 Wolf von Glanvell's "Vorläufiger Bericht" (Wien, AÖAW, Savigny-Kommission, Karton 1 / Mappe 7, Akte 409/1902, 1902 March 12). He also contacted Moritz Cantor (1829–1920), professor of the history of mathematics at University of Heidelberg, to learn more about unknown characters (in lib. III, can. 149, possibly vat. lat. 3833, fol. 89r), but to no avail; see Heidelberg, Universitätsbibliothek, Nachlass Moritz Cantor, Heid. Hs. 4028, 144, 1904 October 10 and 1904 October 20.

In 1902, he also tried to expand the manuscript base for his edition by including the Parisian codex lat. 1458 and the Vaticanus Ottobonianus lat. 3057. The Bibliothèque Nationale declined his request to send the Parisian manuscript lat. 1458 to Austria and so Wolf von Glanvell reached out to a photographer and a colleague who could provide him with a description of the manuscript.[159] As for the Vatican manuscript (Ottobon. lat. 3057), the Austrian Historical Institute sent Wolf von Glanvell a transcription, but he found it insufficient.[160]

In order to complete his edition, Wolf von Glanvell made the long-delayed trip to Rome in the spring of 1903, accompanied by his wife Mary.[161] A year later, the edition was finished: in May 1904, Wolf von

159 See Graz, Universitätsarchiv, Jur. Fak., Z. 292 ex 1902/03 (the "Ministerium für Kultus und Unterricht" informed Wolf von Glanvell that his request to have the codex sent was declined); see also Wien, IÖG, Nachlass Mühlbacher, Letter from Viktor Wolf von Glanvell to Engelbert Mühlbacher, 1902 November 26: "Vor Kurzem wurde mir seitens des k.k. Ministerium für Cultus und Unterricht die unerwünschte Verständigung zutheil, dass Cod. Lat. Paris. nat. 1458 welcher auf f. 242–261 Theile der Canonessammlung des Cardinals Deusdedit enthält, nicht ausgeliehen werden könne; bei dem Umstande nun, als er einen besseren Text als wie die vaticanische Handschrift enthalten soll, ist mir die Kenntnis desselben jedoch unbedingt nothwendig und so möchte ich die fraglichen Blätter photographieren lassen. Ich gestatte mir also die Anfrage, an wen ich mich diesbezüglich und wegen einer genauen Beschreibung der Handschrift zu wenden hätte, weil ich die Angelegenheit gerne vor meiner Reise nach Italien (Februar kommenden Jahres) zum Abschluss bringen möchte." It was Henri Omont (1857–1940), a philologist and librarian, who studied the codex for him: "Eine Reihe sehr wertvoller und eingehender Nachrichten verdanke ich der außerordentlichen Liebenswürdigkeit von Mr. Henri Omont, conservateur de la bibliothèque nationale in Paris" (Wolf von Glanvell, *Kanonessamlung des Kardinals Deusdedit*, XXV n. 28). Cf. Wien, IÖG, Nachlass Sickel, Letter from Viktor Wolf von Glanvell to Theodor von Sickel, 1903 December 3 sending pictures of this codex to von Sickel.

160 Cf. letter from the "philosophisch-historischen Klasse" to the "Ministerium für Cultus und Unterricht" (Wien, AÖAW, Savigny-Kommission, Karton 1 / Mappe 7, Akte 428/1901, 1902 July 17) and the transmission of the transcription by the Istituto Austriaco (Wien, AÖAW, Savigny-Kommission, Karton 1 / Mappe 7, Akte 428/1901, 1902 October 6). Wolf von Glanvell (*Kanonessammlung des Kardinals Deusdedit*, XXXVII n. 94), however, was dissatisfied with the quality of the copy: "eine 'Abschrift' wurde [...] vor nicht langer Zeit von Dr. W. v. Ambros hergestellt: da diese jedoch von den meisten Kapiteln nur Anfang und Ende nach dem Originale sowie eine (deutsche) Inhaltsangabe bringt, überdies aber mit Buch IX schließt, konnte sie für unsere Zwecke natürlich nicht in Frage kommen."

161 Cf. the notes in Wien, AÖAW, Savigny-Kommission, Karton 1 / Mappe 26 and above 18. In a letter to Paul Fournier, he mentioned that he had arrived in Rome at the end of February 1903 to study Vat. lat. 3833, Ottobon. lat. 3057, Vat. lat.

Glanvell sent the manuscript to the publisher Schoeningh in Paderborn.[162] Another year later, he had corrected the proofs and completed his preface, which he dated to Easter 1905—just two weeks before his fall from the Fölzstein.[163]

4.2.2. The Edition: Method, Results, Reception

Wolf von Glanvell aimed at a bipartite volume on Deusdedit's *Collectio canonum.* The first volume, the editor acknowledged as early as 1901, was to encompass editorial notes, a description of the manuscript, the edition itself (including the texts preceding and following Deusdedit's collection), a register of the chapter initials, and a register of proper names.[164] Wolf von Glanvell successfully completed this part of the project and had it printed

1984, two manuscripts in the Biblioteca Vallicelliana, namely C19 and C24, and the manuscript Biblioteca Casanatense 2010 (B V 17) (France, Archives nationales, Fonds Gabriel Le Bras, Papiers Paul Fournier (currently being indexed), Letter from Wolf von Glanvell to Paul Fournier, 1903 March 7). According to the obituary by Karl Doménigg (cited according to Richardi, *Erschließung*, 190–191; similar: Doménigg, *Bergsteigerleben*, 217), Wolf von Glanvell met Cardinal Rampolla in Rome: "[Wolf von Glanvell erzählte uns] von seinen Arbeiten im Institute für Österreichische Geschichtsforschung, von den prunkvollen Empfangsabenden in den Salons der vatikanischen Kirchenfürsten, der bestrickenden Liebenswürdigkeit des damaligen Kardinal-Sekretärs Rampol[l]a, aber auch von endlosen Fahrten in der versengenden Sonnenglut der Campagna und mühevollem Wandern auf dem trostlos öden Sandstein-Gehänge des Monte Sibéllin." The Vatican Apostolic Archives ("Segreteria di Stato" and "Segreteria di Stato, Spogli di Cardinali ed Officiali di Curia, Rampolla") do not transmit any records (kind mail from the Vatican Archives, 2021 May 10). Cardinal Rampolla was much interested in the activities of the Austrian Historical Institute, see Rudolf, "Geschichte des Österreichischen Historischen Instituts," 69.

162 Luschin von Ebengreuth to the Academy of Science (Wien, AÖAW, Savigny-Kommission, Karton 1 / Mappe 26, 1904 May 3). The "Savigny-Kommission" granted another 1000 marks to support the Deusdedit-edition (decision of the "Savigny-Kommission:" Wien, AÖAW, Savigny-Kommission, Karton 1 / Mappe 7, Akte 409/1902, 1902 March 14), which was approved by the "philosophisch-historischen Klasse" (Wien, AÖAW, Protokoll der Sitzung der philosophisch-historischen Klasse 1902 April 23 (C. 1582)) and the "Gesamtakademie" (Wien, AÖAW, Protokoll der Sitzung der Gesamtakademie 1902 April 25 (A. 569)). Brief note in: Almanach der kaiserlichen Akademie der Wissenschaften 52, Wien 1902, 291.

163 Short note about the publication: Almanach der kaiserlichen Akademie der Wissenschaften 56, Wien 1906, 359.

164 Cf. "Bericht über die Vorarbeiten" (Wien, AÖAW, Savigny-Kommission, Karton 1 / Mappe 7, Akte 428/1901, s.d. (presumably spring 1901)).

in 1905 (although without the envisaged register of proper names, which was moved to the second volume). The second volume was to contain a thorough analysis of the collection, including sources, subject indices, and name registers:

> "Eine Übersicht über die Quellen Deusdedits, sowie ein Sachregister und ein Verzeichnis der im Texte vorkommenden Eigennamen habe ich dem zweiten Bande vorbehalten, welcher dann auch eine ausführliche Besprechung der Quellen bringen wird: Deshalb wollte ich auch hier ein bloßes Quellenverzeichnis nicht geben."[165]

He intended to analyze the formal sources of Deusdedit and to scrutinize the alterations the author made to his sources.[166] Finally, Wolf von Glanvell's aim was to shed light on the reception of this collection especially by Gratian.[167] In 1902, he was not sure how long this would take: "In welcher Frist dann der 2. Band (die rechtsgeschichtlichen Erörterungen), welcher einen eingehenden Vergleich unserer Sammlung mit verschiedenen anderen, theilweise ungedruckten erfordert, folgen kann, vermag ich allerdings heute noch nicht anzugeben."[168] This second volume, however, was never published due to Wolf von Glanvell's early death. His academic papers, including drafts, notes, and the other preliminary material for volume 2, have not survived.[169]

---

165 Wolf von Glanvell, *Kanonessammlung des Kardinals Deusdedit*, LIV.

166 See Wolf von Glanvell, *Kanonessammlung des Kardinals Deusdedit*, XLVIII: "Im einzelnen soll dabei weniger auf die formelle Herkunft der einzelnen Kapitel Gewicht gelegt, sondern vor allem auf deren Inhalt beziehungsweise auf dessen etwa absichtliche Umgestaltung seitens Deudedit Rücksicht genommen werden, um so der Sammlung nicht, wie bisher üblich, rein formell, sondern vor allem inhaltlich gerecht zu werden." A somewhat similar programm was carried out by Dusil, *Wissensordnungen*, esp. 117–166.

167 Wolf von Glanvell, *Kanonessammlung des Kardinals Deusdedit*, XLVIII.

168 Wolf von Glanvell's "Vorläufiger Bericht" (Wien, AÖAW, Savigny-Kommission, Karton 1 / Mappe 7, Akte 409/1902, 1902 March 12).

169 Academic papers (such as notes, correspondence, etc.) do not seem to have been preserved. I have checked the following institutions: Archiv der Österreichischen Akademie der Wissenschaften, Landesarchiv Steiermark, Staatsarchiv Wien, Stadtarchiv Graz, Universitätsbibliothek Graz, Universitätsarchiv Graz, family Wolf, family Luschin von Ebengreuth, family zur Eck (descendents of Mary Wolf von Glanvell with Moriz Probst, her second husband). The "Verzeichnis der künstlerischen, wissenschaftlichen und kulturpolitischen Nachlässe in Österreich" (online: https://nlv.obvsg.at/primo-explore/search?vid=NLV) has no entry. See also Emil Friedberg, "Review of 'Wolf von Glanvell, Die Kanonessammlung des Kardi-

How was the edition received? Colleagues immediately reacted quite supportively, emphasizing the importance of this collection, "die den Historiker," as Emil Friedberg put it, "vielleicht noch mehr interessiert als den Kanonisten."[170] Friedberg further stated: "Und gleichzeitig hat er [Wolf von Glanvell] den Verdienst, wenn wir von Regino absehn, die erste kritische Ausgabe einer vorgratianischen Sammlung veranstaltet zu haben."[171] Other reviewers emphasized Wolf von Glanvell's care and diligence (Ulrich Stutz),[172] his industriousness and zeal (Emanuel Hirsch),[173] as well as the love, time, and effort he had put into this edition (Paul Fournier).[174] Founier / Le Bras summarized some thirty years later: "En 1905, Wolf von Glanvell a donné du recueil une édition bien supérieure à la précédente [of Martinucci]."[175] Nonetheless, the reviewers also criticized some minor and two more fundamental points. Among the minor issues were the lack of Jaffé-numbers and of the precise identification of the manuscripts (shelf marks) cited by Wolf von Glanvell when comparing Deusdedit's collection to other collections (such as Anselm's); also, the absence of Gratian's *Decretum* in the apparatus criticus received negative criticism.[176]

---

nals Deusdedit,'" in: Deutsche Zeitschrift für Kirchenrecht 15, 1905, 469–472, at 470: "Ob er Materialien für den II. Band hinterlassen hat, erhellt nicht."

170 Friedberg, "Review of 'Wolf von Glanvell, Die Kanonessammlung des Kardinals Deusdedit,'" 472. Brief note on Wolf von Glanvell's edition in Italian: Hans Hirsch, "Pubblicazioni degli anni 1905, 1906 e 1907 sulla storia medioevale italiana," in: Archivio Storico Italiano 45, 1910, 105–146, at 110; a descriptive review by Eduard Eichmann, "Review of 'Wolf von Glanvell, Kanonessammlung,'" in: Kritische Vierteljahresschrift für Gesetzgebung und Rechtswissenschaft 48, 1909, 185–187.

171 Friedberg, "Review of 'Wolf von Glanvell, Die Kanonessammlung des Kardinals Deusdedit,'" 472. 'Regino' refers to Friedrich Wilhelm August Hermann Wasserschleben, *Reginonis abbatis Prumiensis libri duo de synodalibus causis et disciplinis ecclesiasticis*, Leipzig: Engelmann, 1840 (reprint 1964). One may also add Paul Hinschius, *Decretales Pseudo-Isidorianae et Capitula Angilramni*, Leipzig: Bernhard Tauchnitz, 1863.

172 Stutz, "Review of 'Wolf von Glanvell, Kanonessammlung des Kardinals Deusdedit,'" 2274–2275: "Er ist mit größter Gründlichkeit und Sorgfalt zu Werke gegangen."

173 Emanuel Hirsch, "Review of 'Wolf von Glanvell, Die Kanonessammlung des Kardinals Deusdedit,'" in: AKKR 85, 1905, 795–800, at 796: "Das Werk zeigt einen staunenswerten Fleiss und eine peinliche Genauigkeit im ganzen wie im einzelnen."

174 Paul Fournier, "Review of 'Wolf von Glanvell, Die Kanonessammlung des Kardinals Deusdedit,'" in: Revue d'histoire ecclésiastique 8, 1907, 568–575, at 571: "Il demandait quelques années pour achever l'œuvre qu'il avait commencée avec tant d'amour, sans ménager son temps ni sa peine."

175 Fournier / Le Bras, *Collections canoniques II*, 40.

176 Friedberg, "Review of 'Wolf von Glanvell, Die Kanonesssammlung des Kardinals Deusdedit,'" 471.

Two more serious objections were raised against this edition. First, Wilhelm Peitz, who studied the "Originalregister Gregors VII. im Vatikanischen Archiv (Reg. Vat. 2)," reprimanded Wolf von Glanvell for his use of copies of Deusdedit's collection: "Wolf ist sich weder über die Beziehungen der Handschriften zu einander, noch über ihren Wert für die kritische Gestaltung des Textes wirklich klar geworden."[177] He offered a stemma that is missing in Wolf von Glanvell's edition and he remarked on Wolf von Glanvell's inconsistent use of manuscripts to produce the edited text.[178] It is quite difficult to evaluate this criticism without having studied the manuscripts themselves; however, the history of the editorial work may explain this oddity: at the beginning of the editorial process, Wolf von Glanvell focussed on Teige's transcription of Vat. lat. 3833 and the manuscript itself, and it was only much later that he took notice of the other codices. This approach might explain the apparent weakness of his edition in this regard; nevertheless, Wolf von Glanvell was well aware of this issue and explained his readings at length.[179]

Second, all reviewers noted the editor's decision to parse longer canons in smaller parts: Ulrich Stutz, supported by Emil Friedberg, favoured this separation of texts because of its increased readability ("wodurch die neue Ausgabe an Brauchbarkeit bedeutend gewann").[180] Other reviewers, however, were more reluctant to praise this editorial principle. This issue is central to the interpretation of Deusdedit's collection and deserves a more thorough investigation. In general, canonical collections before Gratian were organized either chronologically or systematically. In a chronological collection, the canons (papal decrees, conciliar decisions, etc.) are presented according to their time of origin and thus allow the reader to learn about the evolution of rules and to contextualize the canons. In a systematic

177 Wilhelm M. Peitz, *Das Originalregister Gregors VII. im Vatikanischen Archiv (Reg. Vat. 2) nebst Beiträgen zur Kenntnis der Originalregister Innozenz' III. und Honorius' III. (Reg. Vat. 4–11)* (Sitzungsberichte der philosophisch-historischen Klasse, vol. 165/5), Wien: Alfred Hölder, 1911, 259.

178 Peitz, *Originalregister*, 256. Fournier, "Review of 'Wolf von Glanvell, Die Kanonessammlung des Kardinals Deusdedit,'" at 573–574 also pointed to the reception of Deusdedit in the *Britannica* which was overlooked by Wolf von Glanvell.

179 Wolf von Glanvell, *Kanonessammlung des Kardinals Deusdedit*, LI–LII.

180 Stutz, "Review of 'Wolf von Glanvell, Die Kanonessammlung des Kardinals Deusdedit,'" 2275; Friedberg, "Review of 'Wolf von Glanvell, Die Kanonesssammlung des Kardinals Deusdedit,'" 470: "Das war eben der grosse Uebelstand der Ausgabe von Martinucci, dass mehrere canones oft zusammen gedruckt waren, so dass sie von dem Suchenden nicht gefunden werden konnten."

collection, the compiler deployed a—more or less cogent—content-based system of organization, such as pope—bishops—clerics—laity, and grouped the canons according to the topic they addressed. The manifold statements in one canon, however, posed a problem for the compiler: Under which topic should this canon be grouped? Or should it be copied over and over again, wasting time and expensive parchment? Deusdedit opted for a combination of both principles, a "Mittelstellung [...] zwischen den früheren chronologischen und den späteren systematischen Sammlungen."[181] He arranged the canons according to their age within specific groups of sources, since Deusdedit started each book with conciliar texts, followed by decretals, excerpts from the Church Fathers, and secular laws.[182] The canons thus gathered were rather indigestible for the reader looking for texts on a specific problem. To overcome this drawback, Deusdedit added a kind of thematic *capitulatio*, similar to a register or index, at the very beginning of the manuscript. He listed specific statements—for instance, *Quod Romanam ecclesiam nemo possit iudicare*—and each of the canons in which they could be found, and thus provided a means to access the whole of his collection; by the same token, one canon was listed as supporting different statements. With this *capitulatio*, Deusdedit strove to eliminate the disadvantages of both the chronological and the systematic structure. A careful copy of this numbering, however, was of paramount importance to Deusdedit, lest the reader become enraged by misleading references.[183]

Deusdedit's decision to leave even longer texts more or less intact resulted in the "famous" canon lib. 3 c. 149, *Ex romano pontificali*, which occupies nearly thirty pages of the printed edition.[184] This was far from usable.

181 Hirsch, "Review of 'Wolf von Glanvell, Die Kanonessammlung des Kardinals Deusdedit,'" 799.

182 Dusil, *Wissensordnungen*, 96 n. 108 (with reference to further literature).

183 Wolf von Glanvell, *Kanonessammlung des Kardinals Deusdedit*, 3 line 3–11 (prologue to the collection): "Singulas autem deflorationes huic operi insertas iuxta ordinem capitulorum minime locavi, quia pene omnes alię bina, alię plura in se negotia continent. Et si secundum numerum negotiorum, de quibus agunt, acciperent sectionem, mihi laborem plurimum et auctoritati afferent derogationem. Ideoque moneo scriptorem, ne lector graviter offendatur, ut non solum in emendatione codicis verum etiam in utrisque numeris recte scribendis et cautissime emendandis diligentiam adhibeat, scilicet in eo, qui subpositus est quibusque capitulis et item in eo, qui per totum codicem prepositus est singulis deflorationibus."

184 Wolf von Glanvell, *Kanonessammlung des Kardinals Deusdedit*, 348–377. On this canon, see, for instance, Przemysław Nowak, "Das Papsttum und Ostmitteleuropa (Böhmen-Mähren, Polen, Ungarn) vom ausgehenden 10. bis zum Beginn des 13.

From the the very start, Wolf von Glanvell intended to break up these long canons and thus increase the usability of his edition:

> "[Z]unächst muss eine neue Capiteleintheilung vorgenommen werden, da in der Handschrift sehr häufig in einem und demselben Capitel ganz verschiedenartiges erscheint; doch werden selbstverständlich, um Vergleichungen zu ermöglichen, die alten Nr. (der Handschrift) in Klammern beigefügt werden. Erst durch diese Neueintheilung wird ein Auffinden der einzelnen Stellen ohne allzu große Mühe möglich werden."[185]

Indeed, Wolf von Glanvell drastically increased the number of canons by subdividing them: his edition counts 1216 canons instead of the original 698; and the aforementioned can. 149 of lib. 3 encompasses 84 canons in the edition.[186] "This was an unfortunate decision," stated Fowler-Magerl in 2005, "the authentic numbering is essential for an understanding [of] the rubrics in the capitulation."[187] Fournier also remained reluctant: "L'introduction de cette numérotation ne serait pas, à mon avis, sans graves inconvénients, si l'éditeur ne s'était imposé la règle de conserver, à côté des numéros nouveaux, les numéros anciens qu'il imprime entre parenthèses."[188] At least, Fournier concluded, Wolf von Glanvell added the original numbers in parentheses, thus allowing for the use of both *capitulatio* and collection. Fournier suspected that the old numbers would be in use for quite a long time: "je crois qu'on se servira longtemps encore de ces anciens numéros."[189]

Why did Wolf von Glanvell change the numbering of the canons? The reason for this editorial decision lies in an unfortunate and misleading

---

Jahrhunderts. Mit einer Neuedition von JL 9067," in: Jochen Johrendt / Harald Müller (ed.), Rom und die Regionen. Studien zur Homogenisierung der lateinischen Kirche im Hochmittelalter, Berlin / Boston: De Gruyter, 2012, 331–369; Przemysław Nowak, "*Dagome iudex* w *Zbiorze kanonów* kardynała Deusdedita," in: Studia Źródłoznawcze–Commentationes 51, 2013, 75–94.

185 Cf. "Bericht über die Vorarbeiten" (Wien, AÖAW, Savigny-Kommission, Karton 1 / Mappe 7, Akte 428/1901, s.d. (presumably spring 1901)).

186 Cf. Wolf von Glanvell, *Kanonessammlung des Kardinals Deusdedit*, XII, LIII; Dusil, *Wissensordnungen*, 95.

187 Fowler-Magerl, *Clavis Canonum*, 160.

188 Fournier, "Review of 'Wolf von Glanvell, Die Kanonessammlung des Kardinals Deusdedit,'" 570.

189 Fournier, "Review of 'Wolf von Glanvell, Die Kanonessammlung des Kardinals Deusdedit,'" 570.

sentence by Deusdedit. He spoke of *deflorationes*, *capitula*, and *negotia* to describe the structure of his collection. Theodor von Sickel assumed a triple numbering of canons in the collection according to the aforementioned terms, although the *negotia*-numbering was no longer extant.[190] Wolf von Glanvell's reading was based on von Sickel's, but he omitted the idea of a *negotia*-level numbering:

> "In der Originalhandschrift war die Einteilung innerhalb des Buches eine andere, als wie sie uns überliefert erscheint: Deusdedit hatte aus seinen Quellen eine Blütenlese (deflorationes) von ihm geeignet erscheinenden Stücken angelegt und diese durch die ganze Handschrift hindurch eigens numeriert; eine derartige 'defloratio' konnte auch mehr als eine Frage behandeln und so auch mehrere Kapitel umfassen, wie denn auch verschiedene kurze deflorationes in ein Kapitel zusammengefaßt wurden."[191]

The assumption that the manuscript Vat. lat. 3833 does not transmit the original version allowed him to regroup canons freely. If, however, one does not interpret *deflorationes* and *capitula* in the sense of a "Doppelzählung,"[192] but rather as one and the same, the numbering in the Vatican manuscript does not need any alteration—the numbers in the *capitulatio* refer to the canons in the manuscript as Deusdedit intended. Emanuel Hirsch was therefore very critical about this change:

> "Darum scheint mir die neue Kapiteleinteilung trotz der dadurch erreichten grösseren Übersichtlichkeit ein schwererer Eingriff in das eigenste Werk des Deusdedit zu sein, als es auf den ersten Blick aussieht. Das der Kanonessammlung vorangeschickte Sachregister, das Deusdedit sicher mit Liebe und Mühe fertigte [...], kommt in der neuen Ausgabe nicht mehr recht zur Geltung."[193]

This misunderstanding of *deflorationes* and *capitula* in the wake of von Sickel's assumption and Wolf von Glanvell's focus on identifying the *fontes* of Deusdedit led to this flaw in his edition (which, however, is not as serious as it seems, since it remains usable due to the preservation of the

190 von Sickel, *Privilegium Otto I.*, 62–63.
191 Wolf von Glanvell, *Kanonessammlung des Kardinals Deusdedit*, XII.
192 Hirsch, "Review of 'Wolf von Glanvell, Die Kanonessammlung des Kardinals Deusdedit,'" 798.
193 Hirsch, "Review of 'Wolf von Glanvell, Die Kanonessammlung des Kardinals Deusdedit,'" 799. Similarly: Peitz, *Originalregister Gregors VII.*, 263–265.

old numbering in parenthesis, as Fournier noted). Despite this weakness, the edition of 1905 is still in use today as one of the oldest editions of pre-Gratian canonical collections.[194] Wolf von Glanvell hoped for a friendly reception:

> "Und wenn in einzelnen Punkten das Werk dem Willen nicht entspricht, so möge nicht vergessen werden, daß hier zum erstenmale der Versuch gemacht wird, eine der großen vorgratianischen Kanonessammlungen in einer wissenschaftlichen Anforderungen entsprechenden Art und Weise herauszugeben. Meine Nachfolger werden es leichter haben; aber aller Anfang ist schwer."[195]

Even with its academic merits, the edition did not sell well. The publisher, Ferdinand Schöningh in Paderborn, wrote only two years after publication that the missing second volume prevented the book from being sold successfully:

> "... daher ist das Werk unvollständig und daraus ergibt sich die natürliche Folge, daß das Werk, das ohnehin schon auf einen kleinen Abnehmerkreis beschränkt ist, in seiner Absatzfähigkeit noch mehr gehemmt wird, da jeder Interessent den Ankauf des Werkes als Torso unterlassen wird; darin wurde ich nun umso mehr bestärkt, als der bisherige Absatz in Wirklichkeit ein nur geringer ist und der gegebenen Verhältnisse zufolge auch für die Zukunft eine größere Absatzfähigkeit nicht zu erwarten ist."[196]

According to his own account, the publisher had expenses of 3806 marks compared to revenues of 1281 marks: a deficit of 2525 marks remained. He urged the "Savigny-Kommission" in Vienna to promote the sale of this book.[197] The "Savigny-Kommission," however, remained reluctant, because

194 Some important editions of canonical collections have not yet been replaced: Wasserschleben's edition of Regino (Wasserschleben, *Reginonis abbatis Prumiensis libri duo* (1840)), although Wilfried Hartmann is currently preparing a new edition of Regino's collection; Friedberg's edition of Gratian's *Decretum* (Emil Friedberg, *Corpus Iuris Canonici*, vol. 1: *Decretum Magistri Gratiani*, Leipzig: Bernhard Tauchnitz, 1879); Hinschius' edition of Pseudo-Isidore's *Decretales* (Hinschius, *Decretales Pseudo-Isidorianae et Capitula Angilramni* (1863)).

195 Wolf von Glanvell, *Kanonessammlung des Kardinals Deusdedit*, VI.

196 Ferdinand Schöningh to the "Savigny-Kommission" (Wien, AÖAW, Savigny-Kommission, Karton 1 / Mappe 26, 1907 December 13).

197 Ferdinand Schöningh to the "Savigny-Kommission" (Wien, AÖAW, Savigny-Kommission, Karton 1 / Mappe 26, 1907 December 13): "Unter diesen Umständen

it could not find a replacement for Wolf von Glanvell, although the "Savigny-Stiftung" in Berlin had already granted 1800 marks for the completion of the second volume.[198] Emanuel Hirsch's brief prayer ("Möge nun eine andere Kraft das trefflich begonnene Werk glücklich zu Ende führen!"[199]) remained unheard. Luschin von Ebengreuth, as a member of the "Savigny-Kommission," wrote to Ferdinand Schöningh: "Da die Versuche der Akademie, einen geeigneten Bearbeiter für die Fortsetzung des Werkes zu finden, bisher ergebnislos waren, so stellt die Kommission es der geehrten Verlagsbuchhandlung frei, ihr einen solchen, wenn möglich, in Vorschlag

möchte ich mir die ganz ergebene Anfrage gestatten, ob Sie mir nicht Mittel und Wege zur Herbeiführung eines weiteren Absatzes zu bezeichnen in der Lage wären, damit ich nicht einen so bedeutenden Schaden erleide."
In the "Todfalls-Aufnahme," the inheritance of Wolf von Glanvell was valued by experts, among them Julius Meyerhoff, a bookseller from Graz. According to the minutes, the two contracts with Ferdinand Schöningh were dated to 1899 June 26 ("Die letztwilligen Verfügungen") and 1900 May 30 ("Collectio canonum"). The expert noted that there were no claims against the publisher (Graz, Steiermärkisches Landesarchiv, Bezirksgericht Graz-I, Verlässe P-XIV-202/1905): "[fol. 19r] 1. Der Verfasser Herr Dr. Wolf Edler von Glanvell hat das Honorar für die 1.te [fol. 19v] Auflage seines Werkes "Die letztwilligen Verfügungen etc." bereits vor Jahren erhalten und ist eine neue Auflage wohl ausgeschlossen. 2. Was das Werk des Erblassers "Die Collectio canonum des Kardinals Deusdedit" anbelangt, so liegt von diesem auf zwei Bände berechneten Werkes nur der 1.ste Band vor, wodurch infolge des Verklausulierungsvertrages die Erben besten Falles an den Verleger nichts daraufzahlen müssen."

198 Stutz, "Die Savigny-Stiftung seit 1901," XIV: "1800 Mark an Professor Dr. Wolf v. Glanvell für die Vorarbeiten zum zweiten Bande seiner Deusdedit-Ausgabe. Der Bedachte verunglückte kurz darauf tödlich in den Alpen. Die Wiener Akademie bemühte sich, allerdings umsonst, einen anderen Bearbeiter zu finden, und behielt zunächst für diesen den Betrag vor."

199 Hirsch, "Review of 'Wolf von Glanvell, Die Kanonessammlung des Kardinals Deusdedit,'" 800. Cf. Friedberg, "Review of 'Wolf von Glanvell, Die Kanonesssammlung des Kardinals Deusdedit,'" 2276: "... es möge bald eine andere, nicht minder tüchtige und aufopferungsfähige Kraft in die Bresche springen, um würdig zu vollenden, was Wolf v. Glanvell so schön begonnen hat." Fournier, "Review of 'Wolf von Glanvell, Die Kanonessammlung des Kardinals Deusdedit,'" 571: "Un terrible accident de montagne a tranché prématurément la carrière, si bien remplie, de M. Wolf von Glanwell." and, at 575: "Quoi qu'il en soit, le volume publié par M. de Glanwell [sic] sera d'un grand secours pour tous ceux qui s'occupent de l'histoire du droit et des institutions ecclésiastiques au moyen âge. Pourquoi faut-il que ce soit le dernier service que l'auteur leur ait rendu!"

zu bringen."[200] It was to no avail: a canon-by-canon analysis of Deusdedit's *Collectio canonum* is still lacking.[201]

4.3. Wolf von Glanvell's Two Editions: Summary

Wolf von Glanvell dedicated his academic time to two medieval single-manuscript collections (if one may call Deusdedit's collection that, although fragments of Deusdedit's collection are extant in other manuscripts). He produced two editions that have stood the test of time, were in keeping with contemporary scholarly practices, and, with respect to his edition of Deusdedit, even our practices today. Both editions also reveal the fundamental influence of Theodor von Sickel: the edition of the first collection, Vat. lat. 1348, resulted from a research stay at von Sickel's institute in Rome and the second was initiated by him. By editing these texts from around 1100, Wolf von Glanvell sought to fill the gap that then existed between the scholarship of Maassen and Schulte and to shed light on the pivotal period of the "Gregorian Reform," as Paul Founier had done a few years earlier.[202] Both editions of pre-Gratian canonical collections also highlight Wolf von Glanvell's skills in paleography, codicology, and the other ancillary sciences that he acquired during his early years as a student in Graz—he was thus a skilled scholar able to cope with the difficulties of editorial work.[203]

200 Luschin von Ebengreuth to Schöningh (Wien, AÖAW, Savigny-Kommission, Karton 1 / Mappe 26, 1907 December 27, concept).

201 Although much has been published about him and his collection, see Kéry, *Canonical Collection*, 230–233; Dusil, *Wissensordnungen*, esp. 93–106.

202 Basdevant-Gaudemet / Domingo, "Paul Fournier (1853–1935)," 312–313.

203 On his studies in Graz, see above 14.

5. Studies on Institutional History

Wolf von Glanvell also wrapped his mind around the history of legal institutions. He dedicated two books to this topic. His first was entitled "Die Negotia inter vivos," in which he presented canonical rules on contracts, such as those for land loans, safe custody, leases and sales agreements, contracts for work, and other such contracts. The second book deals with testamentary dispositions and statutory rules, that is, questions of successions in a general sense. He entitled this book "Die letztwilligen Verfügungen nach gemeinem kirchlichen Rechte." Both books deal with a nowadays often forgotten aspect of canon law, namely the impact of the Church on "private relations" between individuals. Canon law before 1917, and especially in the Middle Ages, is permeated with rules concerning interactions between individuals, hence the term canonical private law ("kanonisches Privatrecht").[204] Many of these rules are part of Book 3 of the traditional five-book scheme of the *Liber Extra*, which deals with clerics, their rights, and their duties. Due to the scarcity of archival material, it is not possible to reconstruct the making of these two books, what influenced their ultimate shape, or the discussions Wolf von Glanvell had with academic colleagues from first hand accounts; the two books must speak for themselves.

5.1. "Die Negotia inter vivos"

Wolf von Glanvell's first book on the ecclesiastical rules pertaining to private law was first published in 1897 with a second, slightly altered edition following in 1898.[205] Wolf von Glanvell selected some titles of Book 3 of the *Liber Extra*, namely titles 14 through 24, which deal with the loan of land (title 14: *De precariis*—similar to the Roman emphyteusis), loans (title 15: *De commodato*), safe custody (title 16: *De deposito*), sales agreements

204 Although many aspects of canonical private law have fallen into oblivion, there is one exception: marriage law. In Austria, marriage law was at Wolf von Glanvell's time an exception as the Church claimed to rule on marriages.

205 Wolf von Glanvell, *Studien aus dem canonischen Privatrechte. I. Die negotia inter vivos*, 1st edition, Graz: Styria, 1897, 2nd edition, Graz: Leuschner & Lubensky, 1898. On the second edition, see 68–69.

(title 17: *De emptione et venditione*), lease agreements (title 18: *De locato et conducto*), bartering (title 19: *De rerum permutatione*), fiefs (title 20: *De feudis*), securities (title 21: *De pignoribus et aliis cautionibus*), guarantors (title 22: *De fideiussoribus*), redemptions of debts (title 23: *De solutionibus*), and donations (title 24: *De donationibus*).

By choosing these topics, Wolf von Glanvell addressed the important crossroad of canon law and economy in the Middle Ages. Some chapters invited Wolf von Glanvell to elaborate on agricultural economy in the early Middle Ages, which relied heavily on the renting of land to peasants in return for crops or regular payments; others encouraged him to explain usury and fair price, the *iustum pretium*. In particular, the rules on usury and the prohibition of interest required convoluted legal constructions, such as the *contractus trinus*, to reconcile ecclesiastical requirements with economic necessities.[206]

Wolf von Glanvell dealt with these questions in a rather peculiar way: he wrote a commentary on the chapters of the relevant titles of the *Liber Extra*, or, to use his own words, he followed "in einer Art moderner Glosse den einzelnen Titeln des Corpus iuris canonici."[207] This decision was borne out of the following consideration: canon law was fragmentary, lacking titles on property rights and partnership agreements, and thus the "modern" divisions between property law, law of obligations, family and inheritance law were inappropriate.[208] With this in mind, Wolf von Glanvell decided to comment on each chapter separately. A methodological introduction and a summarizing chapter are consequently missing, as is an articulation of the overarching research question, apart from his quest to identify the influence of Roman and Germanic law on church law and to carve out the Church's own contribution to its legal system.[209]

His comments on the chapters of the *Liber Extra* reveal him as a legal historian well versed in three legal systems, namely Roman, canon, and

206 See Christian Neschwara, "Darlehen," in: Albrecht Cordes et al. (ed.), Handwörterbuch zur Deutschen Rechtsgeschichte, 2nd edition, vol. 1, Berlin: Erich Schmidt, 2008, 930–932; Mathias Schmoeckel / Matthias Maetschke, Rechtsgeschichte der Wirtschaft. Seit dem 19. Jahrhundert, 2nd edition, Tübingen: Mohr Siebeck, 2016, 16–20. An older study on usury, interests, and bills is from Wilhelm Endemann, Studien in der romanisch-kanonistischen Wirtschafts- und Rechtslehre bis gegen Ende des 17. Jahrhunderts, 2 vols., Berlin: Guttentag, 1874/1883 (reprint 1962).

207 Wolf von Glanvell, *Die negotia inter vivos*, III.

208 Wolf von Glanvell, *Die negotia inter vivos*, III.

209 On the latter point, see 98–100.

Germanic law. He used the classical texts of Roman law, such as the Digest, to point to the differences and similarities between Roman and canon law; he exploited the Monumenta Germaniae Historica to learn more about the *Formulae Andecavenses*, the *Formulae Marculfi*, and other texts;[210] and he used charters to explore the Middle Ages.[211] He also analyzed sources that were considered to be "typically" Germanic, such as the *Codex Euricianus*, the "Saxon Mirror" and the "Swabian Mirror."[212]

He also exploited the authors of the early modern literature of the sixteenth and seventeenth centuries, like Luis de Molina (1535–1600),[213] Giulio Claro (1525–1575),[214] Sigismondo Scaccia (sixteenth / seventeenth century),[215] Leonhardus Lessius (1554–1623),[216] Diego de Covarrubias y Leyva (1512–1577),[217] and others. The works of nineteenth-century authors are used only sporadically[218] and those of well-known representatives of the *Ius Canonicum Universum*, authors such as Ehrenreich Pirhing (1606–

210 E.g., Wolf von Glanvell, *Die negotia inter vivos*, 2 n. 1.

211 E.g., Wolf von Glanvell, *Die negotia inter vivos*, 27.

212 E.g., Wolf von Glanvell, *Die negotia inter vivos*, 63 n. 7, 136 n. 2.

213 Friso Ross, "Molina, Luis de," in: Michael Stolleis (ed.), Juristen. Ein biographisches Lexikon. Von der Antike bis zum 20. Jahrhundert, München: Beck, 1995, 437–438; Wim Decock, "Molina, On Justice and Right," in: Serge Dauchy et al. (ed.), The Formation and Transmission of Western Legal Culture. 150 Books that Made the Law in the Age of Printing, Cham: Springer, 2016, 142–144.

214 Ernst Holthöfer, "Claro (Clarus), Giulio," in: Michael Stolleis (ed.), Juristen. Ein biographisches Lexikon. Von der Antike bis zum 20. Jahrhundert, München: Beck, 1995, 128–129.

215 Christoph Bergfeld, "Scaccia, Sigismondo," in: Michael Stolleis (ed.), Juristen. Ein biographisches Lexikon. Von der Antike bis zum 20. Jahrhundert, München: Beck, 1995, 545.

216 See Toon van Houdt, "Leonardus Lessius," in: Wim Decock / Janwillem Oosterhuis (ed.), Great Christian Jurists in the Low Countries (Cambridge Studies in Law and Christianity), Cambridge: Cambridge University Press, 2021, 64–79.

217 Kurt Seelmann, "Covarubias (Covarruvias) y Leyva, Diego de," in: Michael Stolleis (ed.), Juristen. Ein biographisches Lexikon. Von der Antike bis zum 20. Jahrhundert, München: Beck, 1995, 142–143; Adolfo Giuliani, "Covarrubias y Leyva, Various Solutions," in: Serge Dauchy et al. (ed.), The Formation and Transmission of Western Legal Culture. 150 Books that Made the Law in the Age of Printing, Cham: Springer, 2016, 88–91.

218 E.g., Wolf von Glanvell, *Die negotia inter vivos*, 120 n. 3: Aemilius Richter, *Lehrbuch des katholischen und evangelischen Kirchenrechts*, 6th edition, Leipzig: Bernhard Tauchnitz, 1867; Walter, *Lehrbuch des Kirchenrechts aller christlichen Confessionen* (1861).

1690) or Anaklet Reiffenstuel (1642–1703),[219] seem to have been overlooked. What is missing altogether? The works of the "classical period" of canon law, such as the *summae* of the twelfth and thirteenth centuries, the glosses, the *casus*, and all the other writings of authors such as Panormitanus, Hostiensis, and other late medieval jurists. In this respect, the work seems somewhat unbalanced.[220]

The reception of this book was rather restrained and reviews are scarce. Ulrich Stutz praised the broad analysis of Italian charters and statutes, but lamented the lack of more recent authors. He also pointed out some erroneous interpretations, but concluded positively that the study could be helpful for searching detailed information: "Doch wird, wer mit den betreffenden Materien speziell sich beschäftigt, oder wer etwa in einem kanonistischen Seminar die einschlägigen Dekretalentitel interpretiren lässt, diese Studien nicht ohne Nutzen nachschlagen."[221] Joseph Biederlack SJ, professor in Rome, was more critical in his assessment. First, he ascribed to Wolf von Glanvell an attitude of liberalism ("ökonomischer Liberalismus"); second, he described as ahistorical Wolf von Glanvell's assumption that the Church was driven by economic policy—according to Biederlack, the Church strove for ethical economic behaviour independently of the broader economic framework; and third, he pointed to the methodologically questionable transfer of nineteenth-century liberal ideas to the Middle Ages.[222]

In contrast to the reviewers, Friedrich Thaner and Arnold Luschin von Ebengreuth, who were on the committee of the Faculty of Law of Karl-Franzens-Universität that reviewed his theses as part of the "Habilitation," were more optimistic. Thaner praised the choice of topic, saying that the author explored new ground and gave a decent overview of this topic, considering the limitations of time and library resources:

---

219 See: Stephan Dusil, "Ehrenreich Pirhing," in: Javier Otaduy et al. (ed.), Diccionario general de derecho canónico, vol. 6, Navarra: Aranzadi, 2012, 228–230 and Stephan Dusil, "Anaklet Reiffenstuel," in: Javier Otaduy et al. (ed.), Diccionario general de derecho canónico, vol. 6, Navarra: Aranzadi, 2012, 848–850.

220 Wolf von Glanvell, *Die negotia inter vivos*, IV apologized himself: "Widrige Umstände und Zeitmangel machten es auch unmöglich, im I. Theile die canonistischen Schriftsteller so ausführlich zu behandeln, als sie es eigentlich verdient hätten."

221 Ulrich Stutz, "Review of 'Wolf von Glanvell, Die negotia in vivos,'" in: Deutsche Litteraturzeitung 1898, 1608–1609. Review also by Sägmüller, "Review of 'Wolf von Glanvell, Studien aus dem kanonischen Privatrecht' and 'Wolf von Glanvell, Die Kanonessammlung des Cod. Vatican. lat. 1348,'" 626–629.

222 Joseph Biederlack SJ, "Review of 'Wolf von Glanvell, Die negotia in vivos,'" in: Allgemeines Litteraturblatt 8, 1899, 23–24.

> "Der Verfasser hat sich damit ein Thema gewählt, das bisher so gut wie brach gelegen hat. Wenn man die Kürze der Zeit bedenkt, die ihm zur Bearbeitung derselben zu Gebote stand, sowie die Unzulänglichkeit der Bibliotheksmittel so kann man seiner Arbeitskraft nur volle Anerkennung widerfahren lassen."[223]

He considered the analysis of sources and their treatment to be well done, but he felt Wolf von Glanvell's method was not suited to producing groundbreaking academic insights:

> "Gegen die eingeschlagene Methode der kapitelweisen Interpretation ist allerdings einzuwenden, daß sie zur Gewinnung großer wissenschaftlicher Resultate nicht die geeignetste ist, aber zu Theile wird der Mangel dadurch wett gemacht, daß jedem Titel zum Schluss eine kurze zusammenfassende Darstellung gewidmet ist."[224]

223 Friedrich Thaner in his report to the Faculty of Law in November 1897 (Graz, Universitätsarchiv, Jur. Fak., Z. 303 ex 1897/98); see Appendix 4 (transcription) and Fig. 3.

224 Friedrich Thaner in his report to the Faculty of Law in November 1897 (Graz, Universitätsarchiv, Jur. Fak., Z. 303 ex 1897/98). According to the minutes of the "Professoren-Collegium" held after the "Probevortrag" in early 1898, Thaner was more concerned about the depth of the analysis ("Referent Prof. F. Thaner faßt sein Urtheil über den Habilitationsact dahin zusammen, daß dem Dr. Wolf von Glanvell, obwol die zweite Habilitationsschrift 'Studien aus dem canonischen Privatrecht' unverkennbare Spuren der Eile an sich trägt, die venia legend für Kirchenrecht zu ertheilen sei....;" Graz, Universitätsarchiv, Jur. Fak., Z. 298 ex 1897/98).

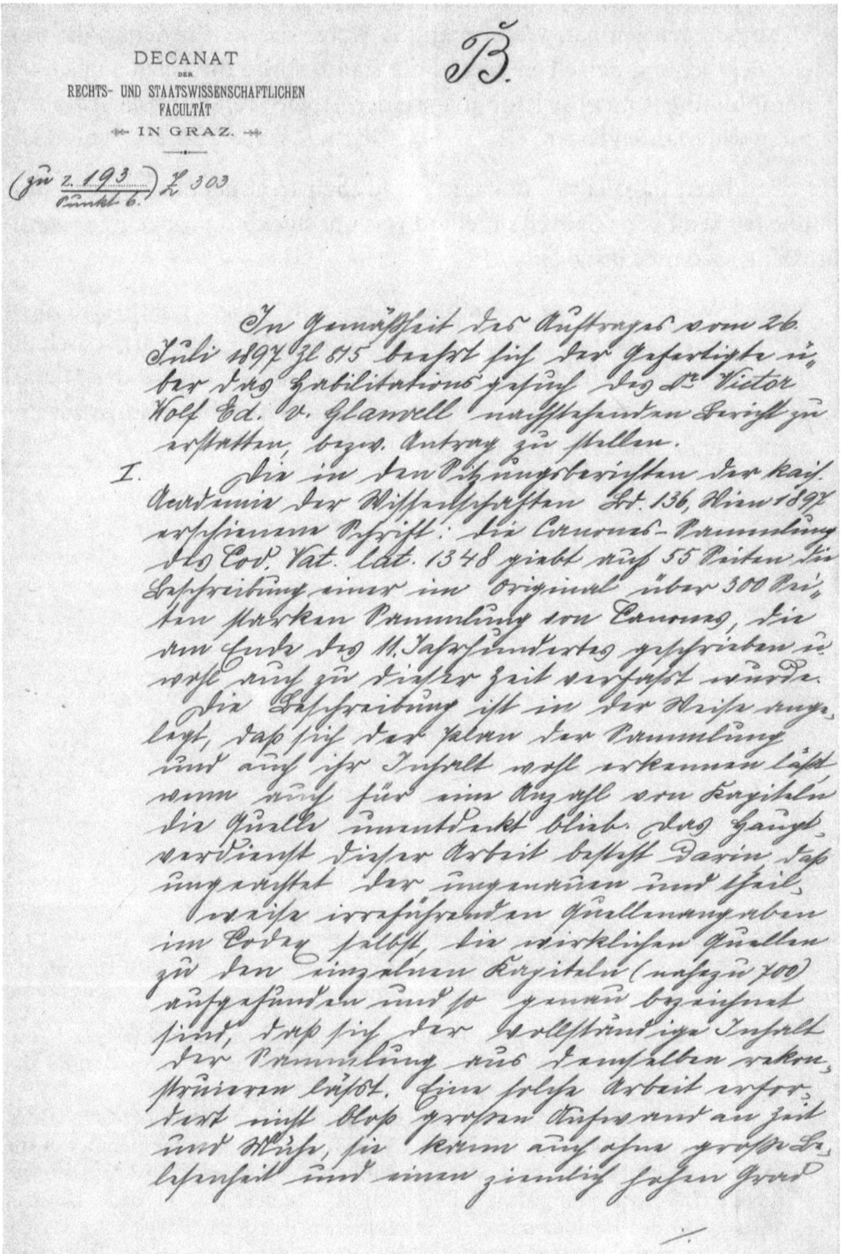

DECANAT
DER
RECHTS- UND STAATSWISSENSCHAFTLICHEN
FACULTÄT
IN GRAZ.

B.

(zu Z. 193 / Punkt 6.) Z. 303

In Gemäßheit des Auftrages vom 26. Juli 1897 Zl 815 beehrt sich der Gefertigte über das Habilitationsgesuch des Dr. Victor Wolf Ed. v. Glanvell nachstehenden Bericht zu erstatten, bezw. Antrag zu stellen.

I. Die in den Sitzungsberichten der kais. Academie der Wissenschaften Bd. 136, Wien 1897 erschienene Schrift: Die Canones-Sammlung des Cod. Vat. lat. 1348 giebt auf 55 Seiten die Beschreibung einer im Original über 300 Seiten starken Sammlung von Canones, die am Ende des 11. Jahrhundertes geschrieben u. wohl auch zu dieser Zeit verfaßt wurde.

Die Beschreibung ist in der Weise angelegt, daß sich der Plan der Sammlung und auch ihr Inhalt wohl erkennen läßt wenn auch für eine Anzahl von Kapiteln die Quelle unentdeckt blieb. Das Hauptverdienst dieser Arbeit besteht darin daß ungeachtet der ungenauen und theilweise irreführenden Quellenangaben im Codex selbst, die wirklichen Quellen zu den einzelnen Kapiteln (nahezu 700) aufgefunden und so genau bezeichnet sind, daß sich der vollständige Inhalt der Sammlung aus denselben reconstruiren läßt. Eine solche Arbeit erfordert nicht bloß großen Aufwand an Zeit und Mühe, sie kann auch ohne große Belesenheit und einen ziemlich hohen Grad

Fig. 3: Report of Friedrich Thaner on Wolf von Glanvell, 1897

The second reviewer, Luschin von Ebengreuth, also emphasized Wolf von Glanvell's quest for Roman, German, and originally canonical elements in the decretals. Furthermore, he checked Wolf von Glanvell's citations ("durchwegs als verläßlich"), esteemed his work on sources and doctrinal evolutions, and saw a promising academic career ahead for Wolf von Glanvell:

> "So zeugen denn die Arbeiten des Habilitierungs[be]werbers sowohl für dessen Befähigung zu quellenkritischen als auch zu dogmengeschichtlichen Arbeiten, sie erwiesen sich durch die ins Einzelne gehende quellenmäßige Begründung als sorgfältig aufgebaut und stellen als Erstlingswerke dem Verfasser eine schöne wissenschaftliche Zukunft in Aussicht."[225]

Reading this book more than 120 years after its publication, one is struck not only by how the intellectual background of the nineteenth century informs the work,[226] but also by two points specific to Wolf von Glanvell's work. The first is how Wolf von Glanvell touched upon the relationship between canon law and economics, which is a pivotal aspect of medieval law as the Church set the framework for economic activities in the Middle Ages. It is interesting that he touched on these topics, even if he did not elaborate on the economic part of the question. The second is how Wolf von Glanvell used works of both jurists and theologians to explain medieval and early modern canon law, for example Sigismondo Scaccia and Leonhardus Lessius. This is not surprising, since the question of "fair trade" was not only a legal issue, but also a question of moral theology. Nonetheless, the close interrelation of jurists and theologians has only recently been rediscovered and more broadly discussed.[227]

These aspects, however, are not explored in a detailed and explicit manner: the lack of a research perspective results in a descriptive study that undoubtedly offered interesting points of departure. Wolf von Glanvell,

---

225 Luschin von Ebengreuth, report to the Faculty of Law (Graz, Universitätsarchiv, Jur. Fak., Z. 304 ex 1897/98); see Appendix 4.

226 On this topic, see 89–100.

227 See, for instance: Wim Decock, *Theologians and Contract Law. The Moral Transformation of the Ius Commune (ca 1500–1650)* (Legal History Library 9 / Studies in the History of Private Law 4), Leiden / Boston: Brill 2013; Wim Decock, "Recht und Finanzen in der Spätscholastik," in: Stefan Grundmann / Jan Thiessen, Religiöse Werte im Recht (Rechtsvergleichung und Rechtsvereinheitlichung 50), Tübingen: Mohr Siebeck, 2017, 19–42.

however, did not use the material to draw more general conclusions, nor did he share with the reader his views pertaining to Roman and Germanic influences on canon law, to medieval law and economics, or to jurists and theologians. An interesting question, for instance, might have been the transformation of ancient Roman law in the early Middle Ages under the influence of Christianity and Christian economic ideas, but the reader remains disappointed.

Although Wolf von Glanvell avoided drawing specific conclusions, he did make pronounced statements about the Church: in the first edition of his "Die negotia inter vivos" he expressed some anticlerical ideas. He described, for instance, the Church as grasping and looking for its own financial advantage: "trotzdem die Kirche als einziges Ziel für ihre Angehörigen das Leben im Jenseits erklärte, wusste sie doch stets sehr gut ihren materiellen Vortheil in dieser Welt wahrzunehmen."[228] A few pages later, he asserted that the Church had acted selfishly, always seeking its own advantage rather than contractual fidelity: "Der eigene Vortheil geht der Kirche über die Vertragstreue. [...] Wir sehen hier wieder einmal jenen starren und anmaßenden Egoismus zum Durchbruche kommen, welcher sich im canonischen Rechte überall dort zeigt, wo der Vortheil der Kirche in Frage kommt."[229] And the last sentence of the entire book summarizes his previous interpretations of the Church as greedy and disloyal. It reads:

> "Der ganze Geist der kirchlichen Vermögensverwaltung aber lässt es ziemlich sicher erscheinen, dass nur bei Zuwendungen, welche der Kirche gemacht wurden, nicht aber bei solchen, welche von ihr ausgiengen, möglichst frei und günstig ausgelegt werden sollte, um ja nur soviel als möglich aus der einzelnen Verleihung herauszuschlagen."[230]

These strong statements were omitted in the second edition of "Die negotia inter vivos," published just one year later. The first quotation was rewritten[231] and the whole paragraph of the second quotation was replaced by a new one in which he reinterpreted the egoism of the Church as a means

228 Wolf von Glanvell, *Die negotia inter vivos*, 101–102 ad X 3.18.2.

229 Wolf von Glanvell, *Die negotia inter vivos*, 116–117 ad X 3.19.2.

230 Wolf von Glanvell, *Die negotia inter vivos*, 219 ad X 3.24.10. These strong judgments are also noted by Biederlack, "Review of 'Wolf von Glanvell, Die negotia in vivos,'" 24.

231 Wolf von Glanvell, *Die negotia inter vivos*, 2nd edition, 101: "eine Bestimmung, welche auch im cap. 2, Tit. XIX wiederkehrt."

to protect the Church from harm.[232] Finally, the concluding sentence of the second edition reads:

> "Die ganzen Verhältnisse des Mittelalters lassen es aber als ziemlich sicher erscheinen, dass die Kirche weit öfter in die Lage kam, diese freie und günstige Auslegung bei Zuwendungen vorzunehmen, welche ihr gemacht wurden, als bei solchen, welche sie zu leisten hatte."[233]

The impression of a greedy Church seeking its own advantage was replaced by the image of a defensive Church seeking protection from damage.

The archival material does not reveal any discussions about the book and its immediate reception, nor the friendly—or unfriendly?—advice colleagues may have given to rewrite certain passages of the book. Only the Biederlack review of 1899 uncovers the harsh statements by Wolf von Glanvell about the Church and stigmatises them as ahistorical and anticlerical. It is also not known how Wolf von Glanvell financed the second edition. In any case, the only differences between the first and the second editions, apart from the correction of some typographical errors, are the above-mentioned softened passages. It is likely, but cannot be proven, that Wolf von Glanvell did not mean to put his academic career at risk and therefore published a more ecclesiastically friendly version of his study on the private law of the Church. This idea does not seem to so far-fetched, for the "Culture Controversy" also shook Austria around 1900. In 1908, a speech by the canonist Ludwig Wahrmund on "Katholische Weltanschauung und freie Wissenschaft" sparked a heated and even violent dispute between Catholics and German-nationalists (the so-called "Wahrmund-Affäre").[234] It is very likely that Wolf von Glanvell strove to avoid such a conflict in Graz by smoothening harsh statements in the second edition.

---

232 Wolf von Glanvell, *Die negotia inter vivos*, 2nd edition, 116: "die Tendenz ist auch hier offenbar die, vornehmlich die Kirche vor Schaden zu bewahren, aber auch dem Missbrauche der Gewalt von Seite der mit der kirchlichen Vermögensverwaltung betrauten Persönlichkeiten entgegenzuwirken." He also dedicated a separate article to this chapter of the *Liber Extra*, see 102.

233 Wolf von Glanvell, *Die negotia inter vivos*, 2nd edition, 219.

234 See Wolfgang Forster, "Wahrmund, Ludwig," in: Neue Deutsche Biographie 27, 2020, 263–264; Hermann J. W. Kuprian, "'Machen Sie diesem Skandal ein Ende. Ihre Rektoren sind eine nette Gesellschaft.' Modernismusdiskussion, Kulturkampf und Freiheit der Wissenschaft: Die Wahrmund-Affäre 1907/08," in: Michael Gehler / Hubert Sickinger (ed.), Politische Affären und Skandale in Österreich. Von Mayerling bis Waldheim, Wien / Thaur / München: Studien Verlag, 1995, 99–127.

5.2. "Die letztwilligen Verfügungen nach gemeinem kirchlichen Rechte"

The second book Wolf von Glanvell authored is very similar in content and methodology to his first one. Here, he offered a detailed explanation of some other titles of Book 3 of the *Liber Extra*, namely those dealing with inheritance law.[235] By analyzing these titles, he shed light on the right of clerics to own property and the ensuing tension with the principle of poverty (cf. title 25: *De peculio clericorum*). He also discussed, among other topics, whether clerics—especially bishops—were entitled to bequeath their property to their relatives (or if it was bound to the Church) and whether monks could make a will.[236] He presented the requirements of a testament in canonical form, namely the parish priest and two witnesses,[237] and elaborated on the different recipients of a testamentary disposition (title 26: *De testamentis et ultimis voluntatibus*).[238] In the last title on intestacy rules, Wolf von Glanvell elucidated the question of whether a prelate of the Church (like the Metropolitan bishop) or someone else (like a secular ruler) was entitled to the inheritance of a deceased cleric.[239] This right to claim the inheritance was called *ius spolii* and led to continuous discussions in the Middle Ages (title 27: *De successionibus ab intestato*).[240]

This second book makes an overall more refined impression than the first volume. In addition to the works he had already used in "Die negotia in vivos," he included works from the "classical period" of canon law, such as the *Summa* by Johannes Faventinus (codex München, Staatsbibliothek, lat. 3873[241]) and the *Summa decretorum* by Huguccio (codex München, Staatsbibliothek, lat. 10247[242]), and he cited Goffredus de Trano, Hostiensis, and Durantis.[243] He explored the positions of early modern canonists like Pirhing, Schmalzgrueber, and Reiffenstuel[244] and he drew from papal

235 Wolf von Glanvell, *Die letztwilligen Verfügungen nach gemeinem kirchlichen Rechte*, Paderborn: Schöningh, 1900.

236 Wolf von Glanvell, *Die letztwilligen Verfügungen*, 34–60.

237 Wolf von Glanvell, *Die letztwilligen Verfügungen*, 110–124.

238 Wolf von Glanvell, *Die letztwilligen Verfügungen*, 158–165.

239 Wolf von Glanvell, *Die letztwilligen Verfügungen*, 251–262.

240 Hans-Jürgen Becker, "Spolienrecht," in: Adalbert Erler et al. (ed.), Handwörterbuch zur Deutschen Rechtsgeschichte, vol. 4, Berlin: Erich Schmidt, 1990, 1779–1780.

241 Wolf von Glanvell, *Die letztwilligen Verfügungen*, 24 n. 2.

242 Wolf von Glanvell, *Die letztwilligen Verfügungen*, 33 n. 2, 51 n. 5.

243 Wolf von Glanvell, *Die letztwilligen Verfügungen*, 25 n. 2 and n. 5 and 6.

244 Wolf von Glanvell, *Die letztwilligen Verfügungen*, 234 n. 6 and 7.

bulls,[245] concordats,[246] and the state legislation of Austria in the eighteenth and nineteenth centuries.[247] Finally, he included writers such as the Tübingen jurist of the *usus modernus*, Wolfgang Adam Lauterbach,[248] and municipal statutes like the Wrocław Statutes of 1588.[249] Again, he does not present a coherent explanation of canon law, but rather a modern gloss that included discussions of more far-reaching topics.[250] The multitude of sources, works, and authors used, are condensed in the footnotes in order to mirror the different discussions.

The second book was better received than the first. Reviewers, however, remained quite ambivalent. On the one hand, they praised the content of this study, describing it as "ausgezeichnete und gründliche Bearbeitung,"[251] "sehr gelehrt,"[252] "klare und ungekünstelte Erklärung der einzelnen Capitel,"[253] "nirgends willkürliche Behauptungen,"[254] "Anerkennung des Fleisses und der Kenntnisse des Verfassers,"[255] and even: "mit wahrem Bienenfleiss."[256] The study was considered to be a source-based analysis, which explored older research well, and the points Wolf von Glanvell made seemed well-founded. One reviewer, Franz Heiner, was particularly drawn to the discussion of the executors and whether or not legally invalid testaments were morally binding: "Nicht bloss Kanonisten, sondern auch Moralis-

---

245 See, for instance, Wolf von Glanvell, *Die letztwilligen Verfügungen*, 58.

246 E.g., the Austrian Concordat of 1855, see Wolf von Glanvell, *Die letztwilligen Verfügungen*, 58.

247 E.g., Wolf von Glanvell, *Die letztwilligen Verfügungen*, 48 n. 1, 59–60.

248 Wolf von Glanvell, *Die letztwilligen Verfügungen*, 234 n. 4.

249 Wolf von Glanvell, *Die letztwilligen Verfügungen*, 199 n. 2.

250 Wolf von Glanvell, *Die letztwilligen Verfügungen*, III: "Dass die Ausführungen dabei über den Rahmen einer 'modernen Glosse' meist wesentlich hinausgehen, werden z.B. die Behandlung des clericalen Peculiums, die Entwicklung des Erbrechtes der Bischöfe oder die Lehre von den Testamentsvollziehern und der Portio funeralis zeigen."

251 Franz Heiner, "Review of 'Wolf von Glanvell, Die letztwilligen Verfügungen,'" in: AKKR 80, 1900, 640–642, at 640.

252 Ulrich Stutz, "Review of 'Wolf von Glanvell, Die letztwilligen Verfügungen,'" in: Deutsche Litteraturzeitung 1901, 811–812, at 811.

253 Michael Hofmann, "Review of 'Wolf von Glanvell, Die letztwilligen Verfügungen,'" in: Zeitschrift für katholische Theologie 24, 1900, 723–724, at 723.

254 Hofmann, "Review of 'Wolf von Glanvell, Die letztwilligen Verfügungen,'" at 723–724.

255 Emil Friedberg, "Review of 'Wolf von Glanvell, Die letztwilligen Verfügungen,'" in: Deutsche Zeitschrift für Kirchenrecht 10, 1901, 398–399, at 398.

256 Stutz, "Review of 'Wolf von Glanvell, Die letztwilligen Verfügungen,'" 811.

ten können gerade hier in manchen Fragen Aufschluss und Belehrung finden."[257]

On the other hand, the form of this study, namely a commenting gloss, was almost unanimously criticized. Franz Heiner, for example, stated that the literary genre of a gloss might be helpful to introduce students to the *Corpus iuris canonici* or to satisfy the needs of some academics, but a more thematic and thus more readable presentation would have attracted a wider circle of readers.[258] Emil Friedberg expressed a similar idea: "In diesem Kommentar ist viel Gelehrsamkeit aufgespeichert und namentlich die kanonistische Literatur eingehend berücksichtigt; aber wer wird sich durch diesen Kommentar durchwinden?" He continued: "Wir glauben, der Verf. hat sich selbst mit seiner Methode das grösste Unrecht zugefügt." And he predicted a very reluctant reception of this study: "Seine Arbeit wird nicht die Beachtung finden, die er doch wünschen muss."[259] According to Ulrich Stutz, Wolf von Glanvell lacked the ability and the courage to digest the historical material and to present it in a comprehensive and coherent form. Thus, his study can best serve as a treasure trove for other canonists, as a "Fundgrube," as the reviewer Heiner put it.[260] Despite these drawbacks, the Tübingen canonist Johannes Baptist Sägmüller saw some positive aspects: "Auf der anderen Seite treten aber auch die Vorzüge der alten Manier hervor, allseitige minutiöse Behandlung des Stoffes, tiefes Eindringen in das Detail."[261] And Heiner concluded, somewhat conciliatorily, that content

257 Heiner, "Review of 'Wolf von Glanvell, Die letztwilligen Verfügungen,'" 641.

258 Heiner, "Review of 'Wolf von Glanvell, Die letztwilligen Verfügungen,'" 642: "Leider können wir aber unsere Uebereinstimmung mit der *Art* oder der *Methode* der Behandlung des Gegenstandes nicht so ohne weiteres erklären. So ganz von aller Systematisirung absehen, Kapitel nach Kapitel einfach interpretiren und das nach einem bestimmten Schema, einschlägige Fragen einfach in die Besprechung hineinziehen, wo dies gerade das Verständniss des Gegenstandes erheischt, das ist wohl die Art, wie man Schüler im Seminar in das Corpus iuris can. einführt, aber die Testamente als Ganzes ‚nach gemeinem kirchlichem Rechte' in dieser Weise behandeln, indem man die einzelnen Rechtssätze einfach nebeneinanderstellt und sie erläutert, das dürfte denn doch wohl wenig Anklang finden."

259 Friedberg, "Review of 'Wolf von Glanvell, Die letztwilligen Verfügungen,'" 398–399.

260 Heiner, "Review of 'Wolf von Glanvell, Die letztwilligen Verfügungen,'" 642 and also Hofmann, "Review of 'Wolf von Glanvell, Die letztwilligen Verfügungen,'" 724.

261 Sägmüller, "Review of 'Wolf von Glanvell, Studien aus dem kanonischen Privatrecht' and 'Wolf von Glanvell, Die Kanonessammlung des Cod. Vatican. lat. 1348,'" 627: "Auch hier treten die unausbleiblichen Fehler der alten Glosse zu Tage, daß Zusammengehöriges auseinandergerissen, bereits Dagewesenes wiederholt wird, daß keine Systematik und keine volle Ein- und Übersicht über die geschichtliche

trumps form: "Wer die Wissenschaft sucht, muss sie eben auch in diesem Gewande hinnehmen. Der Kern ist ein guter, die Schale ist Nebensache."[262]

5.3. Wolf von Glanvell's Two "Studien aus dem canonischen Privatrechte": Summary

The two studies by Wolf von Glanvell, "Die negotia inter vivos" and "Die letztwilligen Verfügungen," must be considered as a unit. Even if the title page does not indicate the connection between the two studies,[263] Wolf von Glanvell clearly expressed this connection in letters to Theodor von Sickel. In May 1899, he called the "letztwilligen Verfügungen" the "2. Theile meiner 'Studien aus dem canonischen Privatrechte'"[264] and, one year later, he announced to von Sickel that he had completed his studies on ecclesiastical private law: "Mit dem vorliegenden Buche sind, die Form ist allerdings etwas geändert worden, nun meine Studien aus dem canonischen Privatrecht beendigt."[265]

In both studies, he chose to expound several titles from Book 3 of the *Liber Extra*. In his study on the canonical aspects of inheritance law, he focused on universal canon law ("nach gemeinem kirchlichen Rechte"), concentrating primarily on ecclesiastical rules that applied to the whole Church, and only secondarily on local or regional developments or state legislation.[266] He addressed the various aspects of canon law in kind of

Entwicklung und das Ganze erreicht wird trotz der vielen historischen Ausführungen des Verf. Auf der anderen Seite treten aber auch die Vorzüge der alten Manier hervor, allseitige minutiöse Behandlung des Stoffes, tiefes Eindringen in das Detail."

262 Heiner, "Review of 'Wolf von Glanvell, Die letztwilligen Verfügungen,'" 642.

263 "Die negotia inter vivos" is part I. of his "Studien zum kanonischen Privatrechte," the study on inheritance law, however, does not appear as part II. This missing link already lead to confusion: Friedberg, "Review of 'Wolf von Glanvell, Die letztwilligen Verfügungen,'" 399: "Ein kleines Räthsel bietet auch das Register dem Benutzer. Dort wird Bd. I u. II unterschieden. Der letztere ist der vorliegende. Aber nirgends ist dieser weder auf dem Titelblatt noch in der Vorrede als solcher II. bezeichnet und über die Existenz des I. wird in jener Registernotiz nichts gesagt."

264 Wien, IÖG, Nachlass Sickel, Letter from Viktor Wolf von Glanvell to Theodor von Sickel, 1899 May 8.

265 Wien, IÖG, Nachlass Sickel, Letter from Viktor Wolf von Glanvell to Theodor von Sickel, 1900 May 24.

266 Wolf von Glanvell, *Die letztwilligen Verfügungen*, III: "[...] es will also darstellen den Inbegriff aller jener Rechtssätze, welche sich mit den letztwilligen Verfügungen beschäftigen und von der katholischen Kirche mit der Geltung für dieselbe in

a gloss, scrutinizing the text, explaining terms and concepts, and placing the chapters in a broader doctrinal context. Although the content of his discussion was widely appreciated, its form as a gloss was harshly criticized as inaccessible and indigestible. Above all, his studies did not start with an overarching question and thus did not yield new, far-reaching insights. Not only is his method remarkable, but also his narrow focus on the influence of Roman, Germanic, and canon law on the law of the Church. Nevertheless, he could have also focused on economic history, but he did not explore this connection by drawing from other areas of inquiry, such as the Historical School of Economics, or by articulating the connection as part of an overarching research question.[267] His studies on the impact of canon law on economy, trade, and private life stand alone.

With his publications, Wolf von Glanvell hoped to contribute to a future code of canon law.[268] The Code of 1917, however, did not take up older legal discussions in their entirety. For example, the specific inheritance rules for clerics were left out and can. 1513 CIC / 1917, which allowed one to relinquish goods for pious reasons, was no more than a remembrance of older debates.[269] Although the subject of loaning land was taken up in

ihrer ganzen Ausdehnung erlassen worden sind. Demzufolge sich örtliche Rechtsbildungen, durch welche einzelne Verhältnisse in für den ganzen Bereich der Kirche mannigfach verschiedener Weise geregelt wurden, erst in zweiter Linie zu berücksichtigen; ja die durch Gewohnheitsrecht erfolgte, vom gemeinen kirchlichen Erbrechte abweichende Regelung der erbrechtlichen Verhältnisse der Geistlichen in Österreich-Ungarn, Deutschland und Frankreich muss einem weiteren Buche vorbehalten bleiben."

267 Surprisingly, he was not the only one to study canon law in this way, as other studies were published in a similar vein, see 88–89. On economic history, see Roman Köster, *Einführung in die Wirtschaftsgeschichte. Theorien, Methoden, Themen*, Leiden: Ferdinand Schöningh, 2020, 11–19; erner Plumpe, "Wirtschaftsgeschichte zwischen Ökonomie und Geschichte–ein historischer Abriss," in: Werner Plumpe (ed.), Wirtschaftsgeschichte (Basistexte Geschichte 2), Stuttgart: Franz Steiner, 2008, 7–39, at 8–12.

268 See 92–94.

269 *Codex Iuris Canonici. Pii X Pontificis Maximi iussu digestus, Benedicti Papae XV auctoritate promulgatus*, Rome 1917, can. 1513 § 1 *Qui ex iure naturae et ecclesiastico libere valet de suis bonis statuere, potest ad causas pias, sive per actum inter vivos sive per actum mortis causa, bona relinquere.* § 2 *In ultimis voluntatibus in bonum Ecclesiae serventur, si fieri possit, sollemnitates iuris civilis; hae si omissae fuerint, heredes moneantur ut testatoris voluntatem adimpleant.* Translation: Edward Peters, *The 1917 or Pio-Benedictine code of Canon Law in English translation*, San Francisco: Ignatius, 2001, 505: "§ 1 Whoever by natural and ecclesiastical law can freely dispose of his goods can relinquish goods for pious causes, whether through a living act or

can. 1541 and can. 1542 CIC / 1917 (and even later, as a kind of a surviving fragment, in can. 1290–1298 and again in can. 1299–1310 CIC / 1983[270]), it was of much less importance than it had been previously. This was a consequence of a new understanding of canon law established in can. 1529 CIC / 1917: "Whatever the civil law establishes in a territory concerning contracts [...] and about resolution, is to be observed in canon law in ecclesiastical materials with the same effects, unless this is contrary to divine law or canon law provides otherwise."[271] In this regard, the previous legal distinction between the laity and the clergy was leveled out and rules on successions harmonized, and the older tradition of canonical private law slowly but surely came to an end. Wolf von Glanvell's wish to contribute to the future codification of canon law was not fulfilled.

through a will. / § 2 In final wills in favor of the Church, there should be observed insofar as it is possible the formalities of civil law; if these are omitted, the heirs are to be advised that they should fulfill the will of the testator."

270 *Codex Iuris Canonici / Codex des Kanonischen Rechts*, 9th edition, Kevelaer: Butzon & Bercker, 2018. On can. 1290, see Matthias Pulte, *Vermögensrecht der katholischen Kirche. Ein Handbuch für Studium und Praxis* (Mainzer Beiträge zum Kirchen- und Religionsrecht 6), Würzburg: Echter, 2019, 155–161.

271 can. 1529 CIC / 1917 *Quae ius civile in territorio statuit de contractibus tam in genere, quam in specie, sive nominatis sive innominatis, et de solutionibus, eadem iure canonico in materia ecclesiastica iisdem cum effectibus serventur, nisi iuri divino contraria sint aut aliud iure canonico caveatur.* Translation: Peters, *The 1917 Pio-Benedictine Code of Canon Law*, 511–512.

6. Wolf von Glanvell as Researcher in His Time

Wolf von Glanvell edited two single-manuscript canonical collections of the Middle Ages and focused on the content of Book 3 of the *Liber Extra* in his two institutional studies and one shorter journal article. The previous two chapters focused on these contributions, their production, content, methodology, and reception. This chapter considers Wolf von Glanvell as a legal historian around 1900 and asks two questions. First, what intellectual influences can be discerned, including colleagues within his academic network and books he consulted (6.1.)? Second, how can we understand his research in the context of the nineteenth century? That is to say, to what extent is he a representative of nineteenth-century research and to what extent is he independent (6.2.-4.)?

6.1. Colleagues, Networks, Library

It is an arduous, if not impossible task, to shed light on the academic background of Wolf von Glanvell, his networks, his colleagues, and how they influenced him.[272] The lack of academic papers is a first reason why his network is difficult to reconstruct; the fact that important aspects may

272 The dazzling term "network" is used for a wide-range of analyses, including quantitative historical research. In this context, "network" is used modestly, aiming at academic dialog partners, regardless of the length and the intensity of the contact. The scarcity of primary sources does not allow for an in-depth analysis of Wolf von Glanvell's contacts. On networks and their analysis see, e.g., Marten Düring / Florian Kerschbaumer, "Quantifizierung und Visualisierung. Anknüpfungspunkte in den Geschichtswissenschaften," in: Marten Düring et al. (ed.), Handbuch Historische Netzwerkforschung. Grundlagen und Anwendungen (Schriften des Kulturwissenschaftlichen Instituts Essen zur Methodenforschung 1), Berlin: Lit, 2016, 31–43 and Christian Marx, "Forschungsüberblick zur Historischen Netzwerkforschung. Zwischen Analysekategorie und Metapher," in: Marten Düring et al. (ed.), Handbuch Historische Netzwerkforschung. Grundlagen und Anwendungen (Schriften des Kulturwissenschaftlichen Instituts Essen zur Methodenforschung 1), Berlin: Lit, 2016, 63–84. On the application of network theory in historical studies, see for instance: Christian Rollinger, *Amicitia sanctissime colenda.* Freundschaft und soziale Netzwerke in der späten Republik (Studien zur Alten Geschichte 19), Heidelberg: Antike, 2014, at 353–389.

have been discussed in person, namely on the floors of the Karl-Franzens-Universität, is a second reason. Nevertheless, it is obvious that Wolf von Glanvell emerged from an academic atmosphere in Austria that was open to legal history. In the middle of the nineteenth century, the Austrian minister Leo von Thun-Hohenstein (1811–1888) established legal history as the basis for the study of law. Consequently, the first two academic years for a law student were filled with courses on Roman law, canon law, German Imperial and Legal History ("Deutsche Reichs- und Rechtsgeschichte"), and Common German Private Law ("Gemeines Deutsches Privatrecht").[273]

At that time, canon law research in Austria was source-oriented: Friedrich Maassen (1823–1900), who became Ordinarius in Graz in 1860, published his famous survey "Geschichte der Quellen und der Literatur des canonischen Rechts im Abendlande," complementary to Savigny's "Geschichte des römischen Rechts im Mittelalter," in 1870.[274] His successor in Graz was Friedrich Thaner (1839–1915), the academic teacher of Wolf von Glanvell. Thaner had studied at the "Institut für Österreichische Geschichtsforschung" and was thus also influenced by Theodor von Sickel and his source-based method.[275] It is therefore not surprising that Thaner expressed his gratitude to Theodor von Sickel in his *Summa magistri Rolandi*, which was based on his "Habilitationsschrift."[276] Before coming to Graz, Thaner taught at Innsbruck for some years (1871–1888). He joined

273 Ebert, "Die Pflege der Rechtsgeschichte im Zeichen der Historischen Schule," 245–246; more general: Kurt Ebert, *Die Grazer Juristenfakultät im Vormärz. Rechtswissenschaft und Rechtslehre an der Grazer Hochschule zwischen 1810 und 1848* (Grazer rechts- und staatswissenschaftliche Studien 22), Graz: Leykam, 1969; and Thomas Simon, "Die Thun-Hohensteinische Universitätsreform und die 'Geschichtliche Rechtswissenschaft,'" in: Beiträge zur Rechtsgeschichte Österreichs 7, 2017, 132–143. Some remarks also by Schäfer, *Juristische Germanistik*, 306–307, 492.

274 Maassen, *Geschichte der Quellen und der Literatur des canonischen Rechts* (1870). On him: Ebert, "Die Pflege der Rechtsgeschichte im Zeichen der Historischen Schule," 252–254; Grass, "Kirchenrechtslehrer der Universität Graz," 228–233; Puza, "Kirchenrechtslehrer an der Universität Graz," 249–258.

275 Grass, "Kirchenrechtslehrer der Universität Graz," 239–253; Ebert, "Die Pflege der Rechtsgeschichte im Zeichen der Historischen Schule," 255–256; Puza, "Kirchenrechtslehrer an der Universität Graz," 262–263. On Thaners's education at the "Institut für Österreichische Geschichtsforschung" see also Lhotsky, *Geschichte des Instituts für Österreichische Geschichtsforschung*, 97–98.

276 Friedrich Thaner, *Die Summa Magistri Rolandi nachmals Papstes Alexander III., nebst einem Anhange Incerti Auctoris Quaestiones*, Innsbruck: Wagner, 1874, VIII: "Zugleich ergreife ich diesen Anlass, um meinem Lehrer, Herrn Professor Theodor Sickel in Wien, auch dafür, dass er mir bei dieser Arbeit mannigfach fördernd an die Hand gieng, meinen besten Dank auszusprechen."

the Graz faculty in 1888 and remained there until his retirement in 1907. Thaner edited several texts of the tenth and eleventh centuries, including the canonical collection compiled by Anselm of Lucca and some treatises in the MGH-edition *Libelli de Lite.*[277] Thaner's source-oriented legal history and his editorial work influenced Wolf von Glanvell, who heard his lectures on canon law and attended his "Kirchenrechtliches Seminar."[278] Relatively late, Thaner also turned to a more doctrinal approach to legal history, as evidenced by two publications on marriage law (1900, 1907).[279]

Thaner was also one of the two members on Wolf von Glanvell's habilitation committee, the other being Arnold Luschin von Ebengreuth (1841–1932). Luschin von Ebengreuth was a key figure in Austrian legal history around 1900. He published on numismatics, on courts in the late Middle Ages, on German students in Italy, on German and Austrian legal history, and other topics.[280] Von Ebengreuth, like Thaner, was source-oriented, but did not share an interest in doctrinal history. He never read "Deutsches Privatrecht" and was described as a pure historian, as "ganz und gar Historiker,

277 Grass, "Kirchenrechtslehrer der Universität Graz," 246, 250–251. Editions by Thaner, for instance: Friedrich Thaner, *Anselm II., Bischof von Lucca, Collectio Canonum una cum collectione minore*, Innsbruck: Wagner, 1906–1915 (reprint 1965); Friedrich Thaner, "Libelli Bernaldi presbyteri monachi," in: MGH Libelli de lite, tom. II (MGH LdL 2), Hannover: Hahn'sche Buchhandlung, 1892, 1–168.

278 Graz, Universitätsarchiv, Jur. Fak., Nationale Viktor Wolf von Glanvell. Grass, "Kirchenrechtslehrer der Universität Graz," 253 wrote (without any footnotes / further references): "Bei der Bearbeitung [der Sammlung Vat. lat. 1348–SD] wurde Wolf durch Thaners Rat wie durch Hinweise Maassens unterstützt."

279 Friedrich Thaner, "Die literar-geschichtliche Entwicklung der Lehre vom Error qualitatis redundans in personam und vom Error conditionis," in: Sitzungsberichte der Kaiserlichen Akademie der Wissenschaften, philosophisch-historische Klasse 142, 1900 (as Abhandlung 2); Friedrich Thaner, "Simulatae nuptiae nullius momenti sunt," in: Österreichisches Zentralblatt für die juristische Praxis 25, 1907, 277–285.

280 On Luschin von Ebengreuth, see Ebert, "Die Pflege der Rechtsgeschichte im Zeichen der Historischen Schule," 279–282; Wilhelm Brauneder, "Luschin von Ebengreuth, Arnold (1841–1932)," in: Albrecht Cordes et al. (ed.), Handwörterbuch zur Deutschen Rechtsgeschichte, 2nd edition, vol. 3, Berlin: Erich Schmidt, 2016, 1099; Gunter Wesener, "Arnold Luschin von Ebengreuth (1841–1932), Rechtshistoriker und Numismatiker," in: Karl Acham (ed.), Rechts-, Sozial- und Wirtschaftswissenschaften aus Graz. Zwischen empirischer Analyse und normativer Handlungsanweisung. Wissenschaftsgeschichtliche Befunde aus drei Jahrhunderten (Kunst und Wissenschaft aus Graz 3), Wien: Böhlau, 2011, 255–271; Marianne Luschin-Dreier, *Arnold Luschin Ritter von Ebengreuth. Ein Leben im Zeichen der Rechtsgeschichte*, 1992 (typoscript, PhD Graz).

nicht Dogmatiker."[281] The source of inspiration for Wolf von Glanvell's elaboration on institutional history is therefore most likely not Luschin von Ebengreuth. Nonetheless, Luschin von Ebengreuth supported Wolf von Glanvell, because he appreciated his academic merits and promoted him to "Privatdocent."[282]

In addition to Thaner and Luschin von Ebengreuth, a third influential person should be mentioned in this context: Theodor von Sickel. As we have seen, he inspired the edition of Vat. lat. 1348 and initiated the edition of Deusdedit's collection. Wolf von Glanvell even dedicated this masterpiece to him as "Freunde und Meister."[283]

A final person in Wolf von Glanvell's network to consider is Gustav Hanausek (1855–1927), but it is difficult to precisely ascertain his influence. Hanausek taught Roman law in Graz, and, more importantly, current private and commercial law, and he was a famous teacher.[284] Hanausek was one of the witnesses at Wolf von Glanvell's wedding, which may indicate a close, even private relationship between the two. If and how Hanausek influenced Wolf von Glanvell's doctrinal approach, remains uncertain.

In sum, Wolf von Glanvell's editorial activity, his dedication to sources, and his skilled use of paleography are typical of the Austrian and especially the Graz academic scene in the late nineteenth century. Maassen, Thaner, and Wolf von Glanvell shared an interest in editions, and in this respect, Wolf von Glanvell was representative of contemporary trends. After the death of Wolf von Glanvell in 1905 and of Thaner in 1915, source-oriented research in Graz, including editorial activities, came to an end:

> "Für die Kirchenrechtswissenschaft an der Universität Graz bedeutete die Jahrhundertwende insofern einen Einschnitt, als etwa um diese Zeit jene betont quellenkundlich orientierte Forschungsrichtung ihrem Ende zuging, die mit der Berufung Bernhard Maassens in den sechziger Jahren

---

281 Paul Puntschart, cited according to: Ebert, "Die Pflege der Rechtsgeschichte im Zeichen der Historischen Schule," 280.

282 Von Ebengreuth was also personally linked to him, as he was the uncle of Wolf von Glanvell's wife, Mary, the daughter of his brother Eugen Franz; see above 17.

283 Wolf von Glanvell, *Kanonessammlung des Kardinals Deusdedit*, title page.

284 Wesener, *Geschichte der Rechtswissenschaftlichen Fakultät der Universität Graz*, vol. 1: *Römisches Recht und Naturrecht*, 98–101; Ebert, "Die Pflege der Rechtsgeschichte im Zeichen der Historischen Schule," 271–272; Leopold Wenger and Paul Koschaker were, among others, his students.

hier Wurzeln geschlagen und in der Folgezeit zu so bedeutenden wissenschaftlichen Leistungen geführt hatte."[285]

Knowing Wolf von Glanvell's network of colleagues and friends helps to elucidate his academic background. This is a first approach to contextualizing him and ascertaining his influences; a second approach is to examine his library collection. Scrutinizing his preferred authors and their works has the potential to shed further light on his intellectual influences. Although his library is no longer extant, the so-called "Todfalls-Aufnahme," the official inventory of his belongings, his property, and his financial means, including his debts, after his death, makes it possible to reconstruct it.[286] On May 29, 1905, the court-appointed expert on books, Julius Meyerhoff, a bookseller in Graz, listed all of Wolf von Glanvell's academic and non-academic books.[287]

The result, however, is quite disappointing. His library included Georges and Schenkel, the leading Latin and Greek dictionary, the "Rechtslexikon" by Holtzendorf, volume 2 of Scherer's "Kirchenrecht," and the *Summa decretorum* edited by Heinrich Singer. He also owned Schmidt's *Thesaurus iuris ecclesiastici* in seven volumes, and some other books of the eighteenth century, such as Thomassin's *Vetus et nova ecclesiae disciplina circa beneficia et beneficiarios* and Schmier's *Jurisprudentia canonica*. In addition, Wolf von Glanvell seemed to be interested in religious orders, congregations, and regular canons. Does his interest in these topics reflect his involvement with the course on "Ordensrecht," which he taught in the summer terms of 1903,

285 Ebert, "Die Pflege der Rechtsgeschichte im Zeichen der Historischen Schule," 286; similar Ebert, "Die Pflege der Rechtsgeschichte im 19. Jahrhundert," 256: "Mit dem Tod Glanvells und seines ihn noch um ein volles Jahrzehnt überlebenden Lehrers Thaner erlosch die seit der Berufung Maassens in den sechziger Jahren in Graz etablierte, betont quellenkundlich orientierte Forschungsrichtung der Kanonistik." See also Grass, "Kirchenrechtslehrer an der Universität Graz," 253. At the University of Graz, Arnold Pöschl (1880–1959) decided to pursue an academic career in canon law after the death of Wolf von Glanvell. He succeeded Friedrich Thaner and worked intensively on questions of institutional history, thereby following the path of Wolf von Glanvell; see Nikolaus Grass, "Arnold Pöschl †," in: ZRG.KA 46, 1960, 659–662, at 659; Grass, "Kirchenrechtslehrer an der Universität Graz," 259–266; Puza, "Kirchenrechtslehrer an der Universität Graz," 264.

286 Steiermärkisches Landesarchiv, Bezirksgericht Graz-I, Verlässe P-XIV-202/1905, fol. 17v-19r.

287 See Appendix 3.

1904 and 1905?[288] Some canon law books were not listed separately, but only by their value ("Zwanzig diverse kirchenrechtliche Bücher a 50h-10 Kronen"). In sum, the library seems quite limited. He did not own books by Friedrich Thaner or Theodor von Sickel, nor any other edition of a pre-Gratian canonical collection,[289] nor even Friedberg's bipartite *Corpus Iuris Canonici*, which included seminal texts like Gratian's *Decretum* and the *Liber Extra*. This is rather surprising, since the latter was the corner-stone of his institutional studies. Were they not listed because he kept them elsewhere? Or did he use a library copy at the university? It is a riddle that remains unsolved. We do know, however, that he intended to expand his library because shortly before his death, as he ordered books for more than 200 Kronen, which was about two-thirds of a month's income.[290] It is, however, impossible to reconstruct these orders.[291]

Unfortunately, Wolf von Glanvell's personal library does not shed much light on his reading preferences, his underlying ideas, or his assumptions. The questions of why he was interested in institutional history and why he chose the unusual method of a modern gloss remain unanswered. In contrast to his reading preferences, his personal network of colleagues helps to understand him a slightly better. In Rome and in Graz, Wolf von Glanvell was surrounded by source-orientated, edition-prone legal historians, and he lines up well with the other Graz legal historians.

288 See Appendix 3, esp. no 4, no 8, no 11, no 13, and Appendix 2. von Scherer, *Handbuch des Kirchenrechtes II*, covers next to sacraments (esp. marriage law), also "Ordensrecht" (708–880), possibly also pointing to his interest in this topic. Why were religious orders of interest to Wolf von Glanvell? Does his interest reflect the importance of orders in the Kulturkampf, which, as supposedly antiliberal institutions, stood in the way of the free development of the personality? On this point, see Ruppert, "'Nach Canossa gehen wir nicht,'" 708–709.

289 For instance, Martinucci's edition of Deusdedit or Wasserschleben's edition of Regino.

290 Steiermärkisches Landesarchiv, Bezirksgericht Graz-I, Verlässe P-XIV-202/1905, fol. 25v-26r.

291 Wolf von Glanvell owed the bookstore "Meyerhoff" 84 Kronen; this bookstore now belongs to "Buchhandlung Moser;" older documents, however, have not been transmitted (kind mail by Buchhandlung Moser, Graz, 2021 May 4).

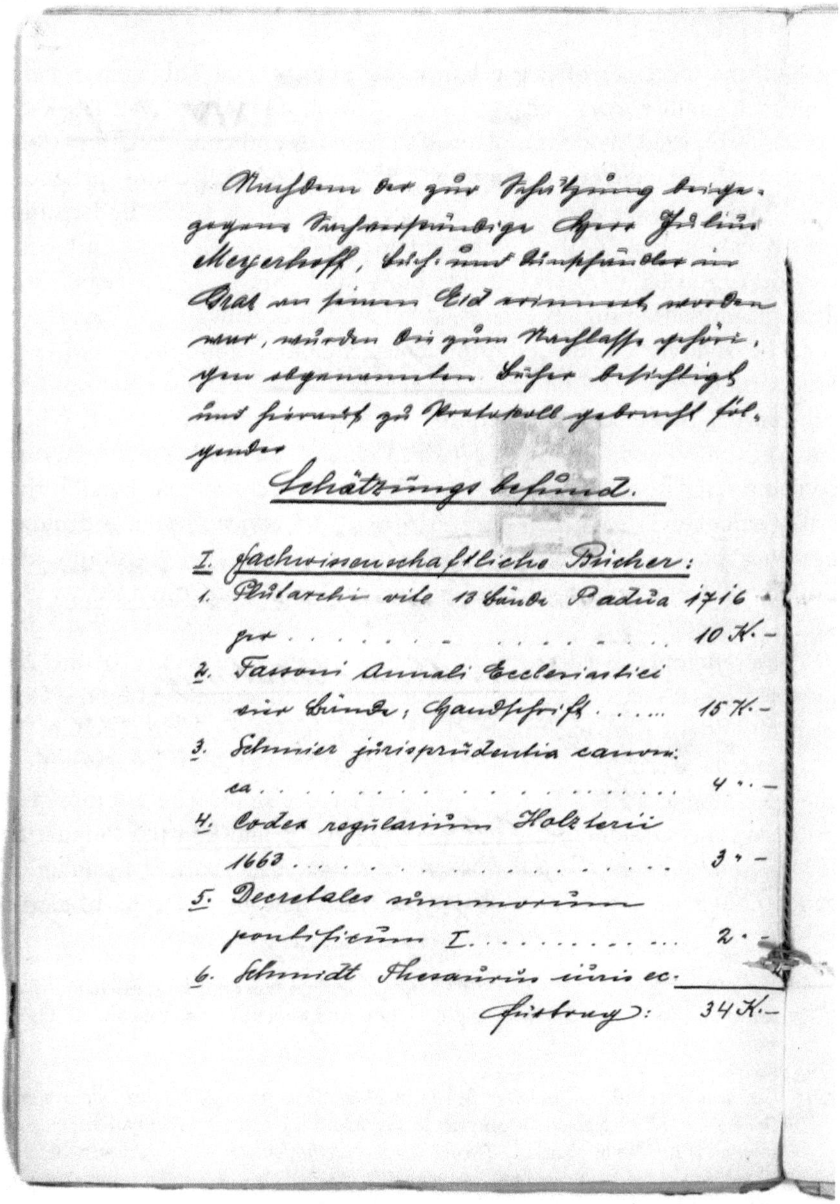

Nachdem der zur Schätzung beigezogene Sachverständige Herr Julius Meyerhoff, Buch- und Kunsthändler in Graz an seinen Eid erinnert worden war, wurden die zum Nachlasse gehörigen, obgenannten Bücher besichtigt und hierauf zu Protokoll gebracht folgender

Schätzungsbefund.

I. Fachwissenschaftliche Bücher:

1. Plutarchi vite 13 Bände Padua 1716 ges. ... 10 K.-
2. Fassoni Annali Ecclesiastici vier Bände; Handschrift ... 15 K.-
3. Schmier jurisprudentia canonica ... 4 .-
4. Codex regularium Holstenii 1663 ... 3 .-
5. Decretales summorum pontificum I. ... 2 .-
6. Schmidt Thesaurus iuris ec.

Fürtrag: 34 K.-

Fig. 4: Beginning of the Inventory of Wolf von Glanvell's Private Library

6.2. The Quest for Canon Law Texts: Editions, Editions, Editions

In 1901, the professor of canon law at the University of Tübingen, Johann Baptist Sägmüller, reviewed Wolf von Glanvell's edition of Vat. lat. 1348. He contextualized Wolf von Glanvell's approach and considered his study as part of the general attempt to edit canonical collections produced after Pseudo-Isidore and before Gratian and to gain a better understanding of canon law in the tenth and especially the eleventh and early twelfth centuries: "Durch Beschreibung und kurzes Inhaltsverzeichnis dieser Kanonensammlung nimmt G. teil an den gegenwärtigen Bestrebungen, die zahlreichen und einflußreichen Kanonensammlungen zwischen Pseudoisidor und Gratian zu entdecken und zu allgemeiner Kenntnis zu bringen."[292] Wasserschleben's edition of Regino's bifold collection (1840) and Martinucci's edition of Deusdedit's *Collectio canonum* (1869) underline contemporary research trends as well as the source-oriented research that was particularly strong in Graz: Friedrich Maassen authored a groundbreaking book on collections and authors before Pseudo-Isidore and Friedrich Thaner edited various writings of Bernold of Constance, as well as Anselm's collection.[293]

These attempts to edit seminal medieval texts were typical of the late nineteenth century. Under the influence of a method outlined by the German philologist Karl Lachmann (1793–1851), research centers, such as the Monumenta Germaniae Historica, expended tremendous energy editing charters, Barbarian law codes, and conciliar decisions. The editions they produced met contemporary academic standards and laid the foundation for the source-based, critical research of (legal) historians.[294] In a similar vein, though on a much smaller scale, the "Savigny-Stiftung" in Berlin

292 Sägmüller, "Review of 'Wolf von Glanvell, Studien aus dem kanonischen Privatrecht' and 'Wolf von Glanvell, Die Kanonessammlung des Cod. Vatican. lat. 1348,'" 629.

293 See 78–79.

294 See, most recently, *Mittelalter lesbar machen. Festschrift. 200 Jahre Monumenta Germaniae Historica*, ed. Monumenta Germaniae Historica, Wiesbaden: Harrassowitz, 2019; Stefan Jordan, *Theorien und Methoden der Geschichtswissenschaft*, 5th edition, Leiden: Brill / Schöningh, 2021, 52–56. On the contribution of Heinrich Brunner to editions see Johannes Liebrecht, "Heinrich Brunner (1840–1915)," in: Stefan Grundmann et al. (ed.), Festschrift 200 Jahre Juristische Fakultät der Humboldt-Universität zu Berlin. Geschichte. Gegenwart und Zukunft, Berlin / New York: De Gruyter, 2010, 305–326, at 314; and Liebrecht, *Brunners Wissenschaft*, 89–96, 188–193.

subsidized editions of, for example, the judgments of the aldermen in Magdeburg ("Magdeburger Schöffensprüche"), the *Libri Feudorum*, the sources of the Roman-canonical process published by Ludwig Wahrmund (1860–1932), and, as we have seen, the edition of Deusdedit's collection.[295] Wolf von Glanvell's editions thus date to the edition-friendly period of the second half of the nineteenth century.

In Austria, Theodor von Sickel, who directed both the "Institut für Österreichische Geschichtsforschung" as well as the Austrian Historical Institute, was the central figure in historical research. Von Sickel not only promoted the ancillary sciences, such as paleography, but he also pointed out the importance of canon law research. Von Sickel claimed, for instance, that even a jurist who intended to work at the Roman Institute had to be a skilled paleographer,[296] and the purpose of his Austrian Historical Institute was to research both Habsburg history and canon law.[297] Moreover, it was von Sickel's analysis of Vat. lat. 3833 and his efforts to find an editor for this manuscript that ultimately led to the publication of Deusdedit's collection in 1905. The influence of Theodor von Sickel on Wolf von Glanvell cannot be underestimated. Even during the editing process, Wolf von Glanvell turned to von Sickel and asked for help, for instance, on how to edit the "e-caudata" and on how to deal with interpunction.[298] He wrote to von Sickel:

> "Im übrigen ist es mein Bestreben, durch die Ausgabe das Original möglichst getreu wiederzugeben; weil ich jedoch noch keine so große derartige Arbeit gemacht habe, kommen mir ab und zu zweifelhafte Fragen vor, welche ich dann Ihnen hochverehrter Herr Sectionschef als zuständigster Autorität vorlegen zu dürfen mir erbitte."[299]

---

295 On these projects, see 44–45; on Wahrmund, see also 69. Ludwig Wahrmund published the writings on procedural law in the series "Quellen zur Geschichte des römisch-kanonischen Prozesses im Mittelalter" (1905–1931). The "Savigny-Stiftung" also supported other studies in the field of legal history, such as the Saxon mirror and Swabian mirror, but it also financed the "Wörterbuch der klassischen Rechtswissenschaft" and research on German students at Italian universities.

296 Rudolf, "Geschichte des Österreichischen Historischen Instituts," 11.

297 Rudolf, "Geschichte des Österreichischen Historischen Instituts," 18.

298 Wien, IÖG, Nachlass Sickel, Letter from Viktor Wolf von Glanvell to Theodor von Sickel, 1901 January 3.

299 See Fig. 5.

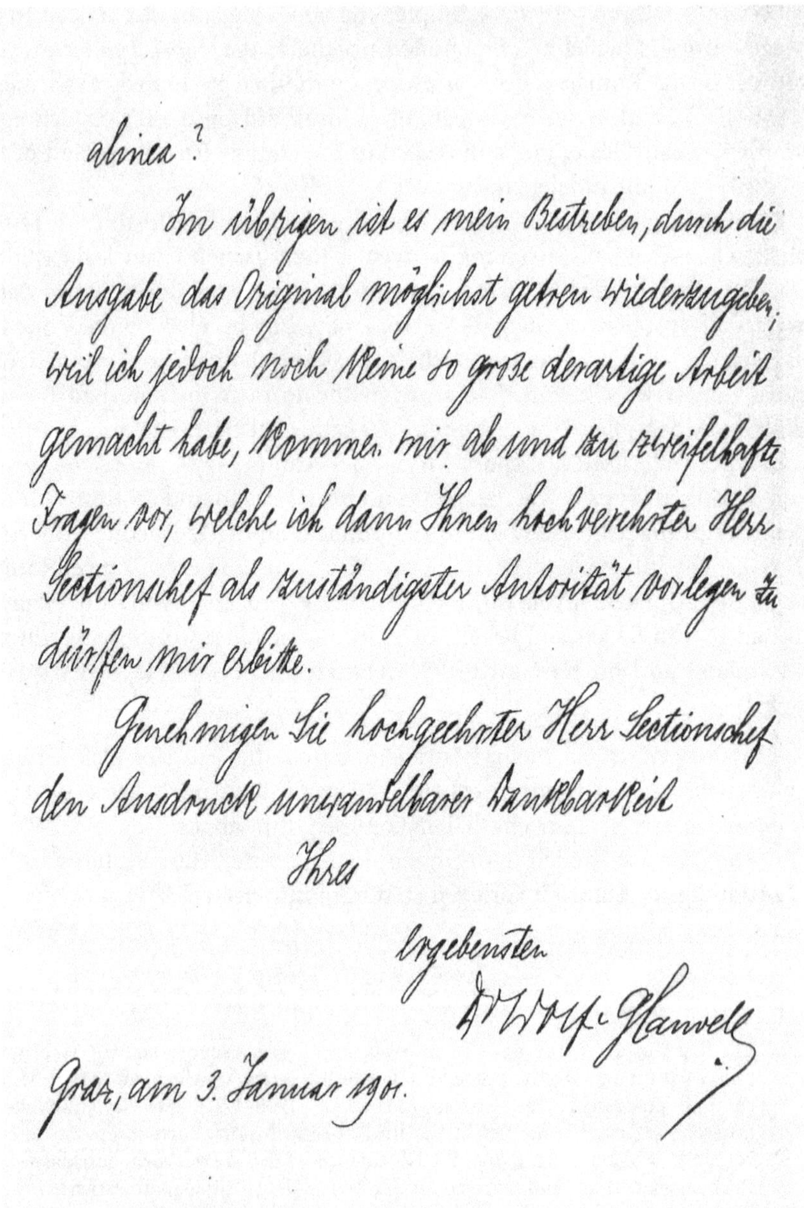

alinea?

Im übrigen ist es mein Bestreben, durch die Ausgabe das Original möglichst getreu wiederzugeben; weil ich jedoch noch keine so grosse derartige Arbeit gemacht habe, kommen mir ab und zu zweifelhafte Fragen vor, welche ich dann Ihnen hochverehrter Herr Sectionschef als zuständigster Autorität vorlegen zu dürfen mir erbitte.

Genehmigen Sie hochgeehrter Herr Sectionschef den Ausdruck unwandelbarer Dankbarkeit

Ihres

ergebensten

DrWolf-Glanvell

Graz, am 3. Januar 1901.

Fig. 5: Viktor Wolf von Glanvell to Theodor von Sickel asking for Advice in Editorial Matters (1901)

Wolf von Glanvell held von Sickel in high esteem, calling him the "geistiger Vater dieser Ausgabe"[300] and dedicating his printed edition to "Theodor von Sickel. Dem Freunde und Meister."[301] Friedrich Thaner and Arnold Luschin von Ebengreuth, the "hochverehrte Lehrer," are also mentioned, but only in the preface.[302] The extent to which von Sickel, Thaner, and Luschin von Ebengreuth influenced the production of Wolf von Glanvell's edition, however, remains obscure, as archival material that could shed light on this question is scarce. Von Sickel's letters, for instance, answering Wolf von Glanvell's questions about editorial matters have been lost. It was von Sickel who pointed to the historical value of charters and inspired Heinrich Brunner to study them.[303] It is possible that he also inspired Wolf von Glanvell to include charters in his institutional studies, thus indirectly influencing him.

In conclusion: It was the goal of many nineteenth-century scholars, including von Sickel and Thaner, to provide the academic public with reliable editions of medieval canon law texts, and Wolf von Glanvell shared their interest in editions. In this respect, too, he was a typical Graz scholar of around 1900.

300 Wien, IÖG, Nachlass Sickel, Letter from Viktor Wolf von Glanvell to Theodor von Sickel, 1901 January 29.

301 Wolf von Glanvell, *Kanonessammlung des Kardinals Deusdedit*, title page. Wolf von Glanvell owed a great deal to Theodor von Sickel and his wife, also on a personal level. His first stay in Rome in 1895/96 was the first time he had left his parents' home for such a long time, and he was warmly welcomed by both: "Es war ja das erstemal, dass ich für lange Zeit von meinem Elternhause weg war; dass ich das Gefühl der Vereinsamung ganz verloren habe, das hochgeehrter Herr Hofrat hat mir die Aufnahme Ihrerseits und Ihrer Frau Gemalin [sic] bewirkt, die es zustande brachte, dass ich mich bei Ihnen wie in einem zweiten Elternhause fühlte." (Wien, IÖG, Nachlass Sickel, Letter from Viktor Wolf von Glanvell to Theodor von Sickel, 1896 March 7).

302 Wolf von Glanvell, *Kanonessammlung des Kardinals Deusdedit*, VI: "Verschiedene dankbarst aufgenommene Ratschläge wurden mir ferner zuteil von meinen hochverehrten Lehrern, den Professoren Dr. Friedrich Thaner und Hofrat Dr. Arnold Luschin von Ebengreuth, ...".

303 On the influence of Theodor von Sickel on Heinrich Brunner: Liebrecht, "Heinrich Brunner (1840–1915)," 306, 314 and Liebrecht, *Brunners Wissenschaft*, 3–7, 98–100.

6.3. Creative Idea or Missed Chance? The Form of a Gloss

Wolf von Glanvell deliberately chose the form of a gloss for his "Studien zum kanonischen Privatrecht." His decision was based on the fragmentary character of the chapters in Book 3 of the *Liber Extra*, which did not allow for a coherent picture of medieval inheritance law of the Church.[304] Although this decision has been much criticized in hindsight, the form of a gloss undoubtedly allowed for a detailed discussion of obscure points.[305]

It is difficult to determine what or who inspired Wolf von Glanvell to adopt the form of a gloss. The use of an expository and annotative gloss is not—as far as I know—known in any other scholarly work of the nineteenth century. Roman and Germanic law researchers tended to develop a "system" of—Roman or Germanic—private law or to explore specific problems, but not to gloss medieval texts. Representatives of the *Ius Canonicum Universum*, like Ehrenreich Pirhing, Anaklet Reiffenstuel, and Franz Schmalzgrueber, explained the decretals title by title (not chapter by chapter!) and freely reordered the topics of the *capitula* in order to present them in a more comprehensible way.[306] Wolf von Glanvell's gloss is reminiscent of the medieval genre of glosses (or, more likely, commentaries)—and, following the medieval model, he even repeated the *lemma* in his commentary to link the original text with the explanation. Such a format is more akin to the *Glossa ordinaria* of the thirteenth century than to the *Ius Canonicum Universum* of the seventeenth and eighteenth centuries. In any case, due to the form of a gloss, Wolf von Glanvell avoided constructing a medieval legal system that never existed. In this respect, he

---

304 Wolf von Glanvell, *Die letztwilligen Verfügungen*, III: "dass das canonische Recht [...] kein vollständiges System eines Erbrechtes aufweist; deshalb war es auch vortheilhafter wieder an die einzelnen Decretalen anzuschließen und gleich an Ort und Stelle den Ausbau der betreffenden Lehre zu verfolgen." Similar idea: Wolf von Glanvell, *Die negotia inter vivos*, III.

305 On reviews, see 64–67 and 71–73.

306 See Georg May / Anna Egler, *Einführung in die kirchenrechtliche Methode*, Regensburg: Friedrich Pustet, 1986, 66–67. The canon-by-canon explanation including the repetition of the words to be explained is reminiscent of the later commentaries on the CIC / 1917; see, for instance, Udalricus Beste, *Introductio in Codicem*, 3rd edition, Collegeville: St. John's Abbey press, 1946. The influential commentary on canon law before the code of 1917 by Franz Xaver Wernz, *Ius decretalium ad usum praelectionum in scholis textus canonici sive iuris decretalium*, 6 vols., Rome: Typographia Polyglotta, 1898–1914, presents the explanation in a continuous text without lemmata.

was a methodologically cautious writer, perhaps even too cautious to draw more far-reaching conclusions from his research.

While the form of a gloss was unusual, producing a commentary on individual chapters of the *Liber Extra* was not uncommon around the time Wolf von Glanvell was working. Various authors explored the juridical meaning of a *capitulum* by tracing its interpretations through the centuries.[307] Even Thaner explained a chapter of the *Liber Extra* in such a way in 1908.[308] The main difference between Wolf von Glanvell and other authors is the predominantly descriptive, summarizing approach of the former, in contrast to the latter's use of a concrete problem as starting point for their analysis.

To summarize, Wolf von Glanvell took up an older, medieval form of commenting to explicate canon law at the very end of the "decretal era," just prior to the dawn of the "codification era."[309] Was this choice anachronistic or postmodern avant la lettre? Whatever the case, Wolf von Glanvell's studies appear to be both a creative idea and a missed opportunity.

6.4. Wolf von Glanvell and the Methodological Approaches of the Nineteenth Century

Wolf von Glanvell did not offer a full-fledged methodological program in his book nor did he express his convictions as legal historian in letters; all attempts to approach his convictions as a scholar thus remain somewhat tentative. Moreover, it is impossible in this study to comprehensively unravel the nineteenth-century melange of historical and doctrinal studies, Catholic and Protestant authors, special studies and literary overviews,

307 See, for instance, Redlich, "Das cap. 11 X de consuetudine (I, 4)," in: Deutsche Zeitschrift für Kirchenrecht 7, 1897, 309–327; Wilhelm Bayer, "Kann ein Bischof Patronat- bzw. Präsentationsrechte auf ein Beneficium erwerben? Zur Erklärung von c. 18 X de iur. patr. III, 38," in: AKKR 82, 1902, 3–16; Rudolf Köstler, "Consuetudo legitime praescripta. Ein Beitrag zur Lehre vom Gewohnheitsrecht und vom Privileg," in: ZRG.KA 8, 1918, 154–194.

308 Friedrich Thaner, "Das Kapitel: Tua nos, Decret. Greg. IX, L. IV. T. I, c. 26," in: Mélanges Hermann Fitting, vol. 1, Montpellier: Imprimerie générale du Midi, 1907, 465–478.

309 "Decretal era" is understood as the period between 1234 and 1917, when the five book-scheme *iudex, iudicium, clerus, connubium, crimen* was the dominant structural order. "Codification era" means the period after 1917.

editions and analyses, and their underlying assumptions.[310] However, even a cursory glance at research in the nineteenth century reveals different strands of methodological approaches and perspectives in the study of canon law and its history. Disentangling these allows us to locate, albeit tentatively, Wolf von Glanvell on the academic map of the late nineteenth century.

The first methodological strand can be seen in the combination of current law and historical approach. Writing about current ecclesiastical law in the nineteenth century inevitably meant writing about history. Not only was the current law of—Catholic, Protestant, and other Christian—churches an extension of medieval and early modern traditions, but older texts, such as the medieval *Liber Extra*, the decisions of the Council of Trent, and the eighteenth-century papal bulls, remained the current law of the Catholic Church until the codification of canon law in 1917. A prime example of this combination of contemporary and historical law in scholarly works is Paul Hinschius' "Das Kirchenrecht der Katholiken und Protestanten in Deutschland," in which he added to the dogmatic skeleton—ordination, pope, patriarchs, etc.—a thorough presentation of the historical evolution of these institutions.[311]

In this context, it is noteworthy that Wolf von Glanvell based his institutional studies on a doctrinal distinction, namely that between private and public law, as the titles of his two doctrinal books indicate: "Studien aus dem kanonischen Privatrechte."[312] The term "kanonisches Privatrecht" is rarely used today. Some modern textbooks employ this term to refer to marriage law in the early modern period or to usury and testaments, but otherwise the term seems to have vanished.[313] It was more common in the nineteenth century when the terms "ecclesiastical public law" and "ecclesiastical private law" structured the presentation of ecclesiastical law

310 Again, a "Wissenschaftsgeschichte" of canon law research is a desideratum, see 11 n. 5.

311 Paul Hinschius, *Das Kirchenrecht der Katholiken und Protestanten in Deutschland*, 6 vols., Berlin: Guttentag, 1869–1897; in a manner akin: Georg Phillips, *Kirchenrecht*, 8 vols., Regensburg: Georg Joseph Manz, 1845–1889.

312 See esp. 73–75.

313 See Wilhelm Brauneder, *Europäische Privatrechtsgeschichte*, Wien / Köln / Weimar: Böhlau, 2014, 81: "Kanonisches Privatrecht: Eherecht / In der frühen Neuzeit war das Kanonische Recht im Privatrecht auf ein einziges Rechtsgebiet beschränkt, das Eherecht." and Mathias Schmoeckel, *Kanonisches Recht*, München: Beck, 2020, 233–240 ("Kanonisches Zivilrecht").

in the past and present. The term "ecclesiastical public law" referred to the constitution of the Church, including the pope, the bishops, the clergy, their ordination, and the means by which the Church was governed (legislation, visitations, etc.). Contrary to "ecclesiastical public law," the term "ecclesiastical private law" referred either to the position of individuals in the Church ("Privatrecht in der Kirche") or to the influence of the Church on private relationships, such as marriages, successions, properties, and commercial affairs ("Privatrecht der Kirche").[314] Canon law, especially Book 3 of the *Liber Extra*, provided rules for private relations and exerted—at least according to nineteenth-century authors—a strong influence on the relation between private parties.[315] The regulation of inheritances was particularly important for the Church, including—to name just a few aspects—whether clerics were free to bequeath their property and who could be installed as statutory heir.[316] Wolf von Glanvell took up the older discussions and

314 See Johann Friedrich von Schulte, *Lehrbuch des katholischen und evangelischen Kirchenrechts nach dem gemeinen Rechte, dem Rechte der deutschen Länder und Oesterreichs*, 4th edition, Gießen: Emil Roth, 1886, 8; Friedrich Vering, *Lehrbuch des katholischen und protestantischen Kirchenrechts, mit besonderer Rücksicht auf das Vaticanische Konzil sowie auf Deutschland, Oesterreich und die Schweiz*, Freiburg im Breisgau: Herder, 1876, 4–5 sees ecclesiastical private law as rights granted to the individuals by the Church.

315 An almost radical stance was taken by Conrad Franz Roßhirt, *Lehrbuch des Kirchenrechts*, 3rd edition, Schaffhausen: Hurter'sche Buchhandlung, 1858, § 133, 55: "Oft wird freilich das canonische Recht von unsern philosophirenden Juristen und manchen engherzigen Practikern, auch modernen Gesetzgebern für abgestorben angesehen, so daß man im besten Fall sporadisch einen oder den andern Grundsatz der Billigkeit zuläßt. Namentlich haben die Germanisten sehr nachtheilig auf das canonische Recht gewirkt. Hier gilt es, darzuthun, daß das canonische Recht in allen Verhältnissen des Privatrechts von festen Grundsätzen christlicher Sittlichkeit und des herkömmlichen germanischen Rechts ausgegangen ist, sonst die Consequenz des römischen Rechts anerkennend. In diesem Sinne muß man das dritte Buch der Decretalen auffassen, wo außer den Standesrechten der Geistlichen, die wir oben schon dargestellt haben, das Güterrecht der Kirche und der Geistlichen ganz in denselben Beziehungen, wie das Vermögensrecht der Laien begründet wird."

316 A reflection of this debate can be found, e.g., in: Walter, *Lehrbuch des Kirchenrechts aller christlichen Confessionen*, § 252, 553–556 (ad X 3.26), § 262, 572–574 (ad X 3.25–27), § 263, 574–575 (*ius spolii*), § 349, 746–747 (testaments), § 350, 747–748 (possession), § 351, 749–750 (interests), etc.; furthermore: Richter, *Lehrbuch des katholischen und evangelischen Kirchenrechts*, § 316, 971–975; George Phillips, *Lehrbuch des Kirchenrechts*, 2nd edition, Regensburg: Georg Joseph Manz, 1871, § 216, 460–464; Friedrich Vering, *Lehrbuch des katholischen, orientalischen und protestantischen Kirchenrechts, mit besonderer Rücksicht auf Deutschland, Oesterreich und die Schweiz*, 3rd edition, Freiburg im Breisgau: Herder, 1893, 795–797

wrote his two dogmatic studies of canon law in light of this distinction, going so far as to explicitly contrast the public and procedural context of the articles he analyzed with aspects of ecclesiastical private law.[317] In this regard, Wolf von Glanvell's "kanonisches Privatrecht" fits in well with research in the nineteenth century and shows how embedded his studies were in the doctrinal research framework of that time.

The combination of doctrine and history in Wolf von Glanvell's work is based not only on the nature of uncodified canon law and on his doctrinal starting point, but also on the approach of the "Historical School of Law" ("Historische Rechtsschule"). This is the second methodological strand that needs consideration when approaching Wolf von Glanvell. In the nineteenth century, legal historians in general were interested in history, as they intended to contribute to the future codification of national law, for example to the German Code of Private Law ("Bürgerliches Gesetzbuch"). In this respect, they foresaw that future codes would be historically rooted, born out of the past, and not an arbitrary decision of a legislator. They considered their studies of ancient and medieval law to be significant additions to the unification of private law in the nineteenth century. This school of thought is called the "Historical School of Law."[318] This school was widespread in the nineteenth century and extended beyond Germany, as it also shaped legal historical research in Austria,[319] and beyond private law, as canon lawyers also committed themselves to the principles of the Historical School, thereby focusing on the historical development of canon law institutions and finding arguments for the structure of the Church in

esp. on the difference between *peculium clericale* and *peculium patrimoniale;* Johannes Baptist Sägmüller, *Lehrbuch des katholischen Kirchenrechts*, vol. 2, 3rd edition, Freiburg im Breisgau: Herder, 1914, 461–467 on the freedom to dispose of property upon death. Publications that do not address canonical private law include: Emil Friedberg, *Lehrbuch des katholischen und evangelischen Kirchenrechts*, Leipzig: Bernhard Tauchnitz, 1879; Philipp Hergenröther, *Lehrbuch des katholischen Kirchenrechts*, 2nd edition, Freiburg im Breisgau: Herder, 1905.

317 Wolf von Glanvell, *Die Negotia inter vivos*, III: "Es lässt sich zwar keineswegs leugnen, dass sich canonisches Privatrecht noch an gar vielen anderen Stellen des Corpus iuris canonici vorfindet [...,] es wäre jedoch ganz unthunlich gewesen, den im großen und ganzen doch öffentlich-rechtlichen oder processualen Inhalt dieser Titel vollständig hier zu behandeln."

318 See, most recently, Hans-Peter Haferkamp, *Die Historische Rechtsschule* (Studien zur Europäischen Rechtsgeschichte 310), Frankfurt am Main: Klostermann, 2018.

319 See above 77–80; even if the Austrian "Allgemeines Bürgerliches Gesetzbuch" (ABGB) dates to 1812.

history.[320] Georg Phillips' multi-volume study on "Kirchenrecht" is a prime example of this historically-rooted approach to canon law.[321] Among the scholars who committed themselves to the Historical School was Friedrich Thaner, Wolf von Glanvell's teacher.[322]

It is obvious that Wolf von Glanvell was influenced by the Historical School's approach to canon law. The title of his "Probevortrag" gives a first hint at this: "Das kirchliche Gewohnheitsrecht." The importance of ecclesiastical customary law, the relation between history and legislation, and the question of whether *consuetudo* formed a source of law, were widely debated issues in the nineteenth century.[323] Although the content of Wolf von Glanvell's "Probevortrag" and his stance on customary law remain unreconstructed, it is obvious that he was engaged with a highly controversial topic, namely the role of history in the Church.

Moreover, Wolf von Glanvell explicitly alluded to the practical relevance his studies on the history of succession law might have in the future, namely in the codification of canon law which in fact took place in 1917:[324]

> "Ob zum Schlusse eine Darstellung des gemeinen kirchlichen Erbrechtes nur ein rechtsgeschichtliches Interesse hat, nachdem ja vieles davon durch Gewohnheitsrecht oder staatliche Gesetzgebung längst praktisch

---

320 See, for instance, the remarks on Johann Wilhelm Bickell and Aemilius Ludwig Richter by Landau, "Evangelische Kirchenrechtswissenschaft im 19. Jahrhundert," 255–258; Peter Landau, "Johann Wilhelm Bickell als Kanonist und seine Geschichte des Kirchenrechts," in: Zeitschrift für evangelisches Kirchenrecht 32, 1987, 411–422 (cited according to the reprint in: Peter Landau (ed.), Grundlagen und Geschichte des evangelischen Kirchenrechts und des Staatskirchenrechts, Tübingen: Mohr Siebeck, 2010, 269–279), and Peter Landau, "Das Recht der frühen Kirche im Werk Aemilius Ludwig Richters," in: Karl-Hermann Kästner (ed.), Festschrift für Martin Heckel zum siebzigsten Geburtstag, Tübingen: Mohr Siebeck, 1999, 117–132 (cited according to the reprint in: Peter Landau (ed.), Grundlagen und Geschichte des evangelischen Kirchenrechts und des Staatskirchenrechts, Tübingen: Mohr Siebeck, 2010, 280–296).

321 See above 74–75 and Andreas Thier, "Phillips, Georg(e)," in: Neue Deutsche Biographie 20, 2001, 401–402.

322 Puza, "Kirchenrechtslehrer an der Universität Graz," 263.

323 Peter Landau, "Die Theorie des Gewohnheitsrechts im katholischen und evangelischen Kirchenrecht des 19. und 20. Jahrhunderts," in: ZRG.KA 77, 1991, 156–196 (reprint in: Peter Landau (ed.), Grundlagen und Geschichte des evangelischen Kirchenrechts und des Staatskirchenrechts, Tübingen: Mohr Siebeck, 2010, 45–79).

324 *Codex Iuris Canonici. Pii X Pontificis Maximi iussu digestus, Benedicti Papae XV auctoritate promulgatus* (1917). English translation: Peters, *The 1917 or Pio-Benedictine code of Canon Law* (2001). On the lacking impact of his studies, see 75.

> bedeutungslos geworden, manches überdies auch in der Doctrin streitig ist, wäre aber trotzdem zu bezweifeln. Schon seit langem und bis in die jüngste Zeit sprechen sich in Frankreich und Deutschland Männer des Clerus und der Wissenschaft für eine Neucodification des gemeinen kirchlichen Rechtes aus; und dabei wird man den Fragen bezüglich der erbrechtlichen Verhältnisse der Geistlichen wohl kaum aus dem Wege gehen wollen und können."[325]

As this rather vague reference to the program of the Historical School is the only one extant in Wolf von Glanvell's writings, it remains unclear whether he was convinced of his contribution to the development of law or whether he only paid lip service to it. Even if the extent of Wolf von Glanvell's adherence to the convictions of the Historical School remains uncertain, the influence of its approach and its principles is still palpable.

The third strand of nineteenth-century research on medieval canon law relevant to the study of Wolf von Glanvell is the shift in focus from the quest for manuscripts, collections, and editions to institutional history. Until the end of the third quarter of the nineteenth century, many historians of canon law were primarily concerned with the texts of medieval canon law. Their studies aimed at providing access to these texts by identifying authors and publishing catalogues, manuscript descriptions, and critical editions; they were not seeking to provide a thorough analysis of their content or the institutional context in which these texts were deployed. To name but a few researchers: Augustin Theiner disclosed his findings on medieval collections in his *Disquisitiones criticae* (1836);[326] Friedrich Maassen gave groundbreaking overviews of medieval libraries and their holdings, of collections and their authors.[327] Friedrich Wilhelm Wasserschleben shared his insights into, among other sources, the *Collectio duodecim partium* and Ivo's *Decretum*;[328] and Johann Friedrich von Schulte wrote his stunning survey of post-Gratian canonists covering the period up to the nineteenth

325 Wolf von Glanvell, *Die letztwilligen Verfügungen*, 280.

326 Theiner, *Disquisitiones criticae* (1836).

327 Friedrich Maassen, "Bibliotheca Latina juris canonici manuscripta," in: Sitzungsberichte der Kaiserlichen Akademie der Wissenschaften, philosophisch-historische Klasse 53, Wien 1867, 373–427 and 54, Wien 1866, 157–288; Maassen, *Geschichte der Quellen und der Literatur des canonischen Rechts* (1870).

328 Friedrich Wilhelm Wassserschleben, *Beiträge zur Geschichte der vorgratianischen Kirchenrechtsquellen*, Leipzig: Bernhard Taunitz, 1839.

century.[329] Wolf von Glanvell's edition of Deusdedit's *Collectio canonum* follows in their wake.

In the last quarter of the nineteenth century, the focus of research turned to "institutional history." By "institutional history," legal historians mean the analysis of juridical, doctrinal constructions in the past, such as liability for material defects in Roman law, matrimonial property law in late-medieval municipal law, or the inheritance rights of illegitimate children under early modern state law. Legal historians scrutinizing both Roman and Germanic law had already published a plethora of works, including broad overviews and studies on specific questions. Famous overviews included Friedrich Carl von Savigny's "System des heutigen römischen Rechts,"[330] Bernhard Windscheids's "Lehrbuch des Pandektenrechts,"[331] and Otto Stobbe's "Handbuch des deutschen Privatrechts;"[332] more specific studies included, for example, Karl von Amira's "Nordgermanisches Obligationenrecht"[333] and Heinrich Siegel's "Das Versprechen als Verpflichtungsgrund im heutigen Recht."[334]

Institutional history was already broadly practised by "Germanisten" and "Romanisten" when "Kanonisten"—hesitantly—adopted this approach in the last quarter of the nineteenth century. Friedrich Maassen's successor in Graz, Carl Gross, examined "Das Recht an der Pfründe" in 1887,[335] and Ulrich Stutz

329 Johann Friedrich von Schulte, *Die Geschichte der Quellen und Literatur des Canonischen Rechts von Gratian bis auf die Gegenwart*, vol. 1: *Einleitung. Die Geschichte der Quellen und Literatur von Gratian bis auf Papst Gregor IX.*, Stuttgart: Ferdinand Enke, 1875; vol. 2: *Die Geschichte der Quellen und Literatur von Papst Gregor IX. bis zum Concil von Trient*, Stuttgart: Ferdinand Enke, 1877; vol. 3, 1: *Die Geschichte der Quellen und Literatur von der Mitte des 16. Jahrhunderts bis zur Gegenwart / Das katholische Recht und die katholischen Schriftsteller*, Stuttgart: Ferdinand Enke, 1880; vol. 3, 2–3: *Die Geschichte der Quellen und Literatur von der Mitte des 16. Jahrhunderts bis zur Gegenwart / Das evangelische Recht, die evangelischen Schriftsteller, die Geschichte der wissenschaftlichen Behandlung, Übersicht*, Stuttgart: Ferdinand Enke, 1880.

330 Friedrich Carl von Savigny, *System des heutigen römischen Rechts*, 8 vols., Berlin: Veit, 1840–1849.

331 Bernhard Windscheid, *Lehrbuch des Pandektenrechts*, 9th edition, with Theodor Kipp, 3 vols., Frankfurt am Main: Ruetten & Loening, 1906.

332 Otto Stobbe, *Handbuch des deutschen Privatrechts*, 5 vols., Berlin: Hertz, 1871–1885.

333 Karl von Amira, *Nordgermanisches Obligationenrecht*, 2 vols., Leipzig: Veit, 1882 / 1895.

334 Heinrich Siegel, *Das Versprechen als Verpflichtungsgrund im heutigen Recht. Eine germanistische Studie*, Berlin: Vahlen, 1873.

335 Carl Gross, *Das Recht an der Pfründe. Zugleich ein Beitrag zur Ermittlung des Ursprungs des jus ad rem*, Graz: Leuschner & Lubensky, 1887.

published his "Geschichte des kirchlichen Benefizialwesens" alongside his groundbreaking and still controversial study on the "Eigenkirche" in 1895.[336] Earlier, Emil Friedberg had devoted himself to marriage law and its history, a subject of Protestant and Catholic church law that was of vital importance in Germany until 1875, when civil marriage replaced the religious form in the wake of the "Kulturkampf." Friedberg's bulky volume on "Das Recht der Eheschliessung in seiner geschichtlichen Entwicklung" covered not only nearly 1500 years, but also canon, Roman, Germanic, and modern state law, as well as Catholic and Protestant views.[337] Friedrich Thaner, likewise, addressed the topic of marriage in two rather late articles, published in 1900 and 1907.[338] Wolf von Glanvell's studies on commercial and succession law pertain to these institutional studies, in which he took up research perspectives that were quite common in the nineteenth century, but had only just recently been employed in canon law research. Wolf von Glanvell is certainly not at the vanguard of research on institutional history, but he is the first canonist in Graz to apply this approach.[339]

Wolf von Glanvell's starting point, namely the doctrinal division in canonical public and canonical private law, and his interest in institutions, explains a peculiarity of his "Studien:" he tended to reduce historical complexity. He linked the growth of a legal institute, its development and critical reception with the multi-layered literature that stemmed from different epochs, written under different conditions and by authors of diverse academic-intellectual backgrounds. In doing so, he levelled these differences out: Leonhardus Lessius and Thomas Aquinas appear in one and the same

336 Ulrich Stutz, *Die Eigenkirche als Element des mittelalterlich-germanischen Kirchenrechtes*, Berlin: Müller, 1895; Ulrich Stutz, *Geschichte des kirchlichen Benefizialwesens. Von seinen Anfängen bis auf die Zeit Alexanders III.*, Berlin: Müller, 1895. For an introduction to this topic, see: Enno Bünz, "Eigenkirche," in: Albrecht Cordes et al. (ed.), Handwörterbuch zur Deutschen Rechtsgeschichte, 2nd edition, vol. 1, Berlin: Erich Schmidt, 2008, 1267–1269; Peter Landau, "Eigenkirchenwesen," in: Theologische Realenzyklopädie 9, 1982, 399–404.

337 Emil Friedberg, *Das Recht der Eheschliessung in seiner geschichtlichen Entwicklung*, Leipzig: Bernhard Taunitz, 1865; again: Emil Friedberg, *Verlobung und Trauung. Zugleich als Kritik von Sohm, Das Recht der Eheschliessung*, Leipzig: Bernhard Tauchnitz, 1876.

338 See above 79. The study by Edgar Loening, *Geschichte des deutschen Kirchenrechts*, vol. 2: *Das Kirchenrecht im Reiche der Merowinger*, Strassburg: Trübner, 1878, is quite interesting, as he wrote on early medieval property law of the Church (632–750) and on testaments and donations as means of acquiring goods (653–680).

339 Puza, "Kirchenrechtslehrer an der Universität Graz," 264.

footnote,[340] as do Covarrubias de Leyva and the gloss to the Institutions,[341] as well as the *Libri Feudorum* and Saxonian feudal law.[342] In this way, "law" is ultimately reduced to an ahistorical, doctrinal rule that allows authors from different legal epochs and fields to be closely linked. This approach is not uncommon in works on institutional history: Bernhard Windscheid, in his "Lehrbuch des Pandektenrechts," searched for a legal system based on Roman law and excerpted ancient sources as well as nineteenth-century studies (but omitted the period of the Ius Commune, 1150–1800) and Wolf von Glanvell's colleague at Graz, Gustav Hanausek (1855–1927), professor of Roman law, approached his subjects in a similar way.[343]

In short, legal history research around 1900, although based on medieval sources, was doctrinal and to some extent ahistorical.[344] It was doctrinal because scholars constructed a legal system based not on rules inherent to (early) medieval law, but on contemporary nineteenth-century thought.[345] As the legal historian Heinrich Brunner once claimed: "... denn für die Rechtsgeschichte bleibt, was sie dogmatisch nicht erfassen kann, totliegender Stoff."[346] At the same time, Brunner used modern concepts and terms to analyse the past and in this regard his method was ahistorical. Nevertheless, there is a fundamental difference between Brunner and other scholars and Wolf von Glanvell: the latter did not try to pinpoint early medieval evolutions with modern terms, and he did not use a modern doctrine to explain the past, as his focus was to describe the past, not analyse it. That is to say, Wolf von Glanvell did not overstate a constructive analysis, because he skipped analysis for the most part.

A fourth strand of nineteenth-century historical research relevant here is linked to Ulrich Stutz, professor of canon law and its history in Freiburg,

340 Wolf von Glanvell, *Die negotia inter vivos*, 84 n. 4.

341 Wolf von Glanvell, *Die negotia inter vivos*, 84 n. 1.

342 Wolf von Glanvell, *Die negotia inter vivos*, 136 n. 2.

343 See, for instance, Gustav Hanausek, *Die Lehre vom uneigentlichen Nießbrauch nach gemeinem Recht*, Erlangen: Andreas Deichert, 1879.

344 Liebrecht, *Brunners Wissenschaft*, 146–178; Liebrecht, "Heinrich Brunner (1840–1915)," at 312–322. For one example of this "juristische Rechtsgeschichte," see Stephan Dusil, *Die Soester Stadtrechtsfamilie. Mittelalterliche Quellen und neuzeitliche Historiographie* (Forschungen zur Deutschen Rechtsgeschichte 24), Köln / Weimar / Wien: Böhlau, 2007, esp. at 33–36.

345 Liebrecht, *Brunners Wissenschaft*, 151: "rechtsbegrifflich-retrospektive Systembildung," 164: "juristische Rechtsgeschichte."

346 Heinrich Brunner, "Die Landschenkungen der Merowinger und der Agilulfinger," 1885, 2 (cited according to: Liebrecht, *Brunners Wissenschaft*, 159–160).

Bonn, and Berlin. On the eve of the Codex Iuris Canonici / 1917, Stutz transformed the history of canon law into a purely historical discipline.[347] His contribution on "Kirchenrecht" to Franz von Holtzendorff's *Rechtsenzyklopädie*—an article of monographic quality—bears witness to this new approach for here he resolutely broke the link between the study of historical and current law. Furthermore, he promoted the separate discipline of "Kirchenrechtsgeschichte" by establishing a new journal, the "Kanonistische Abteilung," a subdivision of the "Zeitschrift der Savigny-Stiftung für Rechtsgeschichte."[348] The historical perspective is paramount in Stutz's research, but not in that of Wolf von Glanvell: the latter remained on the traditional path, in which the dogmatic and the historical perspectives were mixed. For instance, he had the later code of canon law in mind when writing his institutional history; he pursued institutes from the first millennium to the nineteenth century; and he took up the dogmatic division of public and private canon law and applied it to the Middle Ages. His guiding interest is the doctrine of canon law, not pure history. Against the background of this methodological transition around 1900, Ulrich Stutz appears to represent the methodological vanguard, whereas Wolf von Glan-

347 See Ulrich Stutz, *Die kirchliche Rechtsgeschichte. Rede zur Feier des 27. Januar 1905, gehalten in der Aula der Universität Bonn*, Stuttgart: Ferdinand Enke, 1905, 19: "... daß wir das gesamte historische Material unserer Disziplin vom geltenden Recht scheiden und nach historischen Gesichtspunkten durch- und zusammenarbeiten müssen..." Even before, Stutz, *Eigenkirche*, 5 stated: "Man kann die Rechtsgeschichte wie alle Geschichte auf zwei Arten behandeln. Man kann sich mitten in den Strom der geschichtlichen Entwickelung hineinstellen und ihn als Ganzes in's Auge fassen; auf diese Weise erhält man Antwort auf die Fagen: Was? und Wohin? Man kann aber auch mehr auf die einzelnen Strömungen sein Augenmerk richten und das Ganze als ihre Summe oder als ihr Produkt betrachten; das ist der Weg, um zur Klarheit zu gelangen über das Wie? und das Woher? Im Kirchenrecht ist man bis vor nicht langer Zeit fast ausschließlich nach der ersten Art erfahren. Und dies mit vollem Recht. Die historisch-kritische Kirchenrechtsforschung kann noch nicht auf eine langen Vergangenheit zurückschauen, sie ist jung, so jung, daß es heute noch im Kirchenrecht mehr als ein Gebiet gibt, das mit ihrem Pfluge noch nicht ist gepflügt worden. In Folge dessen mußte sie sich nächst der Sichtung und Bearbeitung des Quellenmaterials in erster Linie die Synthese angelegen sein lassen. Das ist jetzt anders geworden."

348 Ulrich Stutz, "Kirchenrecht," in: Franz von Holtzendorff / Josef Kohler (ed.), Encyklopädie der Rechtswissenschaft in systematischer Bearbeitung, 6th edition, vol. 2, Leipzig / Berlin: Guttentag, 1904, 809–972. Wolf von Glanvell possessed a copy of Holtzendorff's encyclopedia, but it is not known which edition, see Appendix 3 no 14.

vell preserves the traditional approach, and his studies appear somewhat old-fashioned.

Ulrich Stutz is also key to understanding Wolf von Glanvell's methodology in another respect. In October 1894, Stutz gave his inaugural lecture at the University of Basel on "Eigenkirchen" (*ecclesia propria*) in the early Middle Ages, in which he proposed pagan, Germanic roots for these "Eigenkirchen."[349] His study on "Eigenkirchen" is closely linked to his concept of "Germanic Church Law." Stutz put the idea forward that after a period of Roman (legal) influences on the Church, it came under Germanic control until the Church freed itself in the second half of the eleventh century in the so-called Investiture Controversy. This "Germanic church law" was then replaced by "canon law."[350] Stutz intended to explore this "Germanismus" in the Church and how it enriched canon law.[351] The "Eigenkirche" thus appeared as "Element des mittelalterlich-germanischen Kirchenrechtes."[352]

In his preface to "Die negotia inter vivos," Wolf von Glanvell articulated a kind of research question, namely to distinguish the influence of Roman and Germanic law on canon law and to identify proper ecclesiastical creations: "Meine Absicht war, nachzuweisen, was im canonischen Privatrechte auf römisch-rechtlichen, was auf deutsch-rechtlichen Grundlagen beruhe und was endlich als eigene kirchliche Rechtsbildung anzusehen

349 Stutz, *Eigenkirche* (1895). On Stutz, see Andreas Thier, "Stutz, Ulrich Georg," in: Neue Deutsche Biographie 25, 2013, 659–660; Katrin Bayerle, "Ulrich Stutz: Von der Eigenkirche zur 'hinkenden Trennung zwischen Kirche und Staat,'" in: Thomas Holzner / Hannes Ludyga (ed.), Entwicklungstendenzen des Staatskirchen- und Religionsverfassungsrechts. Ausgewählte begrifflich-systematische, historische, gegenwartsbezogene und biographische Beiträge (Kirchen- und Staatskirchenrecht 15), Paderborn / München: Ferdinand Schöningh, 2013, 505–518, at 509–516; Karl Siegfried Bader, *Ulrich Stutz (1868–1938) als Forscher und Lehrer*, Bonn: Peter Hanstein, 1969.

350 See Stutz' groundbreaking article on "Kirchenrecht:" Stutz, "Kirchenrecht," at 828: "Das germanische Kirchenrecht" and at 842: "Das kanonische Recht."

351 Stutz, *Eigenkirche*, 11: "Germanismus in der Kirche" and "Arbeit der Germanen am Kirchenrechte," 25: "Bereicherung des Kirchenrechts." The concept of a Germanic canon law still influenced Stutz's assistant, Hans Erich Feine: Hans Erich Feine, *Kirchliche Rechtsgeschichte. Die katholische Kirche*, 5th edition, Köln / Wien: Böhlau, 1972, 147: "Das germanisch geprägte Kirchenrecht." On the reception of Stutz in Austria, see Nikolaus Grass, "Ulrich Stutz und die österreichische Kirchenrechtswissenschaft," in: ZRG.KA 74, 1988, 27–43.

352 See 96 n. 336.

sei."[353] In this respect, Wolf von Glanvell wrote in the wake of a fundamental division that has characterized legal history research since the nineteenth century, namely the division into "Romanisten," "Germanisten," and "Kanonisten," but he also took up the "Germanic" research perspective put forward by Stutz. Yet there is a fundamental distinction: in Stutz's œuvre the Germanic period is a constitutive element of Church history, whereas in Wolf von Glanvell's work it forms no more than an aspect of his research.

Although Wolf von Glanvell touched upon the question of Germanic influence in various chapters, according to Ulrich Stutz he failed to answer the question definitively. Stutz wrote: "Dagegen ist die Absicht des Vf.s, in ihnen eine Analyse des kanonischen Privatrechts zu geben, und festzustellen, was davon römischen, was deutschen Ursprungs sei, und was sich als Ergebniss selbständiger Entwickelung darstelle, nicht vollkommen erreicht."[354] Wolf von Glanvell's analysis of the Germanic sources was, according to Stutz, too superficial and too fragmentary ("zu wenig tiefgründig und zu fragmentarisch").[355]

These different strands of research in legal history research help to situate Wolf von Glanvell and his research within his nineteenth-century context. In his two "Studien" on the history of canon law institutions, he took up the nineteenth-century distinction between the "public law" and the "private law" of the Church as his guiding perspective. Ultimately, his analysis is rooted in the doctrine of law and compared to Stutz, his approach is traditional, blending the study of history and current canon law rather than approaching them separately. His studies appear more as commentary on medieval law and its current continuation than as purely historical in nature. Wolf von Glanvell is thus representative of a certain type of nineteenth-century scholar: skilled in paleography, well-versed in sources, but with a traditional methodological approach. Only once did he break with the mainstream and try something new, namely to produce a commentary in the form of a "modern gloss." This approach, however, did not persuade his contemporaries.

353 Wolf von Glanvell, *Die negotia inter vivos*, III.
354 Stutz, "Review of 'Wolf von Glanvell, Die negotia in vivos,'" 1609.
355 Stutz, "Review of 'Wolf von Glanvell, Die negotia in vivos,'" 1609.

7. Researching Canon Law Around 1900: Summarizing Observations

It is a challenging task to interpret Wolf von Glanvell's studies against the background of the late nineteenth century and to contextualize his works within their contemporary research landscape. One reason for this is the lack of archival documents impeding a close-up view of him, especially of his studies on "kanonisches Privatrecht." Nonetheless, several aspects link Wolf von Glanvell to other scholars around 1900: the endeavor to edit medieval texts, the interest in institutional and doctrinal history, the search for Germanic influences on the Church, and the aspiration to contribute to a new codification of canon law. Furthermore, Wolf von Glanvell tried to fill the gap that Maassen and Schulte left by focusing on the important eleventh century and its "reform collections." Although he never attended a course at the "Institut für Österreichische Geschichtsforschung," he was connected to this Institute and its focus on ancillary science through von Sickel and Thaner, the director and a graduate of the Institute respectively. In short, Wolf von Glanvell appears as a rather typical representative of canon law research in Austria around 1900.

This also holds true for Wolf von Glanvell's network, which is both national and international at the same time. The key figures—von Sickel and Thaner—were Austrian, but he was also in contact with a German scholar and the Frenchman Paul Fournier.[356] Even if his written correspondence is more concerned with administrative matters than with research questions, it is indicative of the international network of canonists around 1900 which Wolf von Glanvell had started to join.[357]

Although this study sheds light on many aspects of Wolf von Glanvell's life and work, his political views remain obscure. One reason is that he chose subjects that were less political, less controversial than others. But

356 Theodor von Sickel was of course German by birth, but spent his academic life abroad. Contacts to Italy can be assumed, even if written documents are missing.

357 On letters between canonists and their often disappointing content, see, for instance, Louis Carlen, "Briefe französischer Rechtshistoriker an Ulrich Stutz," in: ZRG.KA 74, 1988, 17–26. The published discourse was undoubtedly international, as Wolf von Glanvell's books were reviewed in German, Italian, and French journals.

even here, he remained reluctant to make strong statements, perhaps hampered by the form of a gloss.[358] In the one instance in which we know he took up a controversial topic, he did not persist in his views: When he presented anticlerical remarks in the first edition of "Die Negotia inter vivos," it opened the possibility that he was aligning himself with the "Austrian Kulturkampf,"[359] but the revised second edition reveals this was not the case. Otherwise, Wolf von Glanvell would have belonged to a distinct group of Catholic authors with an anticlerical stance.

There are other aspects of Wolf von Glanvell's work that may offer clues about his political views. In his edition of Vat. lat. 1348, he analyzed the collection and pointed to its tendency to emphasize the bishops of the Roman Church and their supremacy over the lower clergy and laity, which resulted in a tight, centralized institutional structure. He concluded: "Also eine Reformsammlung im besten Sinne des Wortes mit fast modernen Anschauungen."[360] But does this sentence reveal his political point of view in the aftermath of Vatican I and its dogmatic constitution *Pastor Aeternus*, which solidified papal dominance in the Church?[361] It is probably nothing more than a juvenile allusion to the present times. At the same time, it remains remarkable that he published an article in a Protestant journal, namely the "Deutsche Zeitschrift für Kirchenrecht" (and not in the Catholic "Archiv für Katholisches Kirchenrecht").[362] Does this suggest

358 Stutz's idea of "Eigenkirchen" shows how much a strong statement can spark discussion—his clear statement may have contributed to his wide reception in academia.

359 See 68–69. On the "Kulturkampf" in Austria (between 1868 and 1933), especially at the Faculty of Theology in Graz, see Liebmann, "Bewährung im österreichischen Kulturkampf," 256–264.

360 Wolf von Glanvell, "Canonessammlung," 55: "Bemerkenswerth bleibt aber die Tendenz: das scharfe Betonen des Vorranges der römischen Kirche vor allen anderen Bischofsitzen und die hohe Stellung, welche nachher den Bischöfen gegenüber dem anderen Clerus und namentlich gegenüber den Laien eingeräumt wird, wodurch auf eine straffe, centralistische Organisation in der ganzen Kirche hingearbeitet wird. Also eine Reformsammlung im besten Sinne des Wortes mit fast modernen Anschauungen."

361 Klaus Schatz, "Vatikanische Konzilien. A. Vaticanum I.," in: Lexikon für Theologie und Kirche, 3rd edition, vol. 10, 2001, 555–561.

362 Wolf von Glanvell, "Das cap. 2 X de rerum permutatione III 19," in: Deutsche Zeitschrift für Kirchenrecht, 8, 1898, 338–346. It was presumably the focus on canon law in the Middle Ages and legal history in general that made Wolf von Glanvell choose this journal. On these journals and their history, see Peter Landau, "Kirchenrechtliche Zeitschriften im 19. und 20. Jahrhundert," in: Michael Stolleis (ed.), Juristische Zeitschriften. Die neuen Medien des 18.-20. Jahrhunderts (Studien zur Europäischen Rechtsgeschichte 128), Frankfurt am Main: Klostermann, 1999,

some flexibility in Wolf von Glanvell's affiliations or was the choice of journal a purely academic decision? The stance of Wolf von Glanvell in the ongoing debate concerning the relationship between state and Church remains hidden.

This observation of a lack of strong political conviction points to another characteristic of Wolf von Glanvell: his preference for collecting as opposed to analyzing. His two information-rich travel guides, two editions of manuscripts, and two explanatory studies of the *Liber Extra* point to a certain type of scholar: the collector who prefers to gather items rather than analyze them. If this characterization is correct, it may explain the lack of reception his works received in scholarly circles. Strong statements of opinion, even doubtful ones, enhance the reception of a theory and thereby inscribe the author in the memory of an academic discipline. Wolf von Glanvell, however, did not succeed in this.[363]

In sum, Wolf von Glanvell appears more as a representative of mainstream canon law research in Austria and elsewhere around 1900 than as an intellectual outsider. This does not, however, undermine the value of examining his life and works in detail. As we have seen, searching for the methodological strands that linked Wolf von Glanvell with his contemporaries has uncovered many aspects of canon law research around 1900. Thus, this study may serve as a prolegomenon, however preliminary, to the history of canon law research in the nineteenth and early twentieth centuries, shedding light on research in general through the study of one researcher.

331–378, at 340–367 (reprint in: Peter Landau (ed.), Grundlagen und Geschichte des evangelischen Kirchenrechts und des Staatskirchenrechts, Tübingen: Mohr Siebeck, 2010, 211–252, at 218–242).

363 Although he was once remembered as "un grande studioso Austriaco," see Giuseppe Motta, "Il 'Liber canonum diversorum sanctorum patrum' e la disciplina canonica," in: Chiesa, diritto e ordinamento della "Societas Christiana" nei secoli XI e XII. Atti della nona Settimana internazionale di studio Mendola, 28 agosto-2 settembre 1983, Milano: Vita e pensiero, 1986, 331–339, at 332.

8. Epilogue: Fölzstein and Beyond

On Saturday, May 11, 1905, Wolf von Glanvell's family and friends, his colleagues, and his comrades laid him to rest in Neuprags, his favorite place and that where he first undertook his alpine adventures. After the service, his comrades from the "Gilde zum groben Kletterschuh" carried the coffin decorated with alpine flowers to the cemetery: "Bergführer des Pragser Tales unter Vorantritt des Führer-Seniors Appenbichler, des einstigen alpinen Lehrmeisters Wolf-Glanvells, schritten, Kränze und Lichter tragend, zu beiden Seiten."[364] After the coffin was lowered into the grave, Karl Doménigg commemorated his comrade and friend, his alpine achievements and his commitment to other climbers, and the president of the Alpenvereins-Section Hochpustertal expressed his deep-gratitude for Wolf von Glanvell's contributions to mountaineering. "Damit war die erschütternde Totenfeier zu Ende."[365]

His widow, Mary, left their common apartment at Morellenfeldgasse 36 at the end of May and temporarily moved in with her parents on the outskirts of Graz.[366] A year later, she joined a cycling club,[367] and another year later, in April 1907, she married again. Her second husband was Moriz Probst, a well-known psychiatrist, with whom she started a new family.[368]

Only two days before his death, Wolf von Glanvell discussed with the "Österreichischer Touristenklub" the construction of a mountain hut in the

---

364 Grazer Volksblatt 1905 May 13 (Morgenausgabe), 3.

365 Grazer Volksblatt 1905 May 13 (Morgenausgabe), 3. The funeral is also reported in: Salzburger Volksblatt 1905 May 12, 6; Die Zeit 1905 May 13 (Morgenblatt), 6; Neues Wiener Tagblatt 1905 May 12, 4–5. In Graz, his former comrades remembered him in memorial services: the "Grazer Turnerschaft" on May 13, the "Turner Bergsteiger" on May 19, see Grazer Tagblatt 1905 May 15 (Abendausgabe), 2 and Grazer Tagblatt 1905 May 20 (Abendausgabe), 1–2.

366 Stadtarchiv Graz, Meldezettel "Wolf Edle von Glanvell, Marie." On October 4, 1905, she moved back to the Morellenfeldgasse 36.

367 In December 1906, she joined the "Steierischer Radfahrer-Gauverband", see Alpenländische Sportzeitung 1907 January 4 (as "Beilage" of the Grazer Tagblatt 1907 January 4), 2.

368 Grazer Volksblatt 1907 May 18 (Morgenausgabe), 7: marriage in April 1907 in the parish church "Sankt Leonhard" in Graz: "Dr. med. Moriz Probst, Psychiater, mit Maria Theresia Wolf Edle von Glanvell, geborne Luschin von Ebengreuth, k.k. Universitäts-Professorswitwe."

Val Travenanzes.[369] The plan to build such a cabin and to name it after him was agreed upon already in the summer of 1905 and at the end of July 1907, the cabin was officially inaugurated.[370] The cabin and its interior were praised for their sound construction and cozy feel and its location for the beautiful mountain scenery:

> "Das Unterkunftshaus ist solid und wetterfest gebaut, die Innenräume sind luftig und hell. Die Schutzhütte enthält zwei Gastzimmer, vier Zimmer mit zehn Betten, neun Matratzenlager und außerdem Heulager. Eine oberhalb der Hütte gefaßte Quelle liefert prächtiges Trinkwasser. Die Hütte, inmitten einer überwältigend schönen, wild-romantischen Bergszenerie gelegen, macht einen überaus anheimelnden Eindruck."[371]

Fig. 6: "Wolf-Glanvell-Hütte" in Val Travenanzes

369 Die Zeit 1905 July 26, 11; see also: Österreichische Touristenzeitung 26, 1906, 49–51.

370 The inauguration took place July 28, 1907. See Österreichs Illustrierte Zeitung 1907 August 11, 1018 and 1019; the programme of the ceremony is printed: Österreichische Touristenzeitung, Beilage 1907 July 1, 53.

371 Arbeiterzeitung 1907 June 28, 11

The hut served as a base for climbers and hikers who enjoyed the beauty of Val Travenanzes and the surrounding mountains. However, less than ten years later, the Val Travenanzes, Wolf von Glanvell's beloved valley, became a battlefield. Austrian and Italian troops fought in South Tyrol during World War I with Val Travenanzes and the Tofana-group marking the front line between the warring nations.[372] On August 1, 1915, Italian troops destroyed the Wolf-Glanvell-Cabin with their artillery:

> "Auch die Wolf-Glanvell-Hütte im Travenanzestale, ein kleines, nettes Hüttchen der Sektion Dresden des Oesterreichischen Touristenklubs, litt unter dem Granatfeuer der Italiener. Die Hütte war gerade von einer Truppenabteilung der Unseren besetzt, als ein Geschoß kleiner Dimension der Italiener durch die Küche fuhr, es richtete indes kein Unheil an. Da sich aber die Beschießung wiederholte, räumten die Unsern den Platz vor dem Artilleriefeuer des Feindes und verließen das Haus. Später beobachtete man, daß die Italiener mehrmals die Wolf-Glanvell-Hütte als Ziel ihrer Gebirgsartillerie nahmen."[373]

The cabin was never rebuilt and today only the foundation walls remain.

Although the visible memorial to Wolf von Glanvell was destroyed, he continued to be remembered by mountaineers and mentioned in alpine journals until the 1950s. In 1924, for example, the "Illustrierte Kronenzeitung" recalled his first ascent of the Campanile di Val Montanaia,[374] and in 1936, his former comrades remembered the foundation of the "Gilde zum groben Kletterschuh" in 1896.[375] In the autumn of 1945, members of the

372 See, for instance, Oswald Mederle, *Auf den Spuren der Tiroler Front. Wanderungen zu den Kriegsschauplätzen 1915–1918*, Bozen: Athesia, 2013, 148–152.

373 Neues Wiener Tagblatt 1915 September 2, 16. Cf. Österreichische Touristenzeitung 1915 October 1, 143; Neues Wiener Tagblatt 1918 October 7, 13; see also Walther Schaumann, *Schauplätze des Gebirgskrieges 1915–1917*, vol. 1b: *Westliche Dolomiten*, Cortina d'Ampezzo: Ghedina e Tassotti Editori, 1981, 316: "Am 1.8. [1915–SD] zerstörte italienisches Artilleriefeuer die bisherige Unterkunft des österreichischen Abschnittskommandos, die Wolf-Glanvell-Hütte. An diesem Tage übernahm ein Zug der 1. Kompanie des Preußischen Jägerbataillons 14 unter Lt. Grosse die Fontana-Negra-Stellung."

374 llustrirte Kronenzeitung 1924 August 22, 3.

375 Innsbrucker Nachrichten 1936 October 22, 10; Salzburger Volksblatt 1936 October 21, 8; Tiroler Anzeiger 1936 October 22, 7; Der Gebirgsfreund 1936 December 14, 223; Österreichische Turistenzeitung 56, 1936, 92; also: Doménigg, "Ein Getreuer des Oesterreichischen Touristenklubs. Dem Andenken Viktor Wolf-Glanvells," 9–10 (obviously, portraits of Wolf von Glanvell were to be hung in the cabins in the "Hochschwabgebiet" (Fölzstein), but I do not know if this idea was ever realized).

"Bergrettungsdienst" in Graz demonstrated their skills in rescuing climbers in the vicinity of Graz and commemorated Wolf von Glanvell, Gottlieb Stopper, and others, who had practised nearby in the early days of Austrian mountaineering ("Urtage österreichischen Bergsteigens").[376] Today, the "Kleinster Zwölfer," which he climbed for the first time in 1896, is named after him ("Wolf-Glanvell-Turm"[377]) and the regular climbing path winding up to the "Santnerspitze," which Wolf von Ganvell discovered in 1896, also bears his name.[378]

Wolf von Glanvell was both an alpinist and an academic. Is it possible to find recurring elements in both parts of his life? Obviously, he loved the adventure of solving climbing challenges and discovering unexplored mountains. His friend Günther von Saar wrote in his obituary: "Einesteils interessierten ihn die schwersten Probleme [of rock-climbing–SD], die andere ersonnen und ausgeführt, andernteils wieder zog es ihn dorthin, wo keiner noch gewesen, wo alles Erstlingsarbeit war."[379] Is the same true of Vat. lat. 1348, a dusty manuscript that no-one had analyzed before—in the words of Wolf von Glanvell: "über welchen sich meines Wissens in der Literatur keinerlei Notizen vorfinden"?[380] This, too, was "Erstlingsarbeit."

Wolf von Glanvell was, according to his friends, a disciplined and careful climber, who exercised a great deal. The same discipline and dedication applied to his academic endeavors:

> "Sein scharfer, klarer Verstand, der unerbittlich logisch vorging, sein eiserner Fleiß und seine unermüdliche Ausdauer auch in wissenschaftlicher Arbeit waren die Eigenschaften, dank derer er schon wenige Jahre nach seiner 1894 erfolgten Promotion sich als Privatdozent für Kirchenrecht habilitieren konnte; schon im November 1901 ward er außeror-

---

376 Neue Steirische Zeitung 1945 November 10, 6.

377 Doménigg, "Ein Getreuer des Oesterreichischen Turistenklubs," 9–10 (first ascent: 1896 September 6). Whether the name "Wolf-Glanvell-Turm" is official or a nickname, remains unknown to me; it is, however, mentioned in Vavra, "Wolf von Glanvell," 328.

378 Richardi, *Erschließung*, 188. There is also a tourist trail (Themenweg "Viktor Wolf Edler von Glanvell") from Schmieden to Lake Prags.

379 von Saar, "Nachruf," 123.

380 Roma, Istituto Storico Austriaco, Archiv I 3, Glanvell 1, 2 ("Arbeitsbericht der ordentlichen Mitglieder des Istituto Austriaco degli Studi Storici, Dr. Victor Wolf von Glanvell für die Arbeitsperiode vom 10. October bis 10. November 1895," 1895 November 14): "Auf diese Weise habe ich studiert Cod. Vatican. lat. 1341 [...] und mich dann entschlossen, den Cod. Vatican. lat. 1348, über welchen sich meines Wissens in der Literatur keinerlei Notizen vorfinden, zu bearbeiten."

> dentlicher Professor. Bis auf die Minute war die tägliche Arbeitszeit eingeteilt und wurde unverbrüchlich eingehalten. Nur die Sonn- und Feiertage waren voll und ganz der Erholung in seinen geliebten Bergen gewidmet."[381]

Self-discipline, hard work, and diligence, together with academic support in Graz contributed to the formation of a young, promising researcher who, despite his early death, authored several editions and studies on medieval canon law. The same traits, together with a community of like-minded adventurers shaped his achievements in mountaineering. Yet it is as an alpinist that Wolf von Glanvell was remembered, while he was all but forgotten as a scholar of canon law.

381 von Saar, "Nachruf," 123.

Appendix 1: List of Publications and Presentations by Wolf von Glanvell

Academic Publications

"Die Canonessammlung des Cod. Vatican. lat. 1348," in: Sitzungsberichte der philosophisch-historischen Classe der kaiserlichen Akademie der Wissenschaften 136, Wien 1897 as „II. Abhandlung" (1–55) (55p).

"Das cap. 2 X de rerum permutatione III 19," in: Deutsche Zeitschrift für Kirchenrecht, 8, 1898, 338–346 (8p).

Studien aus dem canonischen Privatrechte, vol. 1: *Die negotica inter vivos,* 1st edition: Graz: Styria 1897, 2nd edition: Graz: Leuschner & Lubensky, 1898 (IV + 219p).

Die letztwilligen Verfügungen nach gemeinem kirchlichen Rechte, Paderborn: Schöningh, 1900 (VI + 300 p).

Die Kanonessammlung des Kardinals Deusdedit, Band 1: *Die Kanonessammlung selbst,* Paderborn: Schöningh, 1905 (LIV + 656p).

Popular Scientific Publications

"Österreichisches Eherecht," in: Das Wissen für alle. Volksthümliche Vorträge und populär wissenschaftliche Rundschau 1, 1901, 701–704, 724–728, 744–747, 763–767.

Other Publications

Führer durch die Pragser Dolomiten, Wien: K.K. Hof- und Universitätsbuchhandlung R. Lechner, 1890.

"Aus den Pragser Dolomiten," in: Österreichische Touristenzeitung 11, 1891, 1–5, 13–16, 25–28 and 12, 1892, 37–42, 49–51, 65–69, 77–81 and 13, 1893, 17–19, 29–31, 53–54, 69–71, 141–144, 169–172, and 15, 1895, 1–5, 25–29 and 17, 1897, 99–102.

"Die Technik des Seiles," in: Österreichische Touristenzeitung 12, 1892, 151–153, 162–164.

"Kartographie [review of a map of the Dolomites]," in: Österreichische Touristenzeitung 13, 1893, 137.

"Der Haunold. Eine topographisch-touristische Studie," in: Österreichische Touristenzeitung 13, 1893, 205–209, 217–221.

"Tourenbericht," in: Österreichische Touristenzeitung 14, 1894, 235–236, 272.

"Touristik und Recht," in: Österreichische Touristenzeitung 14, 1894, 153–155, 165–168, 177–180, 189–192.

"Die Croda da Lago," in: Österreichische Touristenzeitung 14, 1894, 261–265.

"Ueber das Eigenthum an den jagdbaren Thieren. Ein Nachwort zu 'Touristik und Recht,'" in: Österreichische Touristenzeitung 15, 1895, 73–76, 89–92.

"Die Thürme von Vajolett," in: Österreichische Touristenzeitung 15, 1895, 161–166, 173–176, 185–188.

"Aus den Sextener Dolomiten," in: Österreichische Touristenzeitung 15, 1895, 269–273, 281–285 and 16, 1896, 53–56, 65–68, 81–85, 109–112.

"Tourenbericht," in: Österreichische Touristenzeitung 15, 1895, 256.

"Review of 'L. Purtscheller / H. Hess, Der Hochtourist in den Ostalpen,'" in: Österreichische Touristenzeitung 15, 1895, 80–81.

"Aus den Grödener Dolomiten," in: Österreichische Touristenzeitung 16, 1896, 213–218, 237–242 and 17, 1897, 13–17, 25–28.

"Review of 'Panorama vom Dürrenstein 2840m,'" in: Österreichische Touristenzeitung 16, 1896, 247.

"Die Croda di pausa marza 2503m," in: Österreichische Touristenzeitung 17, 1897, 261–265.

"Tourenbericht," in: Österreichische Touristenzeitung 17, 1897, 12.

"Tourenbericht," in: Österreichische Touristenzeitung 17, 1897, 47.

Dolomitenführer. Mit einer Übersichtskarte der Dolomiten im Massstabe 1:300.000, Wien: Gerold, 1898.

"Tourenbericht," in: Österreichische Touristenzeitung 18, 1898, 143.

[Tourenbericht], in: Rivista mensile del Club Alpino Italiano 17, 1898, 140–142.

"Tourenberichte," in: Österreichische Touristenzeitung 19, 1899, 168, 180, 215–216.

"Val Travenanzes [map of the valley drawn by Viktor Wolf-Glanvell]," in: Österreichische Alpenzeitung 21, 1899, 261.

"Aus den Pragser Dolomiten [Fortsetzung]," in: Österreichische Alpenzeitung 22, 1900, 137–142, 149–153.

[List of ascents], in: Rivista mensile del Club Alpino Italiano 19, 1900, 396–397.

"Tourenberichte," in: Österreichische Alpenzeitung 23, 1901, 84–86 (together with Günther von Saar).

"Gsellknoten," in: Österreichische Alpenzeitung 23, 1901, 87.

"Die Gruppe des Pomagagnon (Eine topographisch-turistische Studie)," in: Österreichische Alpenzeitung 25, 1903, 49–55, 61–66, 73–77.
"Aus der Fanis-Tofanagruppe," in: Zeitschrift des deutschen und österreichischen Alpenvereins 35, 1904, 338–380.
"Vom Hochthor zum Ödstein," in: Wandern und Reisen 1, 1903, 598–601.
"Winterfahrt," in: Österreichische Touristenzeitung 25, 1905, 41–42.

Popular Scientific Presentations

1901 February 1, 8, 15	"Über Eherecht," Graz[382]
1902 December 14	"Die sogenannten Siebenbürgenehen," Kapfenberg[383]
1904 February 23	"Wie mache ich mein Testament?," Graz[384]

Other Presentations[385]

1899 April 12	*Über die Ersteigung des Ödsteins im Gesäuse*, Graz (Österreichischer Touristenklub)[386]
1900 November	*Über die Ersteigung des Hochthores über die Nordwand*, Graz (Österreichischer Alpenklub)[387]

382 Grazer Volksblatt 1901 January 6 (Morgenausgabe), 7; Grazer Volksblatt 1901 February 8, 3.
383 Grazer Tagblatt 1902 October 19, 21. The term "Siebenbürgische Ehe" denotes a legal construction by which Austrian Catholics circumvented the Catholic understanding of the indissolubility of a marriage by changing residence and citizenship; on this construction: Wilhelm Fuchs, *Die sogenannten Siebenbürgischen Ehen und andere Arten der Wiederverehelichung geschiedener österreichischer Katholiken*, Wien: Manz, 1889; Christian Neschwara, "Eherecht und 'Scheinmigration' im 19. Jahrhundert: Siebenbürgische und ungarische, deutsche und Coburger Ehen," in: Gerald Kohl et al. (ed.), Eherecht 1811 bis 2011. Historische Entwicklungen und aktuelle Herausforderungen (Beiträge zur Rechtsgeschichte Österreichs 1/2012), Wien: Akademie der Wissenschaft, 2012, 101–117.
384 Grazer Volksblatt 1904 February 23 (Abendausgabe), 2
385 Presentations for which I do not know the exact title, but have a rough idea of the content, are italicized in the list.
386 Grazer Tagblatt 1899 April 14 (Morgenausgabe), 4
387 Grazer Tagblatt 1900 November 30 (Morgenausgabe), 14.

1900 December 13	"Die Südostwand des Col Rosa," Wien (Österreichischer Alpenklub)[388]
1901 March 15	"Vom Hochthor zum Oedstein," Graz (Österreichischer Touristenklub)[389]
1901 October 25	*Über die Ostwand der Rosengartenspitze (erste führerlose Durchkletterung)*, Graz (Turner-Bergsteiger)[390]
1902 April 4	"Von Norden auf den Saß-Rigais," Wien (Österreichischer Alpenklub)[391]
1903 November 12	"Antelao von Süden," Wien (Österreichischer Alpenklub)[392]
1905 January 26	"Neues aus der Palagruppe," Wien (Oesterreichischer Alpenklub)[393]
1905 March 24	"Die erste Überschreitung der Santnerspitze (mit Skioptikonbildern)," Wien (Österreichischer Touristenklub)[394]

Unless otherwise mentioned, the aforementioned list of publications is based on library catalogues and a systematic research in the following journals (years: 1890–1907): Archiv für Katholisches Kirchenrecht, Deutsche Zeitschrift für Kirchenrecht, Zeitschrift der Savigny-Stiftung für Rechtsgeschichte (Romanistische and Germanistische Abteilung), Österreichische Touristenzeitung, Mittheilungen des deutschen und österreichischen Alpenvereins, Rivista mensile del Club Alpino Italiano.

The list of presentations is based on a full text search (search word: "Glanvell") of newspapers via https://anno.onb.ac.at/ (years: 1890–1907).

388 Neues Wiener Tagblatt 1900 December 13, 23.

389 Grazer Tagblatt 1901 March 13 (Morgenausgabe), 3.

390 Grazer Tagblatt 1901 October 27 (Morgenausgabe), 5.

391 Ostdeutsche Rundschau 1902 April 2 (Abendausgabe), 4.

392 Neues Wiener Tagblatt 1903 November 12 (Tagesausgabe), 9; Ostdeutsche Rundschau 1903 November 12 (Morgenblatt), 10.

393 Die Zeit 1905 January 26 (Morgenblatt), 7; Österreichische Touristenzeitung 25, 1905, 64.

394 Wiener Zeitung 1905 March 24, 7.

Appendix 2: Courses given by Wolf von Glanvell

The following list is based on the "Vorlesungsverzeichnisse" of the University of Graz, digitized at https://archiv.uni-graz.at/de/bestaende/digitaler-bestand-online/lehrveranstaltungsverzeichnisse-und-personalstaende-der-universitaet-graz-1811-1918/, and amended according to archival notes in the Universitätsarchiv Graz.

sommer term of 1898	*courses were announced after publication of course catalogue; the content, however, remains unknown*[395]
winter term of 1898/99	Exegese ausgewählter Stellen des Corpus iuris canonici (unter besonderer Berücksichtigung der Wucherlehre) (2h)
sommer term of 1899	Repetitorium des Kirchenrechts (3h) Exegese ausgewählter Stellen des corpus iuris canonici (II. Die letztwilligen Verfügungen nach Kirchenrecht) (2h)
winter term of 1899/00	Exegese ausgewählter Stellen des Corpus iuris canonici (unter besonderer Berücksichtigung der Wucherlehre) (2h)
sommer term of 1900	Repetitorium des Kirchenrechts (3h) Exegese ausgewählter Stellen des corpus iuris canonici (II. Die letztwilligen Verfügungen nach Kirchenrecht) (2h) Die Quellen des kirchlichen Rechts (2h)[396]
winter term of 1900/01	Kirchliches Privatrecht (mit Exegese ausgewählter Stellen des Corpus iuris canonici) (3h)

395 See the approval of the courses in Graz, Universitätsarchiv, Jur. Fak., Z. 436 ex 1897/98.

396 Course announced after publication of printed course catalogue; Wolf von Glanvell replaced Friedrich Thaner (Graz, Universitätsarchiv, Jur. Fak., Z. 665 ex 1899/00).

sommer term of 1901	Repetitorium des Kirchenrechts (3h) Die Quellen des kirchlichen Rechtes (2h)
winter term of 1901/02	Ehe- und Ordensrecht (mit Exegese ausgewählter Stellen des Corpus iuris canonici) (2h)
sommer term of 1902	Repetitorium des Kirchenrechts (3h) Ordensrecht (2)[397]
winter term of 1902/03	Das corpus iuris canonici (mit Übungen aus demselben) (3h) Encyklopädie der Rechts- und Staatswissenschaften (2h)
sommer term of 1903	Repetitorium des Kirchenrechts (3h) Ordensrecht (2h)
winter term of 1903/04	Das corpus iuris canonici (mit Übungen aus demselben) (3h) Encyklopädie der Rechts- und Staatswissenschaften (2h)
sommer term of 1904	Repetitorium des Kirchenrechts (3h) Ordensrecht (2h)
winter term of 1904/05	Das Corpus iuris canonici mit Übungen (3h) Encyklopädie der Rechts- und Staatswissenschaften (2h)
sommer term of 1905	Repetitorium des Kirchenrechts (3h) Ordensrecht (2h)

397 Course announced after publication of printed course catalogue (Graz, Universitätsarchiv, Jur. Fak., Z. 632 ex 1902/03). This course was a *Collegium publicum*, thus open for all students.

Appendix 3: Reconstruction of Wolf von Glanvell's Private Library

The following reconstruction of Wolf von Glanvell's private library is based on the "Todfalls-Aufnahme" of May 1905 (Graz, Steiermärkisches Landesarchiv, Bezirksgericht Graz-I, Verlässe P-XIV-202/1905, fol. 17v-19r). I present a transcription of this document; my own comments are in italics. See also Fig. 4.

[17v]

I. Fachwissenschaftliche Bücher

1. Plutarchi vite 13 Bände Padua 1716 — 10 Kronen

   Plutarch, Vitae parallelae

2. Tassoni, Annali Ecclesiastici, vier Bände, Handschrift — 15 Kronen

   possibly: *Alessandro Tassoni who summarized in Latin the first 8 books of the Annales Ecclesiastici by Cesare Baronio*[398]

3. Franz Schmier jurisprudentia canonica — 4 Kronen

   possibly: *Franz Schmier, Iurisprudentia canonico-civilis seu ius canonicum universum iuxta V libros decretalium nova et facili methodo explicatum ... in 3 tomos distinctum, Salzburg, 1716*

4. Codex regularium Holzterii (?) 1663 — 3 Kronen

   possibly: *Lucas Holstenius, Codex regularum, quas Sancti Patres monachis et virginibus sanctimonialibus servandas praescripsere, 1663*

5. Decretales summorum pontificum I — 2 Kronen

   either *Decretales Epistolae Summorum Pontificum, 1555* or *Epistolarum Decretalium Summorum Pontificum, tomus Primus, 1591*

398 Siehe Andrea Lazzarini, "Tassoni, Alessandro," in: Dizionario Biografico degli Italiani–Volume 95 (2019).

6. Schmidt Thesaurus iuris ec[18r]clesiastici 7 Bände Heidelberg 1772 — 7 Kronen

   Antonius Schmidt, Thesaurus iuris ecclesiastici, potissimum Germanici sive dissertationes selectae in ius ecclesiasticum, 1772–1779

7. Ecclesiae disciplina Paris 1688 3 Bände folio — 12 Kronen

   Louis Thomassin, Vetus et nova ecclesiae disciplina circa beneficia et beneficiarios, 3 Bände, 1688

8. Pellizzarii manuale regularium 1665, 2 Bände — 10 Kronen

   Francesco Pallizzari, Manuale Regularium constans ex decem tractatibus, et in duo tomos distributum, 1665

9. Georges, Lateinisches Wörterbuch, 2 Bände — 4 Kronen

   Karl Ernst Georges, Ausführliches latenisch-deutsches Handwörterbuch (multiple editions extant)

10. Schenkel, griechisch-deutsches Wörterbuch — 2 Kronen

    Gustav Eduard Benseler / Karl Schenkl, Griechisch-Deutsches und Deutsch-Griechisches Schulwörterbuch (multiple editions extant)

11. Buix ius regularium, 2 Bände — 4 Kronen

    Dominique Bouix, Tractatus de jure regularium, 1867

12. Scherer, Kirchenrecht Band II — 3 Kronen

    Rudolf von Scherer, Handbuch des Kirchenrechtes, Band 2, 1898

13. Heimbucher, Die Orden und Kongregationen — 3 Kronen

    Max Heimbucher, Die Orden und Kongregationen der katholischen Kirche, 1897

14. Holzendorf, Rechtslexikon 2 Bände 4 Kronen

    Franz von Holtzendorff, Encyclopädie der Rechtswissenschaft in systematischer und alphabetischer Bearbeitung, 2 vols., 1870ss (presumably 5th edition, 1890, or 6th edition, 1904)

15. Randa, Der Besitz 2 Kronen

    Anton Randa, Der Besitz nach österreichischem Recht mit Berücksichtigung des gemeinen Rechtes, des peußischen, französischen und sächsischen Gesetzbuches, 1865

16. Singer, Summa decretorum 2 Kronen

    Heinrich Singer, Summa decretorum des Magister Rufinus, 1902
    [18v]

17. Deutsche Zeitschrift für Kirchenrecht 8.-11. Band 5 Kronen

    vol. 8: 1898, vol. 9: 1900, vol. 10: 1901, vol. 11: 1902

18. Archiv für Kirchenrecht 78 bis 81 Band, gebunden 8 Kronen

    presumbly: *Archiv für katholisches Kirchenrecht (vol. 78: 1897, vol. 79: 1899, vol. 80: 1900, vol. 81: 1901)*

19. Archiv für Kirchenrecht 82 und 83 Band à 2 Kronen 4 Kronen

    presumably: *Archiv für katholisches Kirchenrecht (vol. 82: 1902, vol. 83: 1903)*

20. Monumenta Germaniae legum sectio III concilia tomi II pars prima 3 Kronen

    presumably: *Albert Werminghoff, Concilia aevi Karolini (742–842, part 1) (MGH Conc. 2,1)*; this edition, however, was published in 1906 (preface dates to November 1906!), thus one year after the inventory was made. Was this book delivered in quires, so that the first quire was already published in 1905?
    The other possible edition is *Fridericus Maassen, Concilia Aevi Merovingici, 1893 (MGH Conc. 1)*, but it is inscribed *legum sectio*

III concilia tomus I, which does not fit either. This riddle remains unsolved.

21. Zwanzig diverse kirchenrechtliche Bücher a 50h	10 Kronen
22. Eine Partie Broschüren, Rechtsbücher etc	5 Kronen

II. Belletristische Bücher

23. 25 Bände Universum	15 Kronen

III. Touristische Bücher

24. oesterreichischen Alpen 1897–1901	1 Krone
25. Mitheilungen des deutschen und österreichischen Alpenvereins 1885–1894 [19r]	2 Kronen
26. Zeitschrift der deutschen und österreichischen Alpenvereins 1874–1884	2 Kronen 20
27. dito 1885–1894	2 Kronen
28. Oesterreichische Alpenzeitung	1 Krone
29. Oesterreichische Touristenzeitung 1886–1901	8 Kronen
Summe des Schätzwertes der Bücher des Erblasser 20 h	153 Kronen 20h

Appendix 4: "Habilitationsgutachten" (Friedrich Thaner, Arnold Luschin von Ebengreuth)

The "Habilitationsgutachten" by Friedrich Thaner and Arnold Luschin von Ebengreuth are a prime source for the immediate reception of Wolf von Glanvell's studies. Both are edited here. See Fig. 3.

Friedrich Thaner, report to the Faculty of Law in November 1897 (Graz, Universitätsarchiv, Jur. Fak., Z. 303 ex 1897/98):

"In Gemäßheit des Auftrages vom 26. Juli 1897 Zl. 815 beehrt sich der Gefertigte über das Habilitationsgesuch des Dr. Victor Wolf Ed. v. Glanvell nachstehenden Bericht zu erstatten, bzw. Antrag zu stellen.

I. Die in den Sitzungsberichten der kais. Akademie der Wissenschaften Bd. 136, Wien 1897 erschienene Schrift: Die Canones-Sammlung des Cod. Vat. lat. 1348 giebt auf 55 Seiten die Beschreibung einer im Original über 300 Seiten starken Sammlung von Canones, die am Ende des 11. Jahrhundertes geschrieben u[nd] wohl auch zu dieser Zeit verfasst wurde. Die Beschreibung ist in der Weise angelegt, daß sich der Plan [?] der Sammlung und auch ihr Inhalt wohl erkennen lässt, wenn auch für eine Anzahl von Kapiteln die Quelle unentdeckt blieb. Das Hauptverdienst dieser Arbeit besteht darin, daß ungeachtet der ungenauen und theilweise irreführenden Quellenangaben im Codex selbst, die wirklichen Quellen zu den einzelnen Kapiteln (nahezu 700) aufgefunden und so genau bezeichnet sind, daß sich der vollständige Inhalt der Sammlung aus demselben rekonstruieren läßt. Eine solche Arbeit erfordert nicht bloß großen Aufwand an Zeit und Mühe, sie kann auch ohne große Belesenheit und einen ziemlich hohen Grad an Spürsinn überhaupt nicht zum Ziele führen. Dass der Verfasser diese Gaben besitzt, ist für ihn umso empfehlender, als gerade für das canonische Recht noch vieles handschriftliche Material in Bibliotheken und Archiven unverwerthet begraben liegt. Derselbe unterließ es nicht, die Sammlung nach allgemeinen gut gewählten Gesichtspunkten zu characterisieren und wenn auch gegen Einzelheiten Widerspruch zu erheben ist, so kann sein Urtheil doch im Großen und Ganzen als zutreffend bezeichnet werden.

II. "Die Studien aus dem canonischen Privatrechte" behandeln auf 219 Seiten die Titel XIV–XXIV des dritten Buches der Dekretalen Gregors IX, die von den Rechtsgeschäften unter Lebenden handeln. Der Verfasser hat sich damit ein Thema gewählt, das bisher so gut wie brach gelegen hat. Wenn man die Kürze der Zeit bedenkt, die ihm zur Bearbeitung derselben zu Gebote stand, sowie die Unzulänglichkeit der Bibliotheksmittel so kann man seiner Arbeitskraft nur volle Anerkennung widerfahren lassen. Es ist zur Beleuchtung der einzelnen Kapitel ein großes Quellenmateriale aus Urkunden, zahlreiche Citate aus Schriften der Canonisten, aus dem römischen und deutschen Rechte herbeigezogen, und es lässt sich nicht leugnen, daß dasselbe auch geschickt verwerthet ist. Gegen die eingeschlagene Methode der kapitelweisen Interpretation ist allerdings einzuwenden, daß sie zur Gewinnung großer wissenschaftlicher Resultate nicht die geeignetste ist, aber zu Theile wird der Mangel dadurch wett gemacht, daß jedem Titel zum Schluss eine kurze zusammenfassende Darstellung gewidmet ist. Eine und die andere Behauptung ist nicht genügend erwiesen, wie z.B. zu Tit. XIV c. 3 S. 51, zu Tit. XIX c. 2. S. 116, die Bedeutung mancher Kapitel nicht richtig erkannt, wie die des cap. Odoardus, oder des cap. Consultationibus (T. XXIV, 4); dagegen ist rühmend hervorzuheben, daß der Verfasser sein Augenmerk nicht blos auf den offen zu Tage liegenden Einfluß des römischen Rechts, sondern auch auf die Bedeutung des deutschen Rechts für das canonische Recht gerichtet hat, auch ist es ihm nicht entgangen, wie sehr das geistliche Interesse auf die Gestaltung der Rechtssätze bestimmend eingewirkt hat.

Alles in allem genommen, glaubt der Gefertigte zu dem Schlusse berechtigt zu sein, daß der Gesuchsteller sowohl den Fleiß als die Begabung und den ernsten Eifer besitzt, wissenschaftlich thätig zu sein, und stellt daher den Antrag, daß derselbe zum Colloquium zugelassen werde.

Graz, November 1897
Friedrich Thaner"

Arnold Luschin von Ebengreuth, report to the Faculty of Law (s.d.) (Graz, Universitätsarchiv, Jur. Fak., Z. 304 ex 1897/98):

"Neben Prof. Thaner, dem als Vertreter des canonischen Rechts das erste Urtheil über das von Dr. Victor Wolf von Glanvell eingereichte Habilitationsgesuch zusteht, ist auch dem Unterzeichneten durch den Sitzungsbeschluß vom 26. Juli d. J. die Prüfung der vorgelegten Arbeiten übertragen worden.

Ich vermag nun dem eingesand[t]en Gutachten, daß Prof. Thaner in dieser Sache schon abgegeben hat nur wenig aus Eigenem hinzuzufügen, möchte jedoch hinsichtlich der Abhandlung über die Canonessammlung des Cod. Vaticanus lat. 1348 nur hervorheben, daß sie in den Sitzungsberichten der k. Akademie der Wissenschaften zu Wien erschienen ist, welche bekanntlich die Aufnahme eingereichter Arbeiten von Nichtmitgliedern abhängig macht von einer genauen Prüfung und günstigen Begutachtung durch Fachmänner. Spricht dies zu Gunsten des wissenschaftlichen Gehalts der erwähnten Abhandlung, so liefert dieselbe dadurch, daß sie eine nur handschriftlich vorhandene Quelle zum Gegenstand der Untersuchung macht, zugleich den Beweis, daß Dr. v. Wolf auch mit paläographischen Kenntnissen ausgerüstet ist, welche dem Canonisten zur Vornahme von Quellenstudien geradezu unentbehrlich sind.

Die zweite von Herrn Wolf von Glanvell vorgelegte Arbeit "Studien aus dem canonischen Privatrecht" wird durch den Beisatz I die Negotia inter vivos als der erste Theil eines größeren Werkes bezeichnet, dem später wohl eine zweiter über die Negotia mortis causa folgen soll.

Schon das Vorliegende läßt erkennen, daß der Verfasser bei der Wahl des Themas eine glückliche Hand hatte. Seine Absicht war nachzuweisen, was im canonischen Privatrecht auf römisch-rechtlichen, was auf deutschrechtlichen Grundlagen beruhe, ferner auch den Einfluß zu berücksichtigen, den wirthschaftliche Momente und kirchliche Anschauungen in ihrem Zusammentreffen auf die Ausgestaltung der Rechtssätze genommen haben. Man vgl. z. B. das im Abschnitt de emptione et venditione über die Ansichten der canonischen Rechtswissenschaft bezüglich des iustum pretium Gesagte (S. 75ff) oder S. 134 über den Vorzug den sie dem Tausche vor dem Kaufe gab.

Ich habe die Aufmerksamkeit vor allem auf die meinem Fach näher liegenden Abschnitte de precariis gewandt, in welchen der Verfasser zum Schlusse gelangt, daß die Kirche neben dem nach den Grundsätzen des römischen Rechts behandelten Precarium durch Principien öconomischer Art beeinflußt unter dem Namen der Precarie eine Anzahl ganz verschiedener Rechtsgebilde zusammengefasst hat, die nur durch ihren Zweck (die dauernde Benutzung eines wirtschaftlich belangreichen Gegenstandes) und die formale Ursache zu ihrer Entstehung (das Ansuchen) zusammengehalten wurden.

Bei den Untersuchungen in deren Verlauf der Verfasser zu diesem Ergebnis gelangt, geht er mit großer Gewandtheit zu Werke. Er stützt sich dabei auf ein überraschend reiches Quellenmaterial das theils Zeumer'schen Ausgabe der Formelsammlungen in den Mon. Germaniae, theils verschiedenen Urkundensammlungen entnommen wurde. Stichproben die ich in ziemlicher Anzahl vorgenommen habe, ließen die Citate durchwegs als verläßlich erkennen.

So zeugen denn die Arbeiten des Habilitierungs[be]werbers sowohl für dessen Befähigung zu quellenkritischen als auch zu dogmengeschichtlichen Arbeiten, sie erwiesen sich durch die ins Einzelne gehende quellenmäßige Begründung als sorgfältig aufgebaut und stellen als Erstlingswerke dem Verfasser eine schöne wissenschaftliche Zukunft in Aussicht.

Ich halte daher die genannten Schriften für eine geeignete Grundlage des Gesuchs um Habilitierung fürs kanonische Recht und beantrage:

es sei Dr. Victor Wolf von Glanvell zu den weiteren Habilitierungsschriften [sic, presumably: Habilitierungsschritten], zunächst zum Colloquium und sodann eventuell zur Probevorlesung zuzulassen.

Decanat der rechts- und staatswissenschaftlichen Facultät
Graz am [date missing]

Luschin
d[er]z[eitig] Decan"

Appendix 5: List of Figures

Appendix 6: List of Abbreviations

AKKR	Archiv für Katholisches Kirchenrecht
AÖAW	Archiv der Österreichischen Akademie der Wissenschaften
AVA	Allgemeines Verwaltungsarchiv
BMCL	Bulletin of Medieval Canon Law
CIC / 1917	Codex Iuris Canonici (1917)
CIC / 1983	Codex Iuris Canonici (1983)
IÖG	Institut für Österreichische Geschichtsforschung
MGH	Monumenta Germaniae Historica
LdL	Libelli de lite
MIC	Monumenta Iuris Canonici
B	Corpus collectionum
C	Subsidia
N.N.	*nomen nescio* (name unknown)
phil.-hist.	philosophisch-historisch
s.d.	sine dato
UA	Universitätsarchiv
VuF	Vorträge und Forschungen
X	Liber Extra
Z. / Zl.	Zahl
ZRG	Zeitschrift der Savigny-Stiftung für Rechtsgeschichte
GA	Germanistische Abteilung
KA	Kanonistische Abteilung

Appendix 7: Bibliography

7.1. Archival Material

France [Pierrefitte-sur-Seine], Archives Nationales

Fonds Gabriel Le Bras, Papiers Paul Fournier (currently being indexed)

Graz, Pfarrei "Herz Jesu"

Taufbuch II 1901–1911, Signature 1500 (online: https://data.matricula-online.eu/de/oesterreich/graz-seckau/graz-herz-jesu/1500/?pg=152)

Trauungsbuch II 1896–1902, Signature 1575 (online: https://data.matricula-online.eu/de/oesterreich/graz-seckau/graz-herz-jesu/1575/?pg=228).

Graz, Stadtarchiv

Meldezettel "Wolf Edle von Glanvell, Marie"

Meldezettel "Wolf Edler von Glanvell, Viktor"

Graz, Steiermärkisches Landesarchiv

Bezirksgericht Graz-I, Verlässe P-XIV-202/1905

Graz, Universitätsarchiv

Jur. Fak., Nationale Viktor Wolf von Glanvell

Jur. Fak., Rigorosenprotokolle, vol. 8

Jur. Fak., Sitzungsprotokolle, vol. 3

Jur. Fak., Z. 292 ex 1897/98

Jur. Fak., Z. 298 ex 1897/98

Jur. Fak., Z. 303 ex 1897/98

Jur. Fak., Z. 304 ex 1897/98

Jur. Fak., Z. 305 ex 1897/98

Jur. Fak., Z. 436 ex 1897/98

Jur. Fak., Z. 665 ex 1899/00

Jur. Fak., Z. 508 ex 1901/02

Jur. Fak., Z. 598 ex 1901/02

Jur. Fak., Z. 202 ex 1902/03

Jur. Fak., Z. 292 ex 1902/03

Jur. Fak., Z. 632 ex 1902/03
Jur. Fak., Z. 1520 ex 1902/03
Personalakte Wolf von Glanvell

Heidelberg, Universitätsbibliothek Heidelberg

Nachlass Moritz Cantor, Heid. Hs. 4028, 144

Historisches Alpenarchiv

DAV NAS 23 FF.987.0
OeAV 32 M Laternbilder 909.1
(both online: historisches-alpenarchiv.org)

Roma, Istituto Storico Austriaco

Archiv I 3, Glanvell 1
Archiv I 3, Glanvell 2
Archiv I 3, Glanvell 3
Archiv I 3, Glanvell 4

Weimar, Klassik Stiftung Weimar

Goethe und Schiller Archiv 55/BS 1258 (Bestand Kürschner)

Wien, Archiv der Österreichischen Akademie der Wissenschaften

Protokoll der Sitzung der Gesamtakademie 1899 December 15 (A. 545)
Protokoll der Sitzung der Gesamtakademie 1900 January 25 (A. 546)
Protokoll der Sitzung der Gesamtakademie 1901 May 2 (A. 559)
Protokoll der Sitzung der Gesamtakademie 1902 April 25 (A. 569)
Protokoll der Sitzung der phil.-hist. Klasse 1900 January 3 (C. 1517)
Protokoll der Sitzung der phil.-hist. Klasse 1900 April 4 (C. 1527)
Protokoll der Sitzung der phil.-hist. Klasse 1900 July 4 (C. 1534)
Protokoll der Sitzung der phil.-hist. Klasse 1900 October 17 (C. 1537)
Protokoll der Sitzung der phil.-hist. Klasse 1901 April 24 (C. 1554)
Protokoll der Sitzung der phil.-hist. Klasse 1902 April 23 (C. 1582)
Savigny-Kommission, Karton 1 / Mappe 7, Akte 426/1900
Savigny-Kommission, Karton 1 / Mappe 7, Akte 428/1901
Savigny-Kommission, Karton 1 / Mappe 7, Akte 409/1902
Savigny-Kommission, Karton 1 / Mappe 26

Wien, Institut für Österreichische Geschichtsforschung

Nachlass Mühlbacher
Nachlass Sickel

Wien, Österreichisches Staatsarchiv

Allgemeines Verwaltungsarchiv, Adel, Hofadelsakten, Wolf, Ignaz, Major, Adelsstand
Allgemeines Verwaltungsarchiv, Unterricht-Allg., Ktn. 705
Allgemeines Verwaltungsarchiv, Unterricht-Allg., Ktn. 915.37, PA Wolf-Glanvell

7.2. Newspapers

Agramer Zeitung
Allgemeine Sport-Zeitung
Allgemeine Zeitung
Arbeiterwille
Arbeiterzeitung
Das interessante Blatt
Das Vaterland
Der Gebirgsfreund
Deutsches Südmährerblatt
Die Zeit
Freie Stimmen
Grazer Tagblatt
Grazer Volksblatt
llustrirte Kronenzeitung
Innsbrucker Nachrichten
Kärntner Zeitung
Mährisches Tagblatt
Mährisch-Schlesische Presse
Marburger Zeitung
Münchner Neueste Nachrichten
Neue Freie Presse
Neue Schlesische Zeitung
Neue Steirische Zeitung
Neues Wiener Journal
Neues Wiener Tagblatt
Neuigkeits-Welt-Blatt
Oesterreichische Kronen-Zeitung

Österreichische Land-Zeitung
Österreichische Touristenzeitung
Österreichs Illustrierte Zeitung
Prager Tagblatt
Reichspost
Salzburger Chronik
Salzburger Volksblatt
Tagespost
Tiroler Anzeiger
Volksblatt für Stadt und Land
Voralberger Tagblatt
Wiener Zeitung
Znaimer Wochenblatt

7.3. Other Printed Sources

Codex Iuris Canonici / Codex des Kanonischen Rechts, 9th edition, Kevelaer: Butzon & Bercker, 2018.

Codex Iuris Canonici. Pii X Pontificis Maximi iussu digestus, Benedicti Papae XV auctoritate promulgatus, Rome 1917.

Peters, Edward, *The 1917 or Pio-Benedictine code of Canon Law in English translation*, San Francisco: Ignatius, 2001.

Provisorisches Statut, betreffend die Errichtung von Stipendien zum Betriebe wissenschaftlicher Studien in Rom (römische Stipendien), in: Verordnungsblatt für den Dienstbereich des Ministeriums für Cultus und Unterricht 1883 (1883 August 1), 200–202.

Statut für das Istituto austriaco di studii storici in Rom, in: Verordnungsblatt für den Dienstbereich des Ministeriums für Cultus und Unterricht 1893 (1893 October 15), 294–296.

Publications by Wolf von Glanvell are not listed here (see list of his publications, Appendix 1).

7.4. Secondary literature

Adelson, Howard / Baker, Robert, "The Oath of Purgation of Pope Leo III in 800," in: Traditio 8, 1952, 35–80.

Almanach der kaiserlichen Akademie der Wissenschaften 51, Wien 1901.

Almanach der kaiserlichen Akademie der Wissenschaften 52, Wien 1902.

Almanach der kaiserlichen Akademie der Wissenschaften 56, Wien 1906.

Amira, Karl von, *Nordgermanisches Obligationenrecht*, 2 vols., Leipzig: Veit, 1882 / 1895.

Anderson, Ben, *Cities, Mountains and Being Modern in fin-de-siècle England and Germany*, London: Palgrave Macmillan, 2020.

Anter, Andreas, *Max Weber und die Staatsrechtslehre*, Tübingen: Mohr Siebeck, 2016.

Bader, Karl Siegfried, *Ulrich Stutz (1868–1938) als Forscher und Lehrer*, Bonn: Peter Hanstein, 1969.

Basdevant-Gaudemet, Brigitte / Domingo, Rafael, "Paul Fournier (1853–1935)," in: Olivier Deschamps / Rafael Domingo (ed.), Great Christian Jurists in French History, Cambridge: Cambridge University Press, 2019, 309–323.

Bayer, Wilhelm, "Kann ein Bischof Patronat- bzw. Präsentationsrechte auf ein Beneficium erwerben? Zur Erklärung von c. 18 X de iur. patr. III, 38," in: AKKR 82, 1902, 3–16.

Bayerle, Katrin, "Ulrich Stutz: Von der Eigenkirche zur 'hinkenden Trennung zwischen Kirche und Staat,'" in: Thomas Holzner / Hannes Ludyga (ed.), Entwicklungstendenzen des Staatskirchen- und Religionsverfassungsrechts. Ausgewählte begrifflich-systematische, historische, gegenwartsbezogene und biographische Beiträge (Kirchen- und Staatskirchenrecht 15), Paderborn / München: Ferdinand Schöningh, 2013, 505–518.

Becker, Hans-Jürgen, "Spolienrecht," in: Adalbert Erler et al. (ed.), Handwörterbuch zur Deutschen Rechtsgeschichte, vol. 4, Berlin: Erich Schmidt, 1990, 1779–1780.

Bergfeld, Christoph, "Scaccia, Sigismondo," in: Michael Stolleis (ed.), Juristen. Ein biographisches Lexikon. Von der Antike bis zum 20. Jahrhundert, München: Beck, 1995, 545.

Bernal Palacios, Arturo, "La redacción breve del c. 'In die ressurectionis' en las colecciones canónicas pregracianas," in: Peter Landau / Jörg Müller (ed.), Proceedings of the Ninth International Congress of Medieval Canon Law, Munich, 13–18 July 1992 (MIC C/10), Città del Vaticano: Biblioteca Apostolica Vaticana, 1997, 923–952.

Beste, Udalricus, *Introductio in Codicem*, 3rd edition, Collegeville: St. John's Abbey press, 1946.

Biederlack, Joseph SJ, "Review of 'Wolf von Glanvell, Die negotia in vivos,'" in: Allgemeines Litteraturblatt 8, 1899, 23–24.

Bleek, Wilhelm, *Geschichte der Politikwissenschaft in Deutschland*, München: Beck, 2001.

Brauneder, Wilhelm, *Europäische Privatrechtsgeschichte*, Wien / Köln / Weimar: Böhlau, 2014.

——, "Luschin von Ebengreuth, Arnold (1841–1932)," in: Albrecht Cordes et al. (ed.), Handwörterbuch zur Deutschen Rechtsgeschichte, 2nd edition, vol. 3, Berlin: Erich Schmidt, 2016, 1099.

Brunner, Heinrich, "Die Savigny-Stiftung seit 1880," in: ZRG.GA 22, 1901, III–XV.

Bruns, Georg, "Die Savigny-Stiftung," in: ZRG.GA 1, 1880, III–XIX.

Buchenauer, Lieselotte, "Dr. Viktor Wolf Edler von Glanvell," in: Österreichische Alpenzeitung 100, 1982, 80–83.

Bünz, Enno, "Eigenkirche," in: Albrecht Cordes et al. (ed.), Handwörterbuch zur Deutschen Rechtsgeschichte, 2nd edition, vol. 1, Berlin: Erich Schmidt, 2008, 1267–1269.

Burkhard, Manuel, *Der Mönch und seine Berge. Pater Placidus Spescha (1752–1833) als Pionier und Vertreter des modernen Alpinismus* (Berner Forschungen zur Regionalgeschichte 19), Nordhausen: Traugott Bautz, 2016.

Carlen, Louis, "Briefe französischer Rechtshistoriker an Ulrich Stutz," in: ZRG.KA 74, 1988, 17–26.

Decock, Wim, "Molina, On Justice and Right," in: Serge Dauchy et al. (ed.), The Formation and Transmission of Western Legal Culture. 150 Books that Made the Law in the Age of Printing, Cham: Springer, 2016, 142–144.

——, "Recht und Finanzen in der Spätscholastik," in: Stefan Grundmann / Jan Thiessen (ed.), Religiöse Werte im Recht (Rechtsvergleichung und Rechtsvereinheitlichung 50), Tübingen: Mohr Siebeck, 2017, 19–42.

——, *Theologians and Contract Law. The Moral Transformation of the Ius Commune (ca 1500–1650)* (Legal History Library 9 / Studies in the History of Private Law 4), Leiden / Boston: Brill, 2013.

Depping, André, *Das BGB als Durchgangspunkt. Privatrechtsmethode und Privatrechtsleitbilder bei Heinrich Lehmann (1876–1963)* (Beiträge zur Rechtsgeschichte des 20. Jahrhunderts 34), Tübingen: Mohr Siebeck, 2002.

Doménigg, Karl, *Ein Bergsteigerleben. Einer von der 'Gilde zum groben Kletterschuh,'* Wien: Österreichische Bergsteiger-Zeitung, 1949.

——, "Ein Getreuer des Oesterreichischen Touristenklubs. Dem Andenken Viktor Wolf-Glanvells," in: Österreichische Turistenzeitung 57, 1937, 9–10.

—— / Saar, Günther Freiherr von, "Zur Erschließung der Karnischen Voralpen [II]," in: Zeitschrift des deutschen und österreichischen Alpenvereins 37, 1906, 380–396.

Donahue, Charles Jr., "Roman Canon Law in the Medieval English Church: Stubbs vs. Maitland Re-examined After 75 Years in the Light of Some Records from the Church Courts," in: Michigan Law Review 72, 1974, 647–716.

——, *Why the History of Canon Law is Not Written*, London: Selden Society, 1986.

Düring, Marten / Kerschbaumer, Florian, "Quantifizierung und Visualisierung. Anknüpfungspunkte in den Geschichtswissenschaften," in: Marten Düring et al. (ed.), Handbuch Historische Netzwerkforschung. Grundlagen und Anwendungen (Schriften des Kulturwissenschaftlichen Instituts Essen zur Methodenforschung 1), Berlin: Lit, 2016, 31–43.

Dusil, Stephan, "Anaklet Reiffenstuel," in: Javier Otaduy et al. (ed.), Diccionario general de derecho canónico, vol. 6, Navarra: Aranzadi, 2012, 848–850.

——, *Die Soester Stadtrechtsfamilie. Mittelalterliche Quellen und neuzeitliche Historiographie* (Forschungen zur Deutschen Rechtsgeschichte 24), Köln / Weimar / Wien: Böhlau, 2007.

——, "Ehrenreich Pirhing," in: Javier Otaduy et al. (ed.), Diccionario general de derecho canónico, vol. 6, Navarra: Aranzadi, 2012, 228–230.

——, "Siegel, Heinrich Joseph," in: Neue Deutsche Biographie 24, 2010, 338–339.

——, *Wissensordnungen des Rechts im Wandel. Päpstlicher Jurisdiktionsprimat und Zölibat zwischen 1000 und 1215* (Mediaevalia Lovaniensia I/47), Leuven: Leuven University Press, 2018.

Ebert, Kurt, *Die Grazer Juristenfakultät im Vormärz. Rechtswissenschaft und Rechtslehre an der Grazer Hochschule zwischen 1810 und 1848* (Grazer rechts- und staatswissenschaftliche Studien 22), Graz: Leykam, 1969.

——, "Die Pflege der Rechtsgeschichte an der Grazer Universität im 19. Jahrhundert," in: Einzelne Probleme der Rechtsgeschichte und des römischen Rechts. Referate der internationalen Arbeitskonferenz für Rechtsgeschichte und Römisches Recht (Szeged 18.-20. September 1969) (Acta Universitatis Szegediensis de Attila József nominatae, Acta Juridica et Politica 17), Szeged 1970, 249–260.

——, "Die Pflege der Rechtsgeschichte an der Universität Graz im Zeichen der Historischen Schule," in: ZRG.GA 87, 1970, 239–286.

Eichmann, Eduard, "Review of 'Wolf von Glanvell, Kanonessammlung,'" in: Kritische Vierteljahresschrift für Gesetzgebung und Rechtswissenschaft 48, 1909, 185–187.

Endemann, Wilhelm, *Studien in der romanisch-kanonistischen Wirtschafts- und Rechtslehre bis gegen Ende des 17. Jahrhunderts*, 2 vols., Berlin: Guttentag, 1874 / 1883 (reprint 1962).

Erben, Wilhelm, *Theodor Sickel. Denkwürdigkeiten aus der Werdezeit eines deutschen Geschichtsforschers*, München / Berlin: Oldenbourg, 1926.

Erdö, Peter, "Die Forschung der Geschichte des kanonischen Rechts: ein Dialog zwischen Theologie und Rechtsgeschichte," in: ZRG.KA 91, 2005, 1–16.

——, *Geschichte der Wissenschaft vom kanonischen Recht. Eine Einführung* (Kirchenrechtliche Bibliothek 4), ed. Ludger Müller, Berlin: Lit, 2006.

Fantappiè, Carlo, *Storia del diritto canonico e delle istituzioni della Chiesa*, Bologna: Il Mulino, 2011.

Feine, Hans Erich, *Kirchliche Rechtsgeschichte. Die katholische Kirche*, 5th edition, Köln / Wien: Böhlau, 1972.

Forster, Wolfgang, "Wahrmund, Ludwig," in: Neue Deutsche Biographie 27, 2020, 263–264.

Fournier, Paul, "Le premier manuel canonique de la réforme du XIe siècle," in: Mélanges d'archéologie et d'histoire de l'École française de Rome 14, 1894, 147–223, 285–290 (reprint: Paul Fournier, Mélanges de droit canonique, vol. 2, ed. Theo Kölzer, Aalen: Scientia, 1983, as Nr. 19, 551–633).

——, "Review of 'Wolf von Glanvell, Die Kanonessammlung des Kardinals Deusdedit,'" in: Revue d'histoire ecclésiastique 8, 1907, 568–575.

—— / Le Bras, Gabriel, *Histoire des collections canoniques en occident. Dépuis les fausses décrétales jusqu'au décret de Gratien*, vol. 2, Paris: Sirey, 1932, (reprint 1972).

Fowler-Magerl, Linda, *Clavis Canonum. Selected Canon Law Collections Before 1140. Access with data processing*, Hannover: Hahn'sche Buchhandlung, 2005.

Frank-Döfering, Peter, *Adelslexikon des österreichischen Kaisertums. 1804–1918*, Wien: Herder, 1989.

Friedberg, Emil, *Corpus Iuris Canonici*, vol. 1: *Decretum Magistri Gratiani*, Leipzig: Bernhard Tauchnitz, 1879, vol. 2: *Decretalium Collectiones*, Leipzig: Bernhard Tauchnitz, 1881.

——, *Das Recht der Eheschliessung in seiner geschichtlichen Entwicklung*, Leipzig: Bernhard Taunitz, 1865.

——, *Lehrbuch des katholischen und evangelischen Kirchenrechts*, Leipzig: Bernhard Tauchnitz, 1879.

——, "Review of 'Wolf von Glanvell, Die Kanonessammlung des Kardinals Deusdedit,'" in: Deutsche Zeitschrift für Kirchenrecht 15, 1905, 469–472.

——, "Review of 'Wolf von Glanvell, Die letztwilligen Verfügungen,'" in: Deutsche Zeitschrift für Kirchenrecht 10, 1901, 398–399.

——, *Verlobung und Trauung. Zugleich als Kritik von Sohm, Das Recht der Eheschliessung*, Leipzig: Bernhard Tauchnitz, 1876.

Fuchs, Wilhelm, *Die sogenannten Siebenbürgischen Ehen und andere Arten der Wiederverehelichung geschiedener österreichischer Katholiken*, Wien: Manz, 1889.

Fuhrmann, Horst, *Einfluß und Verbreitung der pseudoisidorischen Fälschungen. Von ihrem Auftauchen bis in die neuere Zeit* (MGH Schriften 24/2), vol. 2, Stuttgart: Hiersemann, 1973.

Gilchrist, John, "The Reception of Pope Gregory VII into the Canon Law (1073–1141) (part 2)," in: ZRG.KA 66, 1980, 192–229.

Giuliani, Adolfo, "Covarrubias y Leyva, Various Solutions," in: Serge Dauchy et al. (ed.), The Formation and Transmission of Western Legal Culture. 150 Books that Made the Law in the Age of Printing, Cham: Springer, 2016, 88–91.

Grass, Nikolaus, "Arnold Pöschl †," in: ZRG.KA 46, 1960, 659–662.

——, "Die Kirchenrechtslehrer der Universität Graz und ihre Bedeutung für die Erforschung des klassischen kanonischen Rechts," in: Studia Gratiana 8, 1962, 195–304.

——, "Österreichische Kanonistenschulen aus drei Jahrhunderten," in: ZRG.KA 41, 1955, 290–411.

——, "Ulrich Stutz und die österreichische Kirchenrechts-issenschaft," in: ZRG.KA 74, 1988, 27–43.

Grimm, Peter, "Saar, Günther Freiherr von," in: Neue Deutsche Biographie 22, 2005, 316–317.

Gross, Carl, *Das Recht an der Pfründe. Zugleich ein Beitrag zur Ermittlung des Ursprungs des jus ad rem*, Graz: Leuschner & Lubensky, 1887.

Grupp, Peter, *Faszination Berg. Die Geschichte des Alpinismus*, Köln / Weimar / Wien: Böhlau, 2008.

Haferkamp, Hans-Peter, *Die Historische Rechtsschule* (Studien zur Europäischen Rechtsgeschichte 310), Frankfurt am Main: Klostermann, 2018.

Hanausek, Gustav, *Die Lehre vom uneigentlichen Nießbrauch nach gemeinem Recht*, Erlangen: Andreas Deichert, 1879.

Hees, Herbert, "Zur Collectio quinque Librorum (Cod. Vat. lat. 1348)," in: BMCL 4, 1974, 63–64.

Heiner, Franz, "Review of 'Wolf von Glanvell, Die letztwilligen Verfügungen,'" in: AKKR 80, 1900, 640–642.

Hergenröther, Philipp, *Lehrbuch des katholischen Kirchenrechts*, 2nd edition, Freiburg im Breisgau: Herder, 1905.

Hinschius, Paul, *Das Kirchenrecht der Katholiken und Protestanten in Deutschland*, 6 vols., Berlin: Guttentag, 1869–1897.

——, *Decretales Pseudo-Isidorianae et Capitula Angilramni*, Leipzig: Bernhard Tauchnitz, 1863.

Hirsch, Emanuel, "Review of 'Wolf von Glanvell, Die Kanonessammlung des Kardinals Deusdedit,'" in: AKKR 85, 1905, 795–800.

Hirsch, Hans, "Pubblicazioni degli anni 1905, 1906 e 1907 sulla storia medioevale italiana," in: Archivio Storico Italiano 45, 1910, 105–146.

Hofmann, Michael, "Review of 'Wolf von Glanvell, Die letztwilligen Verfügungen,'" in: Zeitschrift für katholische Theologie 24, 1900, 723–724.

Holthöfer, Ernst, "Claro (Clarus), Giulio," in: Michael Stolleis (ed.), Juristen. Ein biographisches Lexikon. Von der Antike bis zum 20. Jahrhundert, München: Beck, 1995, 128–129.

Hungerbühler, Andrea, *"Könige der Alpen." Zur Kultur des Bergführerberufs*, Bielefeld: Transcript, 2013.

Jacobsen, Peter Christian, *Die Carmina des Kardinals Deusdedit* (Editiones Heidelbergenses 31), Heidelberg: Winter, 2002.

Jordan, Stefan, *Theorien und Methoden der Geschichtswissenschaft*, 5th edition, Leiden: Brill / Schöningh, 2021.

Keller, Tait, *Apostles of the Alps. Mountaineering and Nation Building in Germany and Austria, 1860–1939*, Chapell Hill: University of North Carolina, 2016.

Kerschbaumer, Arno, *Beamte, Unternehmer, Offiziere. Familien der "Zweiten Gesellschaft" aus Innerösterreich*, Graz, 2018.

Kéry, Lotte, *Canonical Collections of the Early Middle Ages* (History of medieval canon law 1), Washington D.C.: Catholic University of America Press, 1999.

Kiene, H., "Erschließer der Dolomiten (7): Dr. Viktor Wolf von Glanvell," in: Dolomiten. Der Bergsteiger in den Dolomiten, 11. Mai 1989, Nr. 106.

Köster, Roman, *Einführung in die Wirtschaftsgeschichte. Theorien, Methoden, Themen*, Leiden: Ferdinand Schöningh, 2020.

Köstler, Rudolf, "Consuetudo legitime praescripta. Ein Beitrag zur Lehre vom Gewohnheitsrecht und vom Privileg," in: ZRG.KA 8, 1918, 154–194.

Kučera, "Krofta, Kamil," in: Österreichisches Biographisches Lexikon (1815–1950), vol. 4, Wien: Verlag der Österreichischen Akademie der Wissenschaften, 1969, 287.

Kuprian, Hermann J. W., "'Machen Sie diesem Skandal ein Ende. Ihre Rektoren sind eine nette Gesellschaft.' Modernismusdiskussion, Kulturkampf und Freiheit der Wissenschaft: Die Wahrmund-Affäre 1907/08," in: Michael Gehler / Hubert Sickinger (ed.), Politische Affären und Skandale in Österreich. Von Mayerling bis Waldheim, Wien / Thaur / München: Studien Verlag, 1995, 99–127.

Kuttner, Stephan / Elze, Reinhard: *A Catalogue of Canon and Roman Law Manuscripts in the Vatican Library*, vol. 1: *Codices Vaticani latini 541–2299* (Studi e Testi 322), Città del Vaticano: Biblioteca Apostolica Vaticana, 1986.

Landau, Peter, "Das Recht der frühen Kirche im Werk Aemilius Ludwig Richters," in: Karl-Hermann Kästner (ed.), Festschrift für Martin Heckel zum siebzigsten Geburtstag, Tübingen: Mohr Siebeck, 1999, 117–132 (reprint in: Peter Landau (ed.), Grundlagen und Geschichte des evangeli-schen Kirchenrechts und des Staatskirchenrechts, Tübingen: Mohr Siebeck, 2010, 280–296).

——, "Die Quellen der mittelitalienischen Kanonessammlung in sieben Büchern (MS Vat. lat. 1346)," in: Kathleen G. Cushing / Richard F. Gyug (ed.), Ritual, Text and Law. Studies in Medieval Canon Law and Liturgy presented to Roger E. Reynolds (Church, Faith and Culture in the Medieval West), Aldershot: Ashgate, 2004, 255–268.

——, "Die Theorie des Gewohnheitsrechts im katholischen und evangelischen Kirchenrecht des 19. und 20. Jahrhunderts," in: ZRG.KA 77, 1991, 156–196 (reprint in: Peter Landau (ed.), Grundlagen und Geschichte des evangelischen Kirchenrechts und des Staatskirchenrechts, Tübingen: Mohr Siebeck, 2010, 45–79).

——, "Eigenkirchenwesen," in: Theologische Realenzyklopädie 9, 1982, 399–404.

——, "Evangelische Kirchenrechtswissenschaft im 19. Jahrhundert," in: Zeitschrift für Evangelisches Kirchenrecht 48, 2003, 1–16 (reprint in: Peter Landau (ed.), Grundlagen und Geschichte des evangelischen Kirchenrechts und des Staatskirchenrechts, Tübingen: Mohr Siebeck, 2010, 253–268).

——, "Johann Wilhelm Bickell als Kanonist und seine Geschichte des Kirchenrechts," in: Zeitschrift für evangelisches Kirchenrecht 32, 1987, 411–422 (reprint in: Peter Landau (ed.), Grundlagen und Geschichte des evangelischen Kirchenrechts und des Staatskirchenrechts, Tübingen: Mohr Siebeck, 2010, 269–279).

——, "Kirchenrechtliche Zeitschriften im 19. und 20. Jahrhundert," in: Michael Stolleis (ed.), Juristische Zeitschriften. Die neuen Medien des 18.-20. Jahrhunderts (Studien zur Europäischen Rechtsgeschichte 128), Frankfurt am Main: Klostermann, 1999, 331–378 (reprint in: Peter Landau (ed.), Grundlagen und Geschichte des evangelischen Kirchenrechts und des Staatskirchenrechts, Tübingen: Mohr Siebeck, 2010, 211–252).

Lhotsky, Alphons, *Geschichte des Instituts für Österreichische Geschichtsforschung 1854–1954* (Mitteilungen des Instituts für Österreichische Geschichtsforschung, Ergänzungsband 17), Graz / Köln: Böhlau, 1954.

Liebmann, Maximilian, "Bewährung im österreichischen Kulturkampf," in: Karl Amon / Maximilian Liebmann (ed.), Kirchengeschichte der Steiermark, Graz / Wien / Köln: Styria, 1993, 256–308.

Liebrecht, Johannes, *Brunners Wissenschaft. Heinrich Brunner (1840–1915) im Spiegel seiner Rechtsgeschichte* (Studien zur europäischen Rechtsgeschichte 288), Frankfurt am Main: Klostermann, 2014.

——, *Die junge Rechtsgeschichte. Kategorienwandel in der rechtshistorischen Germanistik der Zwischenkriegszeit* (Beiträge zur Rechtsgeschichte des 20. Jahrhunderts 99), Tübingen: Mohr Siebeck, 2018.

——, "Heinrich Brunner (1840–1915)," in: Stefan Grundmann et al. (ed.), Festschrift 200 Jahre Juristische Fakultät der Humboldt-Universität zu Berlin. Geschichte. Gegenwart und Zukunft, Berlin / New York: De Gruyter, 2010, 305–326.

Loening, Edgar, *Geschichte des deutschen Kirchenrechts*, vol. 2: *Das Kirchenrecht im Reiche der Merowinger*, Strassburg: Trübner, 1878.

Löwenfeld, Samuel, "Canonsammlung des Cardinals Deusdedit und das Register Gregors VII.," in: Neues Archiv der Gesellschaft für ältere deutsche Geschichtskunde 10, 1885, 309–329.

Luschin-Dreier, Marianne, *Arnold Luschin Ritter von Ebengreuth. Ein Leben im Zeichen der Rechtsgeschichte*, 1992 (typoscript, PhD Graz).

Maassen, Friedrich, "Bibliotheca Latina juris canonici manuscripta," in: Sitzungsberichte der Kaiserlichen Akademie der Wissenschaften, philosophisch-historische Klasse 53, Wien 1867, 373–427 and 54, 1866, 157–288.

——, *Geschichte der Quellen und der Literatur des canonischen Rechts im Abendlande bis zum Ausgange des Mittelalters*, Graz: Leuschner & Lubensky, 1870.

Martinucci, Pius, *Deusdedit Presbyteri Cardinalis Tituli Apostolorum in Eudoxia Collectio Canonum*, Venice: Typographia Aemiliana, 1869.

Marx, Christian, "Forschungsüberblick zur Historischen Netzwerkforschung. Zwischen Analysekategorie und Metapher," in: Marten Düring et al. (ed.), Handbuch Historische Netzwerkforschung. Grundlagen und Anwendungen (Schriften des Kulturwissenschaftlichen Instituts Essen zur Methodenforschung 1), Berlin: Lit, 2016, 63–84.

May, Georg / Egler, Anna, *Einführung in die kirchenrechtliche Methode*, Regensburg: Friedrich Pustet, 1986.

Mederle, Oswald, *Auf den Spuren der Tiroler Front. Wanderungen zu den Kriegsschauplätzen 1915–1918*, Bozen: Athesia, 2013.

Meister, Richard (ed.), *Geschichte der Akademie der Wissenschaften in Wien 1847–1947* (Österreichische Akademie der Wissenschaften. Denkschriften der Gesamtakademie 1), Wien: Adolf Holzhausens NFG., 1947.

Meyer, Christoph H. F., "Ordnung durch Ordnen. Die Erfassung und Gestaltung des hochmittelalterlichen Kirchenrechts im Spiegel von Texten, Begriffen und Institutionen," in: Bernd Schneidmüller / Stefan Weinfurter (ed.), Ordnungskonfigurationen im Hohen Mittelalter (VuF 64), Sigmaringen: Jan Thorbecke, 2006, 303–411.

Miramon, Charles de, "L'invention de la Réforme grégorienne: Grégoire VII au XIXe siècle entre pouvoir spirituel et bureaucratisation de l'Église," 2017 (online: https://shs.hal.science/halshs-01522071).

Mittelalter lesbar machen. Festschrift. 200 Jahre Monumenta Germaniae Historica, ed. Monumenta Germaniae Historica, Wiesbaden: Harrassowitz, 2019.

Mordek, Hubert, "Kanonistik und Gregorianische Reform. Marginalien zu einem nicht-marginalen Thema," in: Karl Schmid (ed.), Reich und Kirche vor dem Investiturstreit. Vorträge beim wissenschaftlichen Kolloquium aus Anlaß des achtzigsten Geburtstages von Gerd Tellenbach, Sigmaringen: Jan Thorbecke, 1985, 65–82.

——, *Kirchenrecht und Reform im Frankenreich. Die Collectio Vetus Gallica, die älteste systematische Kanonessammlung des fränkischen Gallien. Studien und Edition* (Beiträge zur Geschichte und Quellenkunde des Mittelalters 1), Berlin / New York: De Gruyter, 1975.

——, "Systematische Kanonessammlungen vor Gratian: Forschungsstand und neue Aufgaben," in: Stephan Kuttner / Kenneth Pennington (ed.), Proceedings of the Sixth International Congress of Medieval Canon Law, Berkeley, California, 28 July-2 August 1980 (MIC C/7), Città del Vaticano: Biblioteca Apostolica Vaticana, 1985, 185–201.

Motta, Joseph [Giuseppe], "Il 'Liber canonum diversorum sanctorum patrum' e la disciplina canonica," in: Chiesa, diritto e ordinamento della "Societas Christiana" nei secoli XI e XII. Atti della nona Settimana internazionale di studio Mendola, 28 agosto-2 settembre 1983, Milano: Vita e pensiero, 1986, 331–339.

——, "I rapporti tra la Collezione canonica di S. Maria Novella e quella in Cinque Libri. Firenze, Bibl. Naz. Conventi Soppressi MS A.4.269 e Bibl. Vaticana, Vat. lat. 1348," in: BMCL 7, 1977, 89–94.

——, *Liber canonum diuersorum sanctorum patrum siue Collectio in CLXXXIII titulos digesta* (MIC B/7), Città del Vaticano: Biblioteca Apostolica Vaticana, 1988.

Müller, Jörg, "Raymundus de Penyafort," in: Michael Stolleis (ed.), Juristen. Ein biographisches Lexikon. Von der Antike bis zum 20. Jahrhundert, München: Beck, 1995, 511–512.

Neschwara, Christian, "Darlehen," in: Albrecht Cordes et al. (ed.), Handwörterbuch zur Deutschen Rechtsgeschichte, 2nd edition, vol. 1, Berlin: Erich Schmidt, 2008, 930–932.

——, "Eherecht und 'Scheinmigration' im 19. Jahrhundert: Siebenbürgische und ungarische, deutsche und Coburger Ehen," in: Gerald Kohl et al. (ed.), Eherecht 1811 bis 2011. Historische Entwicklungen und aktuelle Herausforderungen (Beiträge zur Rechtsgeschichte Österreichs 1/2012), Wien: Akademie der Wissenschaft, 2012, 101–117.

N.N., "Wandern, Bergsteigen und das Lied," in: Österreichische Touristenzeitung 39, 1919, 150–152.

N.N., "Glanvell, Viktor Wolf von," in: Franco De Battaglia / Luciano Marisaldi (ed.), Enciclopedia delle Dolomiti, Bologna: Zanichelli, 2000, 75–77.

Nowak, Przemysław, "*Dagome iudex* w *Zbiorze kanonów* kardynała Deusdedita," in: Studia Źródłoznawcze–Commentationes 51, 2013, 75–94.

——, "Das Papsttum und Ostmitteleuropa (Böhmen-Mähren, Polen, Ungarn) vom ausgehenden 10. bis zum Beginn des 13. Jahrhunderts. Mit einer Neuedition von JL 9067," in: Jochen Johrendt / Harald Müller (ed.), Rom und die Regionen. Studien zur Homogenisierung der lateinischen Kirche im Hochmittelalter, Berlin / Boston: De Gruyter, 2012, 331–369.

Ogris, Werner, "Die Savigny-Stiftung 1863–???," in: ZRG.GA 126, 2009, XXXVI–XLVI.

——, "Zum Erscheinen von Band 125 der Zeitschrift der Savigny-Stiftung für Rechtsgeschichte," in: ZRG.GA 125, 2008, XXXI–XLIX.

Panreck, Isabelle-Christine, *Klaus von Beyme. Eine Werkbiographie*, Wiesbaden: Springer, 2021.

Peitz, Wilhelm M., *Das Originalregister Gregors VII. im Vatikanischen Archiv (Reg. Vat. 2) nebst Beiträgen zur Kenntnis der Originalregister Innozenz' III. und Honorius' III. (Reg. Vat. 4–11)* (Sitzungsberichte der phil.-hist. Klasse, vol. 165/5), Wien: Alfred Hölder, 1911.

Petrbok, V., "Teige, Josef," in: Österreichisches Biographisches Lexikon (1815–1950), vol. 14, Wien: Verlag der Österreichischen Akademie der Wissenschaften, 2013, 229–230.

Phillips, Georg, *Kirchenrecht*, 8 vols., Regensburg: Georg Joseph Manz, 1845–1889.

——, *Lehrbuch des Kirchenrechts*, 2nd edition, Regensburg: Georg Joseph Manz, 1871.

Picasso, Giorgio, *Collezioni canoniche Milanesi del secolo XII*, Milano: Vita e Pensiero, 1969.

Plumpe, Werner, "Wirtschaftsgeschichte zwischen Ökonomie und Geschichte–ein historischer Abriss," in: Werner Plumpe (ed.), Wirtschaftsgeschichte (Basistexte Geschichte 2), Stuttgart: Franz Steiner, 2008, 7–39.

Pulte, Matthias, *Vermögensrecht der katholischen Kirche. Ein Handbuch für Studium und Praxis* (Mainzer Beiträge zum Kirchen- und Religionsrecht 6), Würzburg: Echter, 2019.

Puza, Richard, "Kirchenrechtslehrer an der Juridischen Fakultät der Universität Graz aus zwei Jahrhunderten," in: ZRG.KA 70, 1984, 237–270.

Redlich, "Das cap. 11 X de consuetudine (I, 4)," in: Deutsche Zeitschrift für Kirchenrecht 7, 1897, 309–327.

Richardi, Hans-Günter, *Die Erschließung der Dolomiten. Auf den Spuren der Pioniere Paul Grohmann und Viktor Wolf-Glanvell in den Bleichen Bergen*, Bozen: Athesia, 2008.

Richter, Aemilius Ludwig, *Lehrbuch des katholischen und evangelischen Kirchenrechts*, 6th edition, Leipzig: Bernhard Taunitz, 1867.

Rolker, Christof, "Fournier's Model and Its Merits," in: Christof Rolker (ed.), New Discourses in Medieval Canon Law Research. Challenging the Master Narrative (Medieval Law and Its Practice 28), Leiden: Brill, 2019, 4–32.

Rollinger, Christian, *Amicitia sanctissime colenda.* Freundschaft und soziale Netzwerke in der späten Republik (Studien zur Alten Geschichte 19), Heidelberg: Antike, 2014.

Ross, Friso, "Molina, Luis de," in: Michael Stolleis (ed.), Juristen. Ein biographisches Lexikon. Von der Antike bis zum 20. Jahrhundert, München: Beck, 1995, 437–438.

Roßhirt, Conrad Franz, *Lehrbuch des Kirchenrechts*, 3rd edition, Schaffhausen: Hurter'sche Buchhandlung, 1858.

Rudolf, Karl, "Geschichte des Österreichischen Historischen Instituts in Rom von 1881–1938," in: Römische Historische Mitteilungen 23, 1981, 1–137.

Rückert, Joachim, "Review of 'Bernd-Rüdiger Kern, Georg Beseler. Leben und Werk, 1982,'" in: ZRG.GA 104, 1987, 399–405.

Ruppert, Stefan, *Kirchenrecht und Kulturkampf. Historische Legitimation, politische Mitwirkung und wissenschaftliche Begleitung durch die Schule Emil Ludwig Richters* (Ius ecclesiasticum 70), Tübingen: Mohr Siebeck, 2002.

——, "'Nach Canossa gehen wir nicht.' Kirchenrecht und Kulturkampf," in: Zeitschrift für evangelisches Kirchenrecht 49, 2004, 689–717.

Saar, Günther Freiherr von, "Nachruf," in: Österreichische Alpenzeitung 27, 1905, 121–126.

——, "Zur Erschließung der Karnischen Voralpen [I]," in: Zeitschrift des deutschen und österreichischen Alpenvereins 36, 1905, 383–400.

Sackur, Ernst, "Der Dictatus papae und die Canonsammlung des Deusdedit," in: Neues Archiv der Gesellschaft für ältere deutsche Geschichtskunde 18, 1893, 135–153.

——, "Deusdedit Presbyteri Cardinalis Libellus contra invasores et symoniacos et reliquos scismaticos," in: Monumenta Germaniae Historica, Libelli de lite, tom. II (MGH LdL 2), Hannover: Hahn'sche Buchhandlung, 1892, 292–365.

Sägmüller, Johannes Baptist, *Lehrbuch des katholischen Kirchenrechts*, vol. 2, 3rd edition, Freiburg im Breisgau: Herder, 1914.

——, "Review of 'Wolf von Glanvell, Studien aus dem kanonischen Privatrecht' and 'Wolf von Glanvell, Die Kanonessammlung des Cod. Vatican. lat. 1348,'" in: Theologische Quartalschrift 83, 1901, 626–629.

Savigny, Friedrich Carl von, *Geschichte des römischen Rechts im Mittelalter*, vol. VII, Heidelberg: J. C. B. Mohr, 1851.

——, *System des heutigen römischen Rechts*, 8 vols., Berlin: Veit, 1840–1849.

Schäfer, Frank L., *Juristische Germanistik. Eine Geschichte der Wissenschaft vom einheimischen Privatrecht* (Juristische Abhandlungen 51), Frankfurt am Main: Klostermann, 2008.

Schatz, Klaus, "Vatikanische Konzilien. A. Vaticanum I.," in: Lexikon für Theologie und Kirche, 3rd edition, vol. 10, 2001, 555–561.

Schaumann, Walther, *Schauplätze des Gebirgskrieges 1915–1917*, vol. 1b: *Westliche Dolomiten*, Cortina d'Ampezzo: Ghedina e Tassotti Editori, 1981.

Schmaus, Michael, "Denifle, Heinrich Suso," in: Neue Deutsche Biographie 3, 1957, 595–597.

Schmitt, Fritz, "Viktor Wolf von Glanvell. Bezwinger des bizarrsten Campanile," in: Der Bergsteiger 1982 (Heft 7), 44–45.

Schmoeckel, Mathias, *Kanonisches Recht*, München: Beck, 2020.

—— / Maetschke, Matthias, *Rechtsgeschichte der Wirtschaft. Seit dem 19. Jahrhundert*, 2nd edition, Tübingen: Mohr Siebeck, 2016.

Schreiber, Rudolf, "Bretholz, Berthold," in: Neue Deutsche Biographie 2, 1955, 601–602.

Schulte, Johann Friedrich von, *Die Geschichte der Quellen und Literatur des Canonischen Rechts von Gratian bis auf die Gegenwart*, vol. 1: *Einleitung. Die Geschichte der Quellen und Literatur von Gratian bis auf Papst Gregor IX.*, Stuttgart: Ferdinand Enke, 1875; vol. 2: *Die Geschichte der Quellen und Literatur von Papst Gregor IX. bis zum Concil von Trient*, Stuttgart: Ferdinand Enke, 1877; vol. 3, 1: *Die Geschichte der Quellen und Literatur von der Mitte des 16. Jahrhunderts bis zur Gegenwart / Das katholische Recht und die katholischen Schriftsteller*, Stuttgart: Ferdinand Enke, 1880; vols. 3, 2–3: *Die Geschichte der Quellen und Literatur von der Mitte des 16. Jahrhunderts bis zur Gegenwart / Das evangelische Recht, die evangelischen Schriftsteller, die Geschichte der wissenschaftlichen Behandlung, Übersicht*, Stuttgart: Ferdinand Enke, 1880.

——, *Lehrbuch des katholischen und evangelischen Kirchenrechts nach dem gemeinen Rechte, dem Rechte der deutschen Länder und Oesterreichs*, 4th edition, Gießen: Emil Roth, 1886.

Seelmann, Kurt, "Covarubias (Covarruvias) y Leyva, Diego de," in: Michael Stolleis (ed.), Juristen. Ein biographisches Lexikon. Von der Antike bis zum 20. Jahrhundert, München: Beck, 1995, 142–143.

Seinecke, Ralf, *Das Recht des Rechtspluralismus* (Grundlagen der Rechtswissenschaft 29), Tübingen: Mohr Siebeck, 2015.

Siegel, Heinrich, *Das Versprechen als Verpflichtungsgrund im heutigen Recht. Eine germanistische Studie*, Berlin: Vahlen, 1873.

Sickel, Theodor von, *Das Privilegium Otto I. für die römische Kirche vom Jahre 962*, Innsbruck: Wagner, 1883.

Simon, Thomas, "Die Thun-Hohensteinische Universitätsreform und die 'Geschichtliche Rechtswissenschaft,'" in: Beiträge zur Rechtsgeschichte Österreichs 7, 2017, 132–143.

Sohn, Andreas / Verger, Jacques / Zink, Michael (ed.), *Heinrich Denifle (1844–1905). Un savant dominicain entre Graz, Rome et Paris. Ein dominikanischer Gelehrter zwischen Graz, Rom und Paris*, Paris: Académie des Inscriptions et Belles-Lettres, 2015.

Steinacker, Harold, "Die Deusdedithandschrift (Cod. Vat. 3833) und die ältesten gallischen libri canonum," in: Mittheilungen des Instituts für österreichische Geschichtsforschung Innsbruck, VI. Ergänzungsband, Innsbruck: Wagner, 1901, 113–144.

Stelzer, Winfried, "Sickel, Friedrich Adolf Theodor Ritter von," in: Neue Deutsche Biographie 24, 2010, 309–311.

Stobbe, Otto, *Handbuch des deutschen Privatrechts*, 5 vols., Berlin: Hertz, 1871–1885.

Stoy, Manfred, "Steinacker, Harold Eugen Adolf," in: Neue Deutsche Biographie 24, 2013, 159–161.

Stutz, Ulrich, *Die Eigenkirche als Element des mittelalterlich-germanischen Kirchenrechtes*, Berlin: Müller, 1895.

——, *Die kirchliche Rechtsgeschichte. Rede zur Feier des 27. Januar 1905, gehalten in der Aula der Universität Bonn*, Stuttgart: Ferdinand Enke, 1905.

——, "Die Savigny-Stiftung seit 1901," in: ZRG.GA 46, 1926, IX–XXII.

——, *Geschichte des kirchlichen Benefizialwesens. Von seinen Anfängen bis auf die Zeit Alexanders III.*, Berlin: Müller, 1895.

——, "Kirchenrecht," in: Franz von Holtzendorff / Josef Kohler (ed.), Encyklopädie der Rechtswissenschaft in systematischer Bearbeitung, 6th edition, vol. 2, Leipzig / Berlin: Guttentag, 1904, 809–972.

——, "Review of 'Die Kanonessammlung des Kardinals Deusdedit,'" in: Deutsche Literaturzeitung 26, 1905, 2273–2277.

——, "Review of 'Wolf von Glanvell, Die letztwilligen Verfügungen,'" in: Deutsche Litteraturzeitung 1901, 811–812.

——, "Review of 'Wolf von Glanvell, Die negotia in vivos,'" in: Deutsche Litteraturzeitung 1898, 1608–1609.

Taschwer, Klaus, "Das Wissen für Alle. Annäherungen an das populärwissenschaftliche Zeitschriftenwesen um 1900," in: Relation. Medien–Gesellschaft–Geschichte 4, 1997, 17–50.

Thaner, Friedrich, *Anselm II., Bischof von Lucca, Collectio Canonum una cum collectione minore*, Innsbruck: Wagner, 1906–1915 (reprint 1965).

——, "Das Kapitel: Tua nos, Decret. Greg. IX, L. IV. T. I, c. 26," in: Mélanges Hermann Fitting, vol. 1, Montpellier: Imprimerie générale du Midi, 1907, 465–478.

——, "Die literar-geschichtliche Entwicklung der Lehre vom Error qualitatis redundans in personam und vom Error conditionis," in: Sitzungsberichte der Kaiserlichen Akademie der Wissenschaften, phil.-hist. Klasse 142, 1900 (as Abhandlung 2).

——, *Die Summa Magistri Rolandi nachmals Papstes Alexander III., nebst einem Anhange Incerti Auctoris Quaestiones*, Innsbruck: Wagner, 1874.

——, "Libelli Bernaldi presbyteri monachi," in: Monumenta Germaniae Historica, Libelli de lite, tom. II (MGH LdL 2), Hannover: Hahn'sche Buchhandlung, 1892, 1–168.

——, "Simulatae nuptiae nullius momenti sunt," in: Österreichisches Zentralblatt für die juristische Praxis 25, 1907, 277–285.

Theiner, Augustin, *Disquisitiones criticae in praecipuas canonum et decretalium collectiones seu Sylloges Gallandianae dissertationum de vetustis canonum collectionibus continuatio*, Rome: Collegium Urbinum, 1836.

Theiß, Dennis, "Raimund de Peñaforte (1175/80–1275)," in: Albrecht Cordes et al. (ed.), Handwörterbuch zur Deutschen Rechtsgeschichte, 2nd edition, vol. 4, Berlin: Erich Schmidt, 2022, 1000–1002.

Thier, Andreas, "Dictatus Papae," in: Albrecht Cordes et al. (ed.), Handwörterbuch zur Deutschen Rechtsgeschichte, 2nd edition, vol. 1, Berlin: Erich Schmidt, 2008, 1043–1045.

——, "Phillips, Georg(e)," in: Neue Deutsche Biographie 20, 2001, 401–402.

——, "Stutz, Ulrich Georg," in: Neue Deutsche Biographie 25, 2013, 659–660.

Van de Wiel, Constant, *History of Canon Law* (Louvain Theological & Pastoral Monographs 5), Leuven: Peeters, 1991.

Van Houdt, Toon, "Leonardus Lessius," in: Wim Decock / Janwillem Oosterhuis (ed.), Great Christian Jurists in the Low Countries (Cambridge Studies in Law and Christianity), Cambridge: Cambridge University Press, 2021, 64–79.

Vavra, Georg, "Wolf von Glanvell, Viktor Edler," in: Österreichisches Biographisches Lexikon (1815–1950), vol. 16, Wien: Verlag der Österreichischen Akademie der Wissenschaften, 2021, 327–328.

Vering, Friedrich, *Lehrbuch des katholischen und protestantischen Kirchenrechts, mit besonderer Rücksicht auf das Vaticanische Konzil sowie auf Deutschland, Oesterreich und die Schweiz*, Freiburg im Breisgau: Herder, 1876.

——, *Lehrbuch des katholischen, orientalischen und protestantischen Kirchenrechts, mit besonderer Rücksicht auf Deutschland, Oesterreich und die Schweiz*, 3rd edition, Freiburg im Breisgau: Herder, 1893.

Walter, Ferdinand, *Lehrbuch des Kirchenrechts aller christlichen Confessionen*, 13th edition, Bonn: Adolph Marcus, 1861.

Wasserschleben, Friedrich Wilhelm, *Beiträge zur Geschichte der vorgratianischen Kirchenrechtsquellen*, Leipzig: Bernhard Taunitz, 1839.

——, *Reginonis abbatis Prumiensis libri duo de synodalibus causis et disciplinis ecclesiasticis*, Leipzig: Engelmann, 1840 (reprint 1964).

Wernz, Franz Xaver, *Ius decretalium ad usum praelectionum in scholis textus canonici sive iuris decretalium*, 6 vols., Rome: Typographia Polyglotta, 1898–1914.

Wesener, Gunter, "Arnold Luschin von Ebengreuth (1841–1932), Rechtshistoriker und Numismatiker," in: Karl Acham (ed.), Rechts-, Sozial- und Wirtschaftswissenschaften aus Graz. Zwischen empirischer Analyse und normativer Handlungsanweisung. Wissenschaftsgeschichtliche Befunde aus drei Jahrhunderten (Kunst und Wissenschaft aus Graz 3), Wien: Böhlau, 2011, 255–271.

——, *Geschichte der Rechtswissenschaftlichen Fakultät der Universität Graz*, vol. 1: *Römisches Recht und Naturrecht* (Publikationen aus dem Archiv der Universität Graz 9/1), Graz: Akademische Druck- und Verlagsanstalt, 1978.

Windscheid, Bernhard, *Lehrbuch des Pandektenrechts*, 9th edition, with Theodor Kipp, 3 vols.: Frankfurt am Main: Ruetten & Loening, 1906.

Wolkinger, Franz, "Univ.-Prof. Dr. Victor Wolf Edler von Glanvell," in: Alpenverein Graz. Nachrichten 2005 (Heft Nr. 4), 6–7.

All homepages were last accessed on 25 July, 2023.

Appendix 8: Indices

8.1. Index of Manuscripts

8.2. Index of Works and Collections

8.3. Index of Names

FSC
www.fsc.org
MIX
Papier | Fördert
gute Waldnutzung
FSC® C083411

Kolibri 360 GmbH
Ferdinand-Jühlke-Straße 7
99095 Erfurt, Deutschland
produktsicherheit@kolibri360.de